T0311579

"This excellent, beautifully organized introduction provides an accurate and unusually rich entré into a relatively new and still somehow frequently misunderstood religion. The author, Christopher Buck, is a leading scholar of the Bahá'í religion. His book is richly enhanced with quotations from official translations of the Bahá'í sacred writings, insights into the formation of distinctive Bahá'í institutions and rare glimpses of key moments in Bahá'í intellectual history from an introduction to the influential African American Bahá'í philosopher, Alain Locke (d. 1954) known as 'the father of the Harlem Renaissance', to a discussion of the more recent development of the Ruhi Institute process. This introduction goes beyond existing textbooks in both scope and detail. It will be warmly welcomed by researchers and students of the Bahá'í Faith."

Todd Lawson, *University of Toronto, Canada*

BAHÁ'Í FAITH

Bahá'í Faith: The Basics provides a thorough and accessible introduction to a fascinating, independent world religion. Examining its historical development, current "community-building" efforts and the social contributions of the Bahá'í Faith in the world today, this introduction covers:

- Beliefs: Bahá'í spiritual teachings.
- Principles: Bahá'í social teachings.
- History: Bahá'u'lláh and his covenant.
- Scripture: Bahá'í sacred texts and inspired guidance.
- Institutions: The Bahá'í Administrative Order.
- Building community: What Bahá'ís do.
- Social action: Bahá'í social and economic development projects.
- Public discourse: The Bahá'í International Community.
- Vision: Foundations for a future golden age.

With features including a glossary of terms, and references to the Bahá'í writings throughout, this is the ideal text for students and interested readers wanting to familiarize themselves with the Bahá'í Faith.

Christopher Buck is an independent scholar and former professor at Michigan State University, USA; Quincy University, USA; Millikin University, USA; and Carleton University, Canada.

The Basics

For more information about this series, please visit: https://www.routledge.com/The-Basics/book-series/B

BAHÁ'Í FAITH

THE BASICS

Christopher Buck

LONDON AND NEW YORK

First published 2021
by Routledge
2 Park Square, Milton Park, Abingdon, Oxon OX14 4RN

and by Routledge
52 Vanderbilt Avenue, New York, NY 10017

Routledge is an imprint of the Taylor & Francis Group, an informa business

British Library Cataloguing-in-Publication Data
A catalogue record for this book is available from the British Library

Library of Congress Cataloging-in-Publication Data
A catalog record has been requested for this book

ISBN: 978-1-138-34617-8 (hbk)
ISBN: 978-1-138-34616-1 (pbk)
ISBN: 978-0-429-02308-8 (ebk)

DOI: 10.4324/9780429023088

Typeset in Bembo
by Deanta Global Publishing Services, Chennai, India

*Dedicated to my dear wife, Nahzy Abadi Buck,
and our two sons, Takur Buck and Taraz Buck.*

CONTENTS

ACKNOWLEDGEMENTS

Advanced studies of the Bahá'í Faith must first begin with basics, which is one reason why this book, *Bahá'í Faith: The Basics*, may be of interest—not only to those readers who have little familiarity with the Bahá'í Faith, but to those readers who already have some knowledge of the Faith as well.

First and foremost, I wish to acknowledge the Universal House of Justice, the international governing council of the Bahá'í Faith (Bahá'í World Centre, Mount Carmel, Haifa, Israel), for its kind permission (granted on 27 March 2020) to quote rather extensively from the Bahá'í writings and authoritative sources, which are readily available to the interested public—and in the public interest—on the "Bahá'í Reference Library: Authoritative Writings and Guidance" website at bahai.org. Inclusion of a rich array of Bahá'í primary sources will put readers in touch with the heart and soul of the Bahá'í worldview, which is universal and unifying in its vision and mission which, in the words of Bahá'u'lláh (1817–1892, prophet-founder of the Bahá'í Faith), is to "unify the world" (public letter to Napoleon III, quoted in Bahá'u'lláh, *Epistle*, BRL).

Thanks also to fellow Bahá'í attorney, Anton Ware, Esq. (based in Shanghai, China, and who speaks and reads Mandarin Chinese), for directing me (on 26 March 2020) to Nima Masroori, Esq., general counsel and legal affairs contact person at the Bahá'í World Centre

(Mount Carmel, Haifa, Israel), so that my request for permission could be readily considered and timely granted.

Special thanks to Derrick Stone (University of Virginia lecturer in Computer Science and Director of Software Development, UVA Health System) for his valuable work in identifying and providing full bibliographic citations for all quotations in the book. The Bahá'í Reference Library provides downloadable versions of authoritative Bahá'í texts. Prof. Stone wrote a computer program to search the manuscript of this book, find matches in the Bahá'í scriptures and other authoritative texts, and generate the corresponding references for the bibliography.

The cover photograph is courtesy of Getty Images, which provides this caption: "Detail of the flower-shaped dome at the Bahá'í House of Worship in Santiago, October 13, 2016. The temple belonging to the Bahá'í Faith, an independent religion that originated over 150 years ago in Iran and has a temple in each continental area. The Bahá'í House of Worship in South America opens its doors on October 19, 2016. (Photo credit: Martin Bernetti/AFP via Getty Images.)" Martin Bernetti is a photojournalist (Chief of photography for the Agence France Presse), who lives and works in Santiago, the capital and largest city of Chile.

I also had great pleasure of working with my editors at Routledge— Rebecca Shillabeer (Senior Editor, Routledge Religion), Amy Doffegnies, PhD (Editorial Assistant, Routledge Religion) and Rennie Alphonsa (Senior Project Manager at Deanta, a publishing production company based in Dublin, Ireland)—for all their excellent work in bringing this introductory book, *Bahá'í Faith: The Basics*, to each and every one of you, my esteemed readers.

INTRODUCTION
WHAT IS THE BAHÁ'Í FAITH?

A NEW WORLD RELIGION

The Bahá'í Faith is an independent world religion, which began in 19th-century Persia (present-day Iran) and is now established in virtually every country and territory around the world (except for North Korea and the Vatican City State). The Bahá'í Faith therefore is a global community. Although relatively small in numbers, the rapid "diffusion" (or spread) is quite remarkable, given the relatively recent appearance of the Bahá'í religion on the historical horizon. The purpose of the Bahá'í Faith is to "unify the world." This vision and mandate has inspired many to join the Bahá'í religion, in which peace is made sacred, and powerful social principles are promoted and put into practice in order to build and/ or strengthen those institutional foundations upon which world peace and prosperity may be based. "Say: no man can attain his true station except through his justice," wrote Bahá'u'lláh (1817–1892), prophet-founder of the Bahá'í Faith: "No power can exist except through unity. No welfare and no well-being can be attained except through consultation" (quoted by the Universal House of Justice, April 2017, BRL).

True to its purpose, the Bahá'í religion is truly worldwide. Around 2,100 indigenous tribal, ethnic, and racial groups are represented in the worldwide Bahá'í community, which currently has 188 national councils that oversee Bahá'í community life in their respective

DOI: 10.4324/9780429023088-1

regions. Bahá'í scriptures and prayers have been translated into over 800 languages. In September 2018, for instance, a collection of Bahá'í prayers, translated into the Maori language with the assistance of Dr. Tom Roa, professor of Maori and Indigenous Studies at the University of Waikato, was published in New Zealand.

To illustrate the recent growth of the Bahá'í Faith, the following concrete examples may be given. There are now ten Bahá'í Houses of Worship around the world, located in: (1) Wilmette, Illinois, United States (opened in 1953); (2) Kampala, Uganda (1961); (3) Sydney, Australia (1961); (4) Frankfurt, Germany (1964); (5) Panama City, Panama (1972); (6) Apia, Samoa (1984); (7) New Delhi, India (1986); (8) Santiago, Chile (2016); (9) Battambang, Cambodia (2017); and (10) Norte del Cauca, Colombia (2018). Plans are underway to build national Houses of Worship in: Port Moresby, Papua New Guinea (design unveiled on 21 March 2018); and in Kinshaha, Democratic Republic of Congo (DRC, design announced on 2 July 2020). Local Houses of Worship are also being constructed in: Tanna, Vanuatu (design revealed on 18 June 2017); Matunda Soy, Kenya (design disclosed on 15 April 2018); and Bihar Sharif, India (designed publicized on 29 April 2020).

Given its impressive geographic spread as the world's most widely diffused religion in the world today (second only to Christianity), the Bahá'í Faith is increasingly attracting interest. Christianity, of course, remains the world's largest religion, with approximately 2.3 billion followers (as of 2015), while the Bahá'í Faith numbers only around seven million adherents. This notable difference in size is directly related to the relative age of each faith. Christianity is over 2,000 years old, whereas the Bahá'í Faith, as of 20 March 2020, is 177 years old, considering that Bahá'í history began in 1844.

PURPOSE OF THE BAHÁ'Í FAITH

A young, independent world religion—co-founded by the Báb in 1844 and by Bahá'u'lláh in 1863—the Bahá'í Faith claims to have the blueprint to usher in a future golden age of world civilization. Time will tell. Bahá'ís are confident that, over time, the Bahá'í religion will fulfill its purpose, and will contribute greatly to the peace and prosperity of the world. The how and why will be explained further in this book.

Like other world religions, the Bahá'í Faith teaches how to live a better life—morally, ethically, and spiritually. The distinctive feature of the Bahá'í religion is its emphasis on promoting unity, from family relations to international relations. With this in mind, it's easy to see how the Bahá'í Faith also teaches how to live a better life socially and globally. The teachings of the Bahá'í religion originate with Bahá'u'lláh (1817–1892) who was born in Persia (present-day Iran) and who, as a prisoner of the Ottoman Empire, was exiled to Acre (Akka), Palestine (present-day Israel) which is how the Bahá'í World Centre was established on the slopes of Mt. Carmel in Haifa, Israel. The Bahá'í Shrines and Gardens are now a place of pilgrimage for Bahá'ís around the world and was declared a "World Heritage Site" by the United Nations in 2008 (UNESCO 2019). This book will serve as an introduction to the "basics" of the Bahá'í Faith.

THE "ONENESS OF GOD"

"Unity" is the watchword of the Bahá'í religion. In a nutshell, its teachings revolve around the "oneness of God," the "oneness of humankind," and the "oneness of religions."

Briefly, the first of these three onenesses is the belief in one God. Thus, the Bahá'í Faith, along with Judaism, Christianity, Islam, and other religions, is a "monotheistic" religion. God is regarded as an "unknowable essence," beyond the reach and ken of human understanding. In such case, God is the supreme "mystery"—yet with the greatest number of clues throughout the universe. Creation being God's handiwork, Bahá'ís believe, there is nothing in creation that does not reflect some quality or attribute of its maker. Even so, God remains beyond comprehension. After all, the finite cannot comprehend the infinite. In short, God can be apprehended, but not comprehended. In other words, while some things may be known about God, God, who knows all things, cannot be known directly or fully. This may seem paradoxical, especially considering the Bahá'í noonday prayer, which states, in part: "I bear witness, O my God, that Thou hast created me to know Thee and to worship Thee" (Bahá'u'lláh, *Prayers and Meditations*, BRL). That is to say, to know and to love God is possible to the extent that God has revealed something of the divine nature and purpose through the prophets and messengers that God has sent in the course of human history.

Put differently, how is it that Bahá'ís—or anyone, for that matter—can believe in, love, and worship a God who cannot truly be known, fathomed, or otherwise understood? The answer is that God sends prophets, messengers, spiritual teachers (known by different names and terms of reference) to reveal the will of God and divine teachings for the betterment of humankind. These teachers are typically the founders of the world's religions. They appear throughout history and serve to enlighten humanity in their part of the world. Bahá'ís take a bird's-eye view of the world's religious history and call this process "Progressive Revelation." So, not only do spiritual teachers bring timeless—and timely—moral, spiritual, and social truths, their teachings are also typically fuller and more complete than the ones brought before. Bahá'ís believe that the teachings of Bahá'u'lláh represent the will of God for this day and age.

THE ONENESS OF HUMANKIND

The second "oneness" is the idea that humanity is an extended family, to use one metaphor. As Bahá'u'lláh has famously said: "The tabernacle of unity hath been raised; regard ye not one another as strangers. Ye are the fruits of one tree, and the leaves of one branch" (Bahá'u'lláh, *Gleanings*, BRL). Like family, all human beings are related and interrelated. This is understood to be scientifically true, as well as spiritually true. The goal of the Bahá'í religion is to make this socially true as well. Bahá'í social teachings all support this overarching goal of promoting the "consciousness of the oneness of humankind" and of taking practical steps to eliminate prejudices of all kinds—whether racial, religious, ethnic, national, gender-based, class-based, etc.—which pose the major barriers to a united world. As previously mentioned, Bahá'ís believe that the will of God for this day and age is that the world should become unified. Humanity, given its spiritual and social evolution, has reached the threshold of its long-awaited "maturity." So, now is the right time for the world to come together. World unity, therefore, is not simply a utopian dream, but a practical necessity, on which the world's future survival, as well as peace and prosperity, ultimately depends. As Bahá'u'lláh has stated: "The well-being of mankind, its peace and security are unattainable unless and until its unity is firmly established" (Bahá'u'lláh, *Gleanings*, BRL).

THE ONENESS OF RELIGION

The third oneness concerns the essential harmony of the world's religions. This teaching does not overlook the many differences that separate religions today. Sectarianism, religious prejudice, religious persecution, interreligious violence, and even interreligious wars (especially those involving terrorism) remain a seemingly intractable global problem. One approach to solving this problem is to look at similarities among religions, rather than focusing on differences. Differences can also be regarded in a positive light. The Bahá'í Faith and values "unity in diversity" and only criticizes differences if they are the cause of social conflict and injustice.

BAHÁ'Í SOCIAL PRINCIPLES

Social principles may be thought of as the collective morals and ethics of the world. Principles embody values and operate as mandates for social action. The Bahá'í Faith has a number of social principles, a few of which will be described here. Justice, for instance, is highly valued in Bahá'í teachings. Social principles, if they attract widespread consensus and are put into general practice, have the power to transform society, each in their own way. The Bahá'í teachings show a keen awareness of the power of such principles. Social principles can be secular or religious. The Bahá'í religion, renders each secular social principle—that forms part and parcel of the overall Bahá'í social agenda—as sacred. This is a process that the present writer has referred to as "sacralizing the secular."

Among the many Bahá'í social principles, the most well known are world peace and prosperity, the equality of women and men, the harmony of science and religion, spiritual solutions to economic problems (in which economic values should be based on human values), universal education, the adoption of an auxiliary world language, and so forth. The present writer has, in fact, identified over 50 Bahá'í principles of unity (Buck 2015b). This is simply to illustrate how deep and pervasive the Bahá'í teachings on unity actually are.

EQUALITY OF WOMEN AND MEN

The equality of women and men, for instance, is a major Bahá'í social principle. It is said that the Bahá'í Faith may well be the first world religion to have proclaimed the full social and spiritual equality of women and men from the very inception of that religion. Of course, today, most other religions also espouse gender equality. This is a good thing. Bahá'ís do not claim "ownership" of this, or any other, major social principle. Considering that around half of the world's population is comprised of women—a vast reservoir of social capital and potential that remains largely untapped and underdeveloped—this social principle is of huge importance, and should receive far more attention than it currently does.

HARMONY OF SCIENCE AND RELIGION

The harmony of science and religion—another major social principle as well—is also of enormous importance. Another way of looking at this principle is to consider science as the major source of empirical knowledge of the physical universe, and religion as a major source of knowledge of the spiritual dimension of the universe. (Any world-view that denies the spiritual dimension of reality may be referred to as philosophical materialism.) Without science, religion can become superstitious. Without religion, science can become unethical, even destructive. When the two major spheres of human knowledge and social influence—science and religion—exist in perfect harmony with one another, an ideal situation results, whereby spiritual and scientific knowledge work together in perfect concert to promote a better life for all.

SYSTEMATIC GROWTH AND SOCIAL TRANSFORMATION

For the Bahá'í Faith to serve a beneficial influence on societies world-wide, it first has to grow. The greater its growth, the greater its potential influence. To that end, since 1996, Bahá'í institutions have adopted a systematic approach to further expanding the growth of the Bahá'í community—what geographers call "expansion diffusion," or what sociologists have referred to as "generating and applying spiritual capital" (although these academic terms of art never occur in Bahá'í discourse). In other words, Bahá'ís around the world have embarked on a coherent plan of individual and social transformation. Today, Bahá'ís worldwide are engaged in the systematic process of "community building," which is all about establishing a new civilization and diffusing Bahá'í principles throughout society and with the cooperation of others. This is achieved through offering children's classes for moral education, by organizing "junior youth spiritual empowerment programs," by hosting devotional meetings for prayer and worship, and by offering study circles for community consolidation and skill-building to equip Bahá'ís and friends to better serve their local communities. "Service" to humanity is seen as spirituality in action, where the Bahá'í religion, along with other religions, is put to good use for the betterment of the world. Such emphasis on service is the primary way in which Bahá'ís "practice what they preach," as it were. This systematic Bahá'í plan will be explained in some detail later in the book.

BAHÁ'Í ADMINISTRATION

That said, there are no "preachers" in the Bahá'í religion, which has no clergy. Instead, the Bahá'í Faith is organized and run by elected councils. Bahá'í elections, in fact, are rather unique since nominating candidates and campaigning are not allowed. Voting is conducted prayerfully by secret ballot, in which the members of Bahá'í councils are elected by "plurality" vote, meaning that the nine individuals who receive the top number of votes are elected to a given Bahá'í council. There are local, regional, national, and international Bahá'í councils. These are called "Spiritual Assemblies," except for Regional Bahá'í Councils, and the international Bahá'í council known as the Universal House of Justice, first elected in 1963, and based in Haifa, Israel.

ORIGINS OF THE BAHÁ'Í FAITH

The Bahá'í World Centre is based in Israel—a "Holy Land" for several religions. Historically, the Bahá'í Faith has its origins in Islam, in 19th-century Persia, just as Christianity has its origins in Judaism, in the Holy Land. As will be discussed in some detail in the chapter on Bahá'í history, the Bahá'í religion evolved and developed into the independent world religion that it is today. While there are many Islamic terms and concepts to be found in the Bahá'í scriptures, Bahá'ís do not regard themselves as Muslims. (By the same token, Muslims do not regard Bahá'ís as Muslims, either.) That said, Bahá'ís do their best to promote respect for Islam and all Muslims. Unfortunately, this respect is not always reciprocated, as in the case of present-day Islamic Republic of Iran, which continues to persecute Bahá'ís. This problematic situation will be discussed in more detail later in this book.

BAHÁ'Í CONSULTATION

Without clergy, Bahá'ís administer their affairs through consultation, which is a tool for enlightened decision-making and for problem-solving. Bahá'ís have developed the art of consultation in some new and interesting ways. For instance, when offering an idea, an individual does so as a contribution to the general discussion and is not (or should not be) attached either to the idea or to the outcome. In this sense, there is no "ownership" of suggestions or recommendations. In addition to local, regional, national, and international Bahá'í councils, consultation also takes part in the "Nineteen-Day Feast." Typically, a Bahá'í Feast consists of devotional, consultative, and social portions. During the consultative session, Bahá'ís discuss their community affairs and, if so inspired, offer their individual suggestions and collective recommendations for the consideration of their Local Spiritual Assembly. Their local Bahá'í council may then, in turn, consult on these ideas and, if so, may convey its decisions to the Bahá'í community at the next Feast. Bahá'í councils, in general, are not only concerned with the administrative affairs of the Bahá'í communities which they oversee and serve, but have a mandate to contribute to the commonweal and general welfare of the greater communities in which they operate.

THE BAHÁ'Í CALENDAR

Most religions have their own sacred calendars. The Bahá'í Faith is no exception. Its calendar is rather unique, in fact. It consists of 19 months of 19 days each, with several days rounding out the calendar year. Each weekday, each day of the month, each month, each year, and any cycle of years is given a special name, each representing an attribute or quality of God, that can also be expressed as a human virtue. The names of the 19 Bahá'í months, in Arabic and English, are as follows: (1) *Bahá* (Splendor); (2) *Jalál* (Glory); (3) *Jamál* (Beauty); (4) *'Aẓamat* (Grandeur); (5) *Nur* (Light); (6) *Raḥmat* (Mercy); (7) *Kalimát* (Words);

(8) *Kamál* (Perfection); (9) *Asmá'* (Names); (10) *Izzat* (Might); (11) *Mashíyyat* (Will); (12) *Ilm* (Knowledge); (13) *Qudrat* (Power); (14) *Qawl* (Speech); (15) *Masá'il* (Questions); (16) *Sharaf* (Honor); (17) *Sulṭán* (Sovereignty); (18) *Mulk* (Dominion); (19) *Alá* (Loftiness).

The precise name for the Bahá'í calendar is the *Badí'* ("Unique" or "Wondrous") calendar. It originated with the Báb ("the Gate"), who founded the Bábí religion, which soon evolved into the Bahá'í Faith, established by Bahá'u'lláh in 1863. Adopting and modifying the *Badí'* Calendar for use by the Bahá'í community, Bahá'u'lláh invested time itself with spiritual significance. He transformed time by the naming of weekdays, days of the month, months, years, and cycles of years after spiritual perfections that can be translated into goodly virtues, such as *Jamál* (Beauty), *'Ilm* (Knowledge), *Sharaf* (*Honor*), and *'Aẓamat* (Grandeur), which are names of four of the 19 Bahá'í months.

These dynamic "names of God" each highlight a distinctive quality of sterling character and human nobility, in a process of transformation that could be called "theophoric metamorphosis" (Buck and Melton, "Bahá'í Calendar and Rhythms of Worship," 2011). Literally, the term "theophoric," as its Greek root indicates, means "God-bearing." Here, the names of God may be conceived as qualities or, better still, as powers of God that individuals can potentially develop. In the Báb's *Kitáb al-Asmá'* (*Book of [Divine] Names*), which exceeds 3,000 pages and is said to be "the largest revealed book in sacred history" (Saiedi 2008, 36), the Báb treats human beings as reflections of divine names and attributes. To the extent that a person is a "bearer" of one of the "names" (i.e. qualities or powers) of God, that individual is empowered to express that quality in human action. Through the progressive spiritualization of all persons, the Báb wished to transform all of reality into "mirrors" reflecting the perfections represented by these divine names. Of course, the mere fact that the name of a given Bahá'í month suggests a spiritual quality that can be acquired as a human virtue does not, alone, accomplish that result. No burst of insight will emanate from the simple recitation of, say, "Grandeur." Meditating on a virtue and then manifesting it is part and parcel of Bahá'í self-transformation. Each of these godly qualities can be expressed as goodly virtues in our thoughts and actions. This is just one example of how the Bahá'í religion cultivates good character, civic virtues, community service, and unity in all walks of life.

AVOIDANCE OF PARTISAN POLITICS

In this way, Bahá'ís do their part to contribute to society, free of all partisan politics, which Bahá'ís regard as divisive. Since the purpose of the Bahá'í Faith is to promote unity, participation in partisan politics will be contrary to that purpose. That said, Bahá'ís have a healthy patriotism for the countries in which they respectively live, superseded by a wider loyalty as "world citizens." Bahá'ís are concerned with the "body politic," as it were—in other words, with the world at large. The Bahá'í worldview is universal in scope, all-inclusive in its outlook, cosmopolitan in its outreach, and egalitarian in practice.

VISION OF THE FUTURE

Not only do Bahá'ís have a clear purpose and mission to promote unity far and wide, but they have a vision of a future golden age as well. This inspires confidence in the process of promoting unity, with the assurance that "peace is inevitable." That peace is inevitable does not mean that there is a fixed time for it since the conditions for world peace have to be ripe. So, the preconditions for peace can vary, depending on time and circumstance. Peace is a process. It is gradual and, ideally, progressive. The Bahá'í Faith envisions the advent of the "Lesser Peace" (i.e. a political peace, with progressively closer-knit harmony among races, religions, and nations) followed by the "Most Great Peace" (a world commonwealth leading to a golden age of world civilization). This grand vision is not merely visionary, but is a mission, with clear objectives and concrete steps for its realization. In that sense, the Bahá'í religion is an authentic peace movement in which utopia becomes utilitarian. World peace requires world effort. To mobilize the social forces and to optimize the social conditions needed to bring about world peace requires a comprehensive vision and plan, which the Bahá'í Faith offers. In this sense, the Bahá'í concept of "salvation" is both individual and social.

The Bahá'í Faith, from its inception, has precociously anticipated the emergence of a global society. The Bahá'í Faith positively contributes a set of corresponding universal values on which such world unity may solidly be based. Thus, the Bahá'í Faith presents a remarkable case study of a global community in the making, i.e. actively engaging in the process of its own enlightened, self-directed development.

As such, the Bahá'í religion offers a social model that demonstrates that world unity—in which races, religions, and nations prospectively can be united in a common global civilization—can be successfully achieved.

Until fairly recently, the Bahá'í Faith has been little known. But it is emerging from its former obscurity, as readers of this book, *Bahá'í Faith: The Basics*, may well appreciate. Suffice it to say that, if Bahá'ís succeed in promoting peace and prosperity by way of fostering the unity of races, religions, and nations worldwide, then the world will be a better place—and the Bahá'í Faith will be better known and appreciated as well.

MISCONCEPTIONS OF THE BAHÁ'Í FAITH

Those who know of the Bahá'í Faith may have a limited or even incorrect understanding of it. For instance, a common misconception is that the Bahá'í religion is somehow "eclectic" or "syncretic"—that is, a mix of religious teachings adapted from other religions. This is far from the truth, considering that the Bahá'í scriptures are revealed, in large part, by its founder, Bahá'u'lláh, who was quite prolific and wrote a large volume of works that Bahá'ís consider to be sacred texts. Taken together, these texts are estimated to comprise the equivalent of some one hundred books. In addition to Bahá'u'lláh's writings, there are the writings of two other central figures of the Bahá'í Faith: the Báb (1819–1850) who foretold the coming of Bahá'u'lláh, and 'Abdu'l-Bahá (1844–1921), who was Bahá'u'lláh's eldest son and designated successor, interpreter, and exemplar of Bahá'u'lláh's teachings. In addition to these, the writings of Shoghi Effendi (1897–1957), although not considered sacred scripture, are regarded as authoritative. Also authoritative are the letters issued by the Universal House of Justice (1963–present). So, there is no need for anything to be borrowed, as it were, from other religious traditions.

PURPOSE OF *BAHÁ'Í FAITH: THE BASICS*

This book, *Bahá'í Faith: The Basics*, is a primer—a relatively brief introduction. Advanced studies on the Bahá'í Faith must also begin with basics. Routledge's *The Basics* series therefore offers an ideal introduction to the study of world religions, including study of the Bahá'í Faith itself. The Bahá'í religion is relatively new on the historical horizon and has only recently begun to emerge from its former obscurity. In the pages that follow, information is presented in an informal, yet systematic and fairly comprehensive way, that can be easily understood by just about any informed reader who is interested in learning more about the Bahá'í Faith, even if only out of mere curiosity. This book can be read from start to finish, or the chapters may be read in any order desired, as the chapters themselves are more or less self-contained units within this book.

Learning about world religions prepares one for an increasingly globalized world, in which "spiritual literacy" can prove meaningful and possibly useful as well. *Bahá'í Faith: The Basics* offers essential information to assist readers in understanding and appreciating the ways in which the Bahá'í community fits into the larger picture of present and future social development. The information that this book provides on Bahá'í Faith is a contribution to "spiritual literacy," as educators say. Learning about world religions is a useful, and perhaps necessary, part of understanding what our increasingly globalized world is all about. Not only are Bahá'í social principles global in scope, they may even play an auxiliary role in the globalization process itself. As a former professor of world religions, the present writer's objective is to further promote "spiritual literacy" by way of providing some fundamental information about the Bahá'í religion, ideally in an interesting and engaging way.

The present book will include brief selections from representative Bahá'í scriptures throughout (primarily presented in text boxes) so that readers can read and experience the rich quality of these sacred texts. Bahá'u'lláh's writings alone comprise an estimated equivalent of one hundred volumes. One rather unique feature of the present book is that one chapter—Chapter Five: "Bahá'í Scripture and Authoritative Writings: Bahá'í Sacred Texts and Inspired Guidance"—is devoted to Bahá'í scriptures, in which selections are offered to give the reader a first-hand sense of how "the sacred" inspires, motivates, and guides Bahá'ís in their individual and collective lives. In certain parts of this book, the structure closely follows information that is presented on official Bahá'í websites today, in order to better ensure that *Bahá'í Faith: The Basics* offers an accurate and contemporary portrayal of this emerging world religion. Doing so ensures that information presented in this book is consistent with how the Bahá'í Faith is publicly represented on official Bahá'í websites.

Since this chapter is introductory and therefore brief, each of the foregoing Bahá'í precepts and practices will be explained more fully throughout the rest of this book.

SUMMARY

- The purpose of the Bahá'í Faith is to "unify the world."
- The Bahá'í Faith was co-founded by the Báb (1819–1850) in 1844 and by Bahá'u'lláh (1817–1892) in 1863.
- The Bahá'í Faith is the second-most widely diffused religion in the world today.
- Since 1996, Bahá'ís around the world have embarked on a systematic plan of individual and social transformation.

2

BELIEFS
BAHÁ'Í SPIRITUAL TEACHINGS

The Bahá'í Faith, as previously stated, is an independent world religion, with faith-communities established in nearly every country of the world. Bahá'í teachings offer sound principles, precepts, and practices for individuals and society alike. As with world religions generally, beliefs are ultimately a matter of individual faith and reason. So, it is up to the reader's own judgment as to how true, valid, and relevant Bahá'í beliefs and doctrines may be, as well as Bahá'í moral, ethical, and social principles. In any case, it is good to learn about the beliefs of religions generally, as this increases one's own "spiritual literacy," as religious studies professors often say, and enriches one's understanding and outlook as well. Therefore, before presenting Bahá'í beliefs in detail, it may be useful to say a few words about approaching world religions generally, as such an approach may be applied to the Bahá'í Faith particularly.

A USEFUL APPROACH TO THE
STUDY OF WORLD RELIGIONS,
INCLUDING THE BAHÁ'Í FAITH

The following approach to the teaching of all religions has been used by the present writer in the course of teaching world religions survey courses. At the beginning of each semester, an introductory lecture,

DOI: 10.4324/9780429023088-2

"World Religions in a Nutshell," would be presented to students in order to orient them to the "inner logic" (in the informal sense of the term) of world religions, to better understand how religious beliefs and actions cohere as dynamic worldviews. One useful approach to the introductory study of world religions is by way of a "disease/cure" model, which can be conceived as a problem/solution approach to the world.

Religions, simply put, try to cure the world's ills. The "cure" depends on the "illness" being treated. As the diagnoses vary, so do the remedies. The success rates of such cures vary as well. With each new social problem, moreover, a new remedy is needed. The illness/cure approach is an attempt to understand something of the internal logic of each religious system's way of coping with the human existential challenge. Although these paradigms differ, whatever solution, or remedy, a given religion may offer will naturally be in response to the overarching problem that a particular religion may set forth.

The world, after all, is full of problems that cry out for solutions. Religions offer solutions at the level of spiritual, moral, ethical, and social teachings. These solutions, of course, vary, and are often quite distinctive. So an appreciation of how a religion approaches the "human predicament," as scholars refer to it, can offer real insights into the inward rationale that motivates a particular religion's outward beliefs and practices. "Human predicament" means the fundamental problem facing humanity as a whole. How a religion responds to the human predicament, of course, varies, and repays serious study with a deeper understanding and appreciation for each religion's special outlook on life. World religions, seen in this light, are systems of salvation, liberation, or harmony. The salvation, liberation, or harmony that each world religion offers is in direct response to the human predicament, as perceived by each particular religion. The human predicament, as religiously defined, changes over time, and is partly a function of the day and age under consideration. Today's priorities and challenges are not the same as yesterday's.

Three simple (or simplified) examples—that of Christianity, Buddhism, and the Bahá'í Faith—should suffice to illustrate this point. In offering these three examples, no attempt is made to summarily reduce Christianity, Buddhism, or the Bahá'í Faith to the level of the illness/cure analogy itself, which is used primarily for illustrative purposes. Religions, after all, are complex systems and cannot—and therefore should not—be oversimplified. Over time, moreover, religions tend to diversify, often as a result of theological differences that may arise, whether by internal debates or outright schisms. Cultural differences may also play a role in the phenomenological variances that manifest in a particular religion, as it may expand geographically and as it may respond to varying circumstances historically. So, the examples of Christian, Buddhist, and Bahá'í soteriologies (doctrines of salvation, liberation, or harmony) are offered here primarily for illustrative purposes. The main point here is that religions present and promote their own overarching paradigms of salvation, liberation, or harmony, as the case may be. In brief, these three illness/cure paradigms, offered as examples of such an approach, are as follows:

- In Western Christianity, humanity is plagued with the problem of "sin." Therefore, Christianity offers "salvation from sin."
- Similarly, in early Buddhism, the "First Noble Truth" is that all life is suffering. So, it is equally logical that early Buddhism offered "liberation from suffering."
- From the perspective of the Bahá'í Faith—a new world religion that this book introduces—the human predicament is that of profound disunity, from family relations to international relations. A Bahá'í perspective on the human predicament may be further elaborated. On 20 January 1882, Bahá'u'lláh (1817–1892), the prophet-founder of the Bahá'í Faith, framed the world's overarching problem so:

> No two men can be found who may be said to be outwardly and inwardly united. The evidences of discord and malice are apparent everywhere, though all were made for harmony and union. The Great Being saith: O well-beloved ones! The tabernacle of unity hath been raised; regard ye not one another as strangers. Ye are the fruits of one tree, and the leaves of one branch. We cherish the hope that the light of justice may shine upon the world and sanctify it from tyranny.
>
> (Bahá'u'lláh, *Gleanings*, BRL)

Note how both problem and solution are presented here. The statement—"No two men can be found who may be said to be outwardly and inwardly united"—is clear, yet enigmatic. What is obvious is that the human predicament, as defined by Bahá'u'lláh, is that of profound and pervasive disunity. Such worldwide discord represents the gravest social ill facing humanity today. It is also obvious that the solution to this problem—or cure for this illness, to invoke the medical metaphor—is world unity.

BAHÁ'U'LLÁH AS THE DIVINE PHYSICIAN FOR THIS DAY AND AGE

The Bahá'í Faith, as said, has come to unify the world. This will not happen miraculously or magically. It will be the result of hard work, guided and directed by the Bahá'í teachings, which provide a blueprint for building a unified world. This blueprint is clear and compelling. Its focus on unity is profound, yet pragmatic. So, it makes perfect sense that the type of salvation—individual and social—that the Bahá'í Faith offers is that of unity, from family relations to international relations. One representative Bahá'í text that analyzes the human predicament from the standpoint of a disease/cure approach is as follows:

> The Prophets of God should be regarded as physicians whose task is to foster the well-being of the world and its peoples, that, through the spirit of oneness, they may heal the sickness of a divided humanity. To none is given the right to question their words or disparage their conduct, for they are the only ones who can claim to have understood the patient and to have correctly diagnosed its ailments. No man, however acute his perception, can ever hope to reach the heights which the wisdom and understanding of the Divine Physician have attained. Little wonder, then, if the treatment prescribed by the physician in this day should not be found to be identical with that which he prescribed before. How could it be otherwise when the ills affecting the sufferer necessitate at every stage of his sickness a special remedy? ... These are not days of prosperity and triumph. The whole of mankind is in the grip of manifold ills. Strive, therefore, to save its life through the wholesome medicine which the almighty hand of the unerring Physician hath prepared.
>
> (Bahá'u'lláh, *Gleanings*, BRL)

The Bahá'í Faith defines salvation both individually and collectively; both are dynamically interrelated. Each is bound up with the other. The destiny of the individual is connected with the destiny of society, and vice versa. In the "Tablet of the World" (1891), Bahá'u'lláh declared, "Let your vision be world-embracing, rather than confined to your own self" (Bahá'u'lláh, *Tablets*, BRL). Societies are in need of salvation as well. A spiritual solution, at the level of principle, and a practical application, at the level of implementation, is needed to address and resolve each and every pressing social problem that demands attention today. One way to refer to this betterment of society as a whole is "social salvation," although this term is not used in the Bahá'í writings (sacred scriptures) themselves. Bahá'u'lláh expresses the idea of social salvation in this way:

> That which is conducive to the regeneration of the world and the salvation of the peoples and kindreds of the earth hath been sent down from the heaven of the utterance of Him Who is the Desire of the world. Give ye a hearing ear to the counsels of the Pen of Glory.
>
> (Bahá'u'lláh, "Book of the Covenant," *Tablets*, BRL)

In this context, "salvation" is one of individual and social transformation and, as such, is not quite the same as the traditional Christian doctrine of Christ's "atonement" which is said to primarily effect salvation from sin individually. Bahá'u'lláh's mission and purpose, as expressed in terms of salvation, is to bring about world unity. Of course, "unity" is a deep, profound and complex concept.

Suffice it to say that the solutions that the Bahá'í Faith offers to the challenges and crises facing humanity today are both individual and collective in nature. When problems engulf the world as a whole, then solutions must be equally global in scope. Around 1870, Bahá'u'lláh, in his open epistle, or public letter, to Queen Victoria (1837–1901), proclaimed,

> That which the Lord hath ordained as the sovereign remedy and mightiest instrument for the healing of all the world is the union of all its peoples in one universal Cause, one common Faith. This can in no wise be achieved except through the power of a skilled, an all-powerful and inspired Physician.
>
> (Bahá'u'lláh, *Summons*, BRL)

In this passage, Bahá'u'lláh proclaims to Queen Victoria that he is the "skilled, an all-powerful and inspired Physician" whom God has sent for this day and age. This view of Bahá'u'lláh as the divine Physician is an important Bahá'í metaphor, and is a key to understanding and appreciating a core Bahá'í belief.

SEARCH AFTER TRUTH AS A
BASIC BAHÁ'Í TEACHING

Before all else, the Bahá'í teachings encourage search after truth. This is a basic Bahá'í teaching. Search after truth is a duty. Each individual has this duty. No one—not even clergy—can decide for an individual what he or she should believe. Truth, like beauty, is in the eye of the beholder—not in an absolute sense, of course, but relatively speaking. Of what benefit is the truth unless put to good use? How can the truth be known, absent the search for truth? Answers depend on questions. "Questions," in fact, is the name of one of the Bahá'í months in the special and unique Bahá'í Calendar of 19 months of 19 days each. Questing for truth leads to knowledge, which is another divine attribute that can and should be manifested as a human virtue. This brief mention of the Bahá'í principle of "search after truth" (or "independent investigation" of truth) serves as a prelude to the presentation of the basic Bahá'í spiritual teachings in this chapter.

BASIC BAHÁ'Í SPIRITUAL TEACHINGS

Just as science deals with the physical universe, religions deal with the spiritual universe. Both coexist. They are interconnected, one with the other. Reality therefore consists of both physical and metaphysical dimensions. According to Bahá'í belief, each human being lives in both physical and spiritual worlds of experience. The physical world is obvious. It is immediately perceived by the senses. The spiritual world is not so apparent. Perception is needed. Many people deny the existence of life's spiritual dimension. Religions serve to awaken individuals to their own spiritual reality. Consistent with this purpose, the Bahá'í Faith orients individuals and societies to the spiritual dynamic of human existence, and guides humanity morally, ethically, and socially. Without a healthy appreciation of the spiritual reality of the human person, the animal nature will predominate. Each individual, metaphorically speaking, has both angelic and demonic potentials. Spiritual growth and progress—which impacts physical growth and progress—is needed to awaken, activate, and actualize the potential of each person. This, in turn, will impact self and society in the "real world" of human affairs.

The selection and order of Bahá'í spiritual teachings, as presented in this chapter, are more or less based on the way the Bahá'í Faith is publicly presented on official Bahá'í websites, such as bahai.org, bahai. us, bahai.uk, etc. The primary purpose of this method of presentation is so that readers, when visiting these official Bahá'í websites, will already have a working familiarity with their approach and content. To acquaint readers with basic information and to enable them to understanding a formerly unfamiliar topic of interest is what an introductory book is for, after all. That said, the explanations that follow are the present writer's own. Therefore, the reader should understand that, while the author has made every effort to present the basic Bahá'í teachings as accurately as possible, the information offered here represents one individual's perspective. With this disclaimer in mind, this chapter's brief survey of essential Bahá'í teachings begins with a Bahá'í understanding of God and the world.

GOD AND THE WORLD

REVELATION BY AN OTHERWISE UNKNOWABLE GOD

The Bahá'í Faith is a monotheistic religion. "Monotheism" is a belief in one supreme deity. God is the great unknown. That said, God is the supreme mystery, with the greatest number of clues throughout the universe. Bahá'ís speak of God as an "unknowable essence." So how would Bahá'ís know that God is unknowable? For that matter, how is it that Bahá'ís—or anyone else for that matter—can "know" anything at all about God, if God is an unknowable essence? This is a fundamental question of epistemology (theory of knowledge). The answer may be summed up in one word: revelation. According to Bahá'í belief, God sends prophets and messengers, at critical turning points in history. This Bahá'í doctrine is more broadly and formally known as "progressive revelation," according to which God has sent, and will continue to send, spiritual teachers to the world, as needed, to guide humanity. Therefore, whatever the otherwise unknowable God reveals, that much will be knowable.

According to this view of sacred history, the great world religions have been founded by "manifestations of God" (see next section), each of whom brings a new message that conveys God's will for humanity, with renewed spiritual teachings and new social laws, according to the "exigencies" (i.e. specific needs) of the world (or that part of the world) at any given point in historical time. These sets of laws (which include moral and ethical teachings, instructions regarding worship, and other teachings pertaining to community life) necessarily differ, according to the requirements of historical time and place. These phenomenological differences should be respected and not be a cause of religious prejudice or sectarian strife.

God alone is the creator and sustainer of the universe. In a real sense, God is the creator actively and continuously. The universe is part of an ongoing process of creation and recreation. God created—and continues to create and recreate—the universe in order to be known, and did so as an act of love. God, the great unknown, desired to be known. In so saying, Bahá'ís are quick to point out that any and all descriptions of God are subject to human conceptualizations, which are the products of human ideation and imagination, and therefore are limited in scope. After all, God is infinite, while humans are finite. Therefore, by definition, human descriptions of God are subject to limitations. God cannot be defined, but only "apprehended." What is known of God is what God makes known by sending His (not gendered) "Manifestations" to humanity, who reveal certain key qualities about God—known as the "names" or "attributes" of God. These names or attributes, by which God is described, represent energies, powers, and other distinguishing characteristics of God.

The Bahá'í teachings about God are compatible with science and reason. This does not mean that the existence of God can be proved (or disproved) by scientific means or by rational proofs. Yet the Bahá'í doctrine of God is free from anthropomorphism, that is, free of ascribing human attributes to God. Although God can be experienced personally, God is not a person. God is made known primarily through the teachings of the messengers, that is, the manifestations of God as described in the next section.

MANIFESTATIONS OF GOD

A "Manifestation of God" is a special Bahá'í term for prophets and messengers of God who appear at key turning points in history, when humanity is in great need of spiritual renewal and social reform. Manifestations of God can be understood as appearances of God, or theophanies, or revealers of God. The manifestations of God are God's representatives—that is, God's ambassadors to humanity, according to Bahá'í belief. Each Manifestation of God has a special mission, or emphasis, notwithstanding the fact that all divinely revealed religions are "one" in essence. In other words, when Bahá'ís say, "all religions are one in essence," this is not to say that religions are identical or comparatively uniform, but rather that they share some fundamental similarities. This "oneness of religion" should be acknowledged universally, and is a powerful principle for promoting peace among religions.

That said, each religion is distinctive, each in its own way. Yet the Manifestations of God are "one" in spirit: "It is clear and evident to thee that all the Prophets are the Temples of the Cause of God, Who have appeared clothed in divers attire," Bahá'u'lláh explains, while hastening to add, "If thou wilt observe with discriminating eyes, thou wilt behold them all abiding in the same tabernacle, soaring in the same heaven, seated upon the same throne, uttering the same speech, and proclaiming the same Faith" (Bahá'u'lláh, *Gleanings*, BRL).

Bahá'í teachings emphasize the intrinsic spiritual unity of God's messengers over their extrinsic differences. The great Manifestations of God may be thought of as the founders of the world's religions (as well as prophets and messengers who appear later on). These spiritual teachers enlighten the world, illuminating the way. But their influence, no matter how profound, is limited. Just as God has sent a series of Manifestations of God in the past, God will continue to do so in the future. This is the fundamental teaching of the Bahá'í doctrine of progressive revelation. Each of the Manifestations of God has endowed religion with a spiritual and social purpose. (On possible indigenous messengers of God sent to the Americas in the Western Hemisphere, see the entry "Manifestation of God" in the Glossary of this book and see also Buck 2016.)

THE PURPOSE OF RELIGION

Religion has a universal purpose. According to Bahá'í belief, religion is the great civilizing influence—of past, present, and future. Religion is the primary source of moral and ethical teachings, which set the general standards of conduct of individual and social life. That being the case, it stands to reason that the decline of religion is associated with a corresponding decline in social stability, morality, and the overall quality of social life. The stability of all human affairs depends upon the sustained and sustaining moral and social influence of religion.

That said, the Bahá'í teachings also recognize and address the downside of religion. Religions are far from perfect. This is because of the imperfections of their followers. Over time, religions decline, and therefore, from time to time, religions may require spiritual and social renewal.

One of the major purposes of the Bahá'í Faith is to foster peace among religions. In further addressing this problem caused by the decline of religion, the Bahá'í teachings encourage ideal interfaith relations, which can go far in countering the negative influences caused by religious strife. In this respect, the Bahá'í doctrine of progressive revelation may be understood not only as a linear view of sacred history (i.e. that religions appear at key stages in history, and bring progressively new and fuller teachings and practices), but also as a means for advancing civilization in the present. In other words, the Bahá'í teachings, if wisely applied and accepted, can exert a progressive influence on religion in society today.

THE COMING OF AGE OF HUMANITY

Despite all its problems and setbacks, civilization moves forward. One of the purposes of a Bahá'í's life, in fact, is this: "All men have been created to carry forward an ever-advancing civilization" (Bahá'u'lláh, *Gleanings*, BRL). Bahá'ís not only believe in physical evolution (with certain qualifications), but also in spiritual and social evolution. The key developmental task that faces humanity today is to accept and accelerate its fundamental unity, i.e. the consciousness of the oneness of humankind. "In every Dispensation," 'Abdu'l-Bahá explains,

> "the light of Divine Guidance has been focused upon one central theme. ... In this wondrous Revelation, this glorious century, the foundation of the Faith of God, and the distinguishing feature of His Law, is the consciousness of the oneness of mankind.
> (quoted in Shoghi Effendi, *The Promised Day Is Come*, BRL)

As part of this collective maturation process, special attention is paid to international relations. After all, the world's peace and prosperity depend upon ideal international relations, as well as domestic peace and tranquility, based on a common recognition of the fundamental relatedness of all human beings to one another.

Progressive revelation, in fact, is all about spiritual and social evolution. The Bahá'í idea of "progressive revelation" is often explained by way of analogy to the growth and maturity of an individual. Purely as an analogy, compare religious history to a person, who is born as a baby, grows through childhood, becomes a teenager, and then matures as an adult. At each stage in an individual's moral and social development, guidance is needed. In much the same way, humanity progresses through its developmental stages as well, requiring spiritual and social guidance along the way. Religions, ideally, have provided such guidance throughout history. Humanity has now reached its coming of age and is on the verge of its social, institutional, and organic maturity, i.e unity.

THE LIFE OF THE SPIRIT

Religion, from a Bahá'í perspective, is all about spiritual and social transformation. Whatever affects the individual spiritually is bound to have social consequences, even if only as a "butterfly effect" (i.e. minor causes cumulatively contributing to major effects). The betterment of society can therefore be enhanced by actively promoting the spiritual vitality of its citizens. In the Bahá'í world today, a set of training materials is used as part of an initiative called "the institute process," which comprises a series of guided "study circles" in which the participants progress through a series of courses, based on study of these "Ruhi books." The first of these training materials is a small booklet, entitled, "Reflections on the Life of the Spirit" (published by the Ruhi Institute), which consists of three basic "spiritual foundation" sections: "Understanding the Bahá'í writings" (Unit 1), "Prayer" (Unit 2), and "Life and Death" (Unit 3). The subject matter of the following sections is largely addressed in "Reflections on the Life of the Spirit."

THE HUMAN SOUL

INTRODUCTION

The Bahá'í Faith offers spiritual teachings that are both individual and social in nature. A person's essence is the soul. The human soul is a distinct human reality, since it is fundamentally "rational" in nature. This is an important point of distinction, especially considering that many people today conceive of the human being as essentially a higher "animal." Human beings do possess an animal nature, often referred to in the Bahá'í writings as the "lower self." If the carnal "passions" that animate the"lower self predominate—unduly influencing one's thoughts and actions thereby—then the animal nature prevails over the spiritual nature. This is contrary to being truly human—which is to transform selfish passion into unselfish compassion, or empathy for others. The following sections highlight some of the more well-known Bahá'í teachings regarding the human soul.

THE RATIONAL SOUL

Human existence is one of discovery. Self-discovery involves recognition that, at the heart of human existence, is the soul. The soul is a profound mystery. Asked about the nature of the soul, Bahá'u'lláh responded:

> Thou hast asked Me concerning the nature of the soul. Know, verily, that the soul is a sign of God, a heavenly gem whose reality the most learned of men hath failed to grasp, and whose mystery no mind, however acute, can ever hope to unravel. It is the first among all created things to declare the excellence of its Creator, the first to recognize His glory, to cleave to His truth, and to bow down in adoration before Him. If it be faithful to God, it will reflect His light, and will, eventually, return unto Him. If it fail, however, in its allegiance to its Creator, it will become a victim to self and passion, and will, in the end, sink in their depths.
>
> (Bahá'u'lláh, *Gleanings*, BRL)

The distinctive quality of the human soul is that it is "rational" in nature. The ability to ideate—think in the abstract—allows for conceptualization, a capacity that, at best, is profoundly limited in the animal kingdom. That rational quality, although inherent in the soul itself, has to be developed. Rationality is the power of reason. But reason, alone, cannot realize its own intrinsic spiritual nature, unaided. Faith is usually required in order to come to this realization. Such "self-realization," as it is often referred to in popular discourse, has been described in Christian terms as being "born again." In this sense, "salvation" is not a static state of being, but a process of spiritual progress, which is the purpose of life. Connected with spiritual self-discovery is the recognition of God—i.e., the soul is "the first among all created things to declare the excellence of its Creator, the first to recognize His glory," as Bahá'u'lláh has explained in the passage above.

Although each and every human being is endowed with an immortal, rational soul, a person may not know it until the moment of spiritual self-realization, i.e. self-discovery of one's own "true self," as Bahá'u'lláh has put it: "Through the Teachings of this Day Star of Truth every man will advance and develop until he attaineth the station at which he can manifest all the potential forces with which his inmost true self hath been endowed" (Bahá'u'lláh, *Gleanings*, BRL). And further, "True loss is for him whose days have been spent in utter ignorance of his self" (Bahá'u'lláh, *Tablets*, BRL). Here, "true loss" implies its converse—that is, that true gain is to know one's own self in a deep and profound way, especially to fully realize the spiritual nature of one's inner self.

Bahá'u'lláh compares the soul to the sun: "The soul of man is the sun by which his body is illumined, and from which it draweth its sustenance, and should be so regarded" (Bahá'u'lláh, *Gleanings*, BRL). So the soul, by nature, is rational, immortal, and endowed with the potential to be goodly—and therefore godly—in character. That potential, however, has to be developed through spiritual discipline and service to others, which not only is of benefit to others, but also to the development and progress of the soul itself.

HUMAN NATURE

Philosophically, the Bahá'í writings speak of "essence" and "nature." As these terms relate to God, the essence of God can never be known. That said, aspects of the nature of God may be known by divine qualities, often referred to in the Bahá'í texts as the names or attributes of God. Consider this key passage by Bahá'u'lláh, who portrays the potential nobility and grandeur of the human soul:

> Nay, whatever is in the heavens and whatever is on the earth is a direct evidence of the revelation within it of the attributes and names of God, inasmuch as within every atom are enshrined the signs that bear eloquent testimony to the revelation of that most great Light. ... How resplendent the luminaries of knowledge that shine in an atom, and how vast the oceans of wisdom that surge within a drop! To a supreme degree is this true of man, who, among all created things, hath been

invested with the robe of such gifts, and hath been singled out for the glory of such distinction. For in him are potentially revealed all the attributes and names of God to a degree that no other created being hath excelled or surpassed. All these names and attributes are applicable to him. Even as He hath said: "Man is My mystery, and I am his mystery."

(Bahá'u'lláh, *Kitáb-i-Íqán*, BRL)

The human soul, being spiritual, can manifest attributes of God, to varying degrees—but if and only if it aspires and strives to do so. These attributes, moreover, may be regarded as dynamic "energies" or spiritual forces that pervade the entire creation—the soul included:

These energies with which the Day Star of Divine bounty and Source of heavenly guidance hath endowed the reality of man lie, however, latent within him, even as the flame is hidden within the candle and the rays of light are potentially present in the lamp.

(Bahá'u'lláh, *Gleanings*, BRL).

Transforming latency into potency requires a catalyst or synergist, as it were, which is stimulated and energized by the influence of Bahá'í teachings, when taken to heart. In other words, God's attributes or qualities are divine energies that can inspire, empower, and ennoble the human soul.

One way of understanding Bahá'í spirituality is to think of the various ways in which godly attributes can be transformed into goodly "virtues." One of the purposes of human existence, according to the Bahá'í teachings, is to acquire virtues—"to acquire such virtues as will exalt their stations among the peoples of the world" (Bahá'u'lláh, *Tablets*, BRL). Focus on virtues as been a major theme in Bahá'í moral education efforts, especially among children and youth. Virtues are synonymous with transforming godly qualities into a goodly character. The acquisition of virtues is one of the purposes, as well as outcomes, of spiritual development, from a Bahá'í perspective. Just as service to others is a moral compass, unity is a polestar, guiding one's actions in a positive direction, toward a social destination. Godlike attributes can become goodly virtues, where character and conscience combine to produce a life that bears much fruit. The Bahá'í Faith, therefore, contributes greatly to character development.

LIFE AND DEATH

Spirituality is a matter of life and death—that is, spiritual life and death. There may be physical consequences as well, in that a spiritual life is often a more healthy life physically as well as psychologically. The terms "life" and "death" are not literal, binary, either/or terms. Rather, as used in the Bahá'í writings metaphorically, life and death are used in a relative sense, primarily referring to the quality and degree of spiritual life, i.e., of personal and social consciousness. The Bahá'í religion provides resources for enhancing the positive character of human consciousness, which is seen as an overarching purpose—and ideal outcome—of religion itself. Bahá'ís do not believe in reincarnation, since the soul progresses throughout all the worlds of God. Such progress would not be furthered by returning to Earth, time and again.

The soul is intrinsically immortal, as previously said. In other words, there is life after death, according to the Bahá'í teachings. The quality of that afterlife depends largely on the quality of an individual's earthly life. It is not simply a matter of whether one's deeds were predominantly good or bad, but a matter of the consciousness associated with those deeds. Actions, after all, are simply the execution of prior decisions, motivated by intentions, whether noble or ignoble, and for good or for ill. The nature of the afterlife is portrayed by Bahá'u'lláh in exalted terms, as set forth in this well-known passage of Bahá'í scripture:

> And now concerning thy question regarding the soul of man and its survival after death. Know thou of a truth that the soul, after its separation from the body, will continue to progress until it attaineth the presence of God, in a state and condition which neither the revolution of ages and centuries, nor the changes and chances of this world, can alter. It will endure as long as the Kingdom of God, His sovereignty, His dominion and power will endure. It will manifest the signs of God and His attributes, and will reveal His loving kindness and bounty. ... The honor with which the Hand of Mercy will invest the soul is such as no tongue can adequately reveal, nor any other earthly agency describe. ....
> If any man be told that which hath been ordained for such a soul in the worlds of God, the Lord of the throne on high and of earth below, his whole being will instantly blaze out in his great longing to attain that most exalted, that sanctified and resplendent station.
>
> (Bahá'u'lláh, *Gleanings*, BRL)

The most frequent metaphor used in the Bahá'í writings to describe the nature of life after death is that of the child in the womb. Just as the child's life after birth is altogether different than life as a fetus in the womb, life after death is quite impossible to describe in terms that humans can understand and appreciate, since the next world is so far beyond the reach and ken of human experience. Having faith and assurance in an afterlife, moreover, enhances human nobility, since the conviction and confidence that the soul survives death adds a whole new dimension to the purpose of human existence. Physical life here on Earth is seen as a training ground for moral and spiritual development, not only as needed for life in the here and now, but in order to develop spiritual capacities for progress in the afterlife. In other words, the quality of the afterlife depends, in large part, on the quality of this earthly life.

DEGREES OF SPIRIT

There are degrees of existence, both physical and spiritual. Physical existence is limited. Spiritual existence is relatively unlimited. Degrees in the physical world, or levels (i.e. grades or categories) of material existence, are metaphorically described in Bahá'í texts as "kingdoms": i.e. mineral, vegetable, animal, and human realms. There is also the "Kingdom of God," as Jesus taught. In all, there are five categorical degrees of spirit, according to Bahá'í texts: (1) the vegetable spirit; (2) the animal spirit; (3) the human spirit; (4) the spirit of faith; and (5) the Holy Spirit ('Abdu'l-Bahá, *Promulgation*, BRL).

This five-kingdom classification system is not intended as scientific. Rather, it is a general observation that integrates spiritual reality with physical existence. The purpose of human existence is to advance and progress spiritually—little by little, degree by degree—in both this world and throughout the realms above, i.e. the heavenly worlds of being, which are beyond time and space, as discussed in the next section. Spiritual progress is aided by the inspiration of the Holy Spirit, which activates the "spirit of faith," in spiritually awakened individuals. Beyond that, it is up to the individual to progress, both materially and spiritually—and, where possible, to assist others to do likewise.

HEAVEN AND HELL

World religions, in general, teach that there is an afterlife. Christians and Muslims, generally speaking, have popularly regarded "Heaven" and "Hell" as places. This is not literally so, according to the Bahá'í teachings. Rather, Heaven and Hell are spiritual conditions, which are experienced in this life as well as in the afterlife. The quality of that afterlife depends on the quality of an individual's life here on Earth, as previously mentioned. The terms "Heaven" and "Hell" therefore refer to spiritual conditions, including the experience of "reward" (divine confirmations) and punishment (profound and painful regret and remorse), respectively. In the following passage, Bahá'u'lláh briefly explains the nature of heaven and hell:

> As to Paradise: It is a reality and there can be no doubt about it, and now in this world it is realized through love of Me and My good-pleasure. Whosoever attaineth unto it God will aid him in this world below, and after death He will enable him to gain admittance into Paradise whose vastness is as that of heaven and earth. ...
>
> Likewise apprehend thou the nature of hell-fire and be of them that truly believe. For every act performed there shall be a recompense according to the estimate of God, and unto this the very ordinances and prohibitions prescribed by the Almighty amply bear witness. For surely if deeds were not rewarded and yielded no fruit, then the Cause of God—exalted is He—would prove futile. ... However, unto them that are rid of all attachments a deed is, verily, its own reward.
>
> (Bahá'u'lláh, *Tablets*, BRL)

In this passage, the first experience of Heaven—i.e. of "Paradise" itself—is "now in this world" and is "realized" through the love of God (as represented by the Manifestation of God) and through divine "good-pleasure"—i.e. being well-pleasing to God, by living a moral, mindful, and fruitful life. Therefore, Heaven and Hell, not only are spiritual conditions—i.e, respectively, nearness to God and remoteness from God—but also the consequences of good and evil actions. Such spiritual ideas, expressed metaphorically, effectively disenchant traditional and popular Christian and Islamic notions of a celestial Paradise, with all its pleasures, and a literal Hell, with all its torments. This is not meant to criticize such concrete beliefs, but to offer familiar examples by which Bahá'í perspectives may be better understood and appreciated.

DEVOTION

INTRODUCTION

Devotion is love—especially the love of God. The devotional life, therefore, involves prayer, meditation, fasting, pilgrimage, work, and service. Since there is a relationship between the individual and the collective, Bahá'í spiritual teachings can be seen as having a social component. This social dimension often takes the form of service to others. The following sections briefly describe the highlights and hall-marks of the ideal Bahá'í devotional life.

PRAYER

Prayer is regarded as a spiritual form of communication, that is, com-munion with God. Bahá'í prayer has been characterized as "con-versation with God." Although interactive and spiritually dynamic in nature, this is not a two-way conversation in the ordinary sense. Rather, prayer is a supplication to God, ideally followed by reflection and action. Prayer can take many forms. It can be spontaneous, or it can be recited. Bahá'ís have many prayers that have been revealed by the Báb, Bahá'u'lláh, and 'Abdu'l-Bahá. The more popular and/or well-known prayers have been published in the Bahá'í prayer books, and are used during Bahá'í communal worship as well.

From a Bahá'í perspective, the way in which prayer is "answered" is not a matter of asking God for something, and then waiting for an answer. The answer to prayer has as much to do with the individual offering the prayer as it does with God who "hears" (although not lit-erally so) the prayer itself. This is because of how prayer works. The way in which prayer is fulfilled, according to the Bahá'í teachings, is by increasing the capacity of the individual who offers the prayer, as stated in this enlightening explanation by 'Abdu'l-Bahá regarding the nature and dynamics of prayer:

> Know thou, verily it is becoming in a weak one to supplicate to the Strong One, and it behooveth a seeker of bounty to beseech the Glorious Bountiful One. When one supplicates to his Lord, turns to Him and seeks bounty from His Ocean, this supplication brings light to his heart, illumination to his sight, life to his soul and exaltation to his being.
>
> During thy supplications to God and thy reciting, "Thy Name is my healing," consider how thine heart is cheered, thy soul delighted by the spirit of the love of God, and thy mind attracted to the Kingdom of God! By these attractions one's ability and capacity increase. When the vessel is enlarged the water increases, and when the thirst grows the bounty of the cloud becomes agreeable to the taste of man. This is the mystery of supplication and the wisdom of stating one's wants.
>
> ('Abdu'l-Bahá, quoted in Esslemont, BRL)

In the Bahá'í view, prayer is not answered miraculously or capriciously by divine decree. Rather, a prayer requires follow-up for its fulfillment. If prayer is regarded as seeking divine assistance, then such assistance requires that the individual takes action pursuant to the prayer itself. Such assistance does not mean that a prayer will be granted automatically. Rather, in order to fulfill and thereby "complete" the prayer, the individual needs to think about what to do, decide to do so, and then take action. If successful, then the prayer can said to have been answered. Prayer, from this Bahá'í perspective, is dynamic—i.e. active, not passive. In other words, prayer is not a magic formula for invoking a miracle, at will. Prayer mobilizes willpower, and guides it aright, if all goes well. There is no guarantee, of course, that a prayer will be granted as requested. In this sense, all prayer is answered potentially, and only in accordance with the wisdom of God:

> He [God] answers the prayer of this plant. The plant prays potentially, "O God! Send me rain!" God answers the prayer, and the plant grows. God will answer anyone. He answers prayers potentially. ...
>
> But we ask for things which the divine wisdom does not desire for us, and there is no answer to our prayer. His wisdom does not sanction what we wish. We pray, "O God! Make me wealthy!" If this prayer were universally answered, human affairs would be at a standstill. There would be none left to work in the streets, none to till the soil, none to build, none to run the trains. Therefore, it is evident that it would not be well for us if all prayers were answered. The affairs of the world would be interfered with, energies crippled and progress hindered. But whatever we ask for which is in accord with divine wisdom, God will answer. Assuredly!
>
> ('Abdu'l-Bahá, *Promulgation*, BRL)

Prayer, as described above, is all about increasing one's capacity and then activating and actualizing that potential by taking decisive action. In this sense, prayer can have thought, force, and direction—and favorably positive outcomes, if in accordance with divine wisdom, and depending also on the particular facts and circumstances, which, to a great extent, may dictate whether a prayer is realistic or not—that is, whether feasible, or impossible—as well as being practical and beneficial in nature.

MEDITATION

Meditation, as understood from a Bahá'í perspective, is the power of human reflection. Human beings think and reflect as part of their daily lives. Meditation, then, is the discipline of concentrating the power of reflection. In other words, meditation, can take the form of pondering deeply on a particular question or problem, in order to find an answer or solution. Meditation can follow prayer, especially if the prayer is focused on achieving a particular outcome, or developing a quality of character, or virtue. Meditation can therefore lead to a decision, followed by action.

Bahá'ís are free to meditate whatever way they choose. There is no prescribed Bahá'í form of meditation. The Bahá'í encouragement to meditate is general, rather than specific, in nature. Throughout Bahá'í texts, the phrase, "prayer and meditation," is frequently seen as a recurring pair of related terms.

FASTING

Bahá'ís regularly fast from sunrise to sunset each year during the first three weeks of March. In addition to abstaining from food and drink during the fasting period, Bahá'ís are encouraged to focus more intensively on spiritual matters, especially during this time of increased detachment from physical concerns. The Bahá'í Fast is therefore considered an especially important time during the Bahá'í calendar year. Exempt from the Fast are those who are pregnant, ill, elderly, or who are traveling long distances. Bahá'ís may eat breakfast prior to sunrise, and are expected to have dinner after sunset, during the duration of the Fast. It is a time of spiritual devotion, discipline, and meditation. There are special Bahá'í prayers for the Fast.

Fasting is a physical and spiritual discipline. Fasting, ideally, cultivates detachment. Physical detachment—from food, for instance—is good training for spiritual detachment. Detachment does not mean withdrawal from the world or disengagement from it. Rather, detachment entails not being controlled by desires or by passions. This is not to say that desires or passions are intrinsically wrong, in and of themselves. Passions have their place, yet should be kept in check, i.e. in moderation, such that a healthy balance is maintained, especially so that one's actions are not dominated by desires and passions as sole or primary motivations in human conduct.

PILGRIMAGE

Pilgrimage, generally speaking, is religious visitation of holy places. In the Bahá'í religion, pilgrimage, at present, takes the form of praying in the Bahá'í Shrines in Haifa and Akko (Akka), Israel. The Shrine of the Báb, as the name implies, is where the Báb is buried. The Báb (1819–1850) was the prophet-herald who foretold the imminent advent of Bahá'u'lláh (1817–1892), the prophet-founder of the Bahá'í Faith. The Shrine of Bahá'u'lláh, similarly, is where Bahá'u'lláh is buried. What makes these two pilgrimage sites holy is the fact that Báb and Bahá'u'lláh themselves were holy, being the two Messengers of God for this day and age, according to Bahá'í belief.

WORK AND SERVICE

Work is worship, according to the Bahá'í teachings. That is to say, work performed in the spirit of service is accounted as an expression of true piety. In that sense, work is prayer in action. Work is dynamic worship. Taking the work-as-worship analogy further, work becomes a prayer with a positive outcome that benefits both the individual and society.

Since work is livelihood, life is sustained. Beyond working for one's survival, there is a strong Bahá'í work ethic of excellence as well as service. Excellence is relative, of course, to one's abilities. That said, excellence remains a gold standard of the Bahá'í work ethic. This is yet another example of an individual, spiritual obligation that has a social benefit.

CHARACTER AND CONDUCT

INTRODUCTION

The Bahá'í teachings aim to enhance human nobility by refining its character. The development of virtues, i.e. positive moral qualities, is also greatly encouraged. The proof of a sterling character is in exemplary conduct. On the importance of good character, Bahá'u'lláh states:

The third Taráz concerneth good character. A good character is, verily, the best mantle for men from God. With it He adorneth the temples of His loved ones. By My life! The light of a good character surpasseth the light of the sun and the radiance thereof. Whoso attaineth unto it is accounted as a jewel among men. The glory and the upliftment of the world must needs depend upon it.

(Bahá'u'lláh, *Tablets*, BRL)

Character and conduct are interrelated. Cultivating a good character is one of the primary purposes of being a Bahá'í. In so doing, not only does the individual benefit personally, but the wider society as well, as Bahá'u'lláh promises, "Whoso ariseth, in this Day, to aid Our Cause, and summoneth to his assistance the hosts of a praiseworthy character and upright conduct, the influence flowing from such an action will, most certainly, be diffused throughout the whole world" (Bahá'u'lláh, *Gleanings*, BRL)

DIVINE LAW

Law, in common usage, refers to civil and criminal law, as well as statutory and administrative regulations. Obviously, laws are to be obeyed. The same holds true for spiritual "laws." Such laws are considered to be divinely ordained insofar as they represent the will of God for humanity. Bahá'í laws are codified in the Kitáb-i-Aqdas, *The Most Holy Book*, revealed by Bahá'u'lláh in 1873 (Bahá'u'lláh, *Kitáb-i-Aqdas*, BRL). These laws are meant to refine human character, to establish a well-ordered society, and to enhance civilization. Not all of Bahá'u'lláh's laws are currently in force, since some of them may be impracticable where civil, criminal, and administrative laws preclude the practice of some Bahá'í laws for the time being.

LOVE AND KNOWLEDGE

Like character and conduct, the love and knowledge of God go together, like heart and mind. Love of God is an expression of the knowledge of God. In *Some Answered Questions*, in the chapter "Good Deeds and Their Spiritual Prerequisites," 'Abdu'l-Bahá explains that good deeds, standing alone, are praiseworthy, yet are imperfect if not enriched by the knowledge and love of God. Otherwise, such deeds are devoid of spirit. The knowledge and love of God endow all good deeds with an added dimension of significance and influence, which is why the knowledge and love of God are considered spiritual prerequisites in perfecting good deeds, and giving them added effect.

The knowledge and love of God have horizontal as well as vertical dimensions. If the heart is full, it overflows. Like a whirling dervish, expressions of love for God are centrifugal—they radiate, in a broadcast way, to others. If such devotion to God edifies the individual, it surely is worthy of wisely and lovingly sharing with family, friends, and acquaintances, depending on their interest and receptivity. This is one of the primary motivations for Bahá'ís, the world over, to host and to hold devotional gatherings (Bahá'í prayer services) in their homes, to spiritually elevate their neighborhoods in the process of "community building," which is a major emphasis across the Bahá'í world today.

TRUTHFULNESS, TRUSTWORTHINESS, AND JUSTICE

Truthfulness, trustworthiness, and justice are regarded as cardinal Bahá'í virtues, which have pride of place and deserve special mention. On the importance of truthfulness, 'Abdu'l-Bahá has stated,

> Truthfulness is the foundation of all the virtues of the world of humanity. Without truthfulness, progress and success in all of the worlds of God are impossible for a soul. When this holy attribute is established in man, all the divine qualities will also become realized.
>
> (Shoghi Effendi, *Advent*, BRL)

As for trustworthiness, Bahá'u'lláh has emphasized its importance in this remarkable passage:

> The fourth Taráz concerneth trustworthiness. Verily it is the door of security for all that dwell on earth and a token of glory on the part of the All-Merciful. He who partaketh thereof hath indeed partaken of the treasures of wealth and prosperity. Trustworthiness is the greatest portal leading unto the tranquillity and security of the people. In truth the stability of every affair hath depended and doth depend upon it. All the domains of power, of grandeur and of wealth are illumined by its light.
>
> Not long ago these sublime words were revealed from the Pen of the Most High:

"We will now mention unto thee Trustworthiness and the station thereof in the estimation of God, thy Lord, the Lord of the Mighty Throne. One day of days We repaired unto Our Green Island. Upon Our arrival, We beheld its streams flowing, and its trees luxuriant, and the sunlight playing in their midst. Turning Our face to the right, We beheld what the pen is powerless to describe; nor can it set forth that which the eye of the Lord of Mankind witnessed in that most sanctified, that most sublime, that blest, and most exalted Spot. Turning, then, to the left We gazed on one of the Beauties of the Most Sublime Paradise, standing on a pillar of light, and calling aloud saying:

'O inmates of earth and heaven! Behold ye My beauty, and My radiance, and My revelation, and My effulgence. By God, the True One! I am Trustworthiness and the revelation thereof, and the beauty thereof. I will recompense whosoever will cleave unto Me, and recognize My rank and station, and hold fast unto My hem. I am the most great ornament of the people of Bahá, and the vesture of glory unto all who are in the kingdom of creation. I am the supreme instrument for the prosperity of the world, and the horizon of assurance unto all beings'."

Thus have We sent down for thee that which will draw men nigh unto the Lord of creation.

(Bahá'u'lláh, *Tablets*, BRL)

In this remarkable passage, Bahá'u'lláh vividly recounts a vision of "Trustworthiness" which (or who) is suddenly brought to life, animated, and personified. This angelic being—the very incarnation of Trustworthiness—calls out to the denizens of Earth and Heaven. This fascinating passage presents a strong message (especially to all Bahá'ís) of just how important the virtue of trustworthiness is to the integrity of all interpersonal relationships—on which reciprocal confidence, reliability, and mutual trust must ultimately depend. This striking vignette—a dramatic scene in one act—exemplifies the rich tapestry of Bahá'u'lláh's writings—the ethical, moral, and social aspects of which are enriched by such literary devices as personification. As for "justice," the following is Bahá'u'lláh's most well-known and celebrated statement:

O SON OF SPIRIT! The best beloved of all things in My sight is Justice; turn not away therefrom if thou desirest Me, and neglect it not that I may confide in thee. By its aid thou shalt see with thine own eyes and not through the eyes of others, and shalt know of thine own knowledge and not through the knowledge of thy neighbor. Ponder this in thy heart; how it behooveth thee to be. Verily justice is My gift to thee and the sign of My loving-kindness. Set it then before thine eyes.

(Bahá'u'lláh, *Hidden Words*, BRL)

The notion of "justice" here is "fairness," an ethic that can be, and should be, practiced by all individuals. This is not "justice" as to its enforcement, which is not the prerogative of individuals, but of institutions, their role being to investigate specific acts of injustice and, upon a finding of guilt, to pass judgment and then to sentence.

PURITY OF HEART

In the Bahá'í writings, purity of heart primarily refers to intention and the degree to which one is motivated to do good for others. In other words, the purer the heart, the more noble the intention, and the less selfish the action. Purity of heart is a matter of degree. Bahá'í texts commonly compare the heart to a mirror. In 19th-century Persia (present-day Iran) and reaching back into antiquity, mirrors were typically made of polished bronze, which were susceptible to rust. Rust (and dust) obscure the image reflected in the mirror, which must be burnished so that it may once again reflect the light of divine attributes, as Bahá'u'lláh states in these two brief passages:

O My Brother! A pure heart is as a mirror; cleanse it with the burnish of love and severance from all save God, that the true sun may shine within it and the eternal morning dawn.

(Bahá'u'lláh, *Call*, BRL)

O SON OF GLORY! Be swift in the path of holiness, and enter the heaven of communion with Me. Cleanse thy heart with the burnish of the spirit, and hasten to the court of the Most High.

(Bahá'u'lláh, *Hidden Words*, BRL)

Here, the heart—as a mirror of godly attributes transformed into goodly virtues—requires continual burnishing and polishing by way of vigilance, self-reflection, discipline, and a service to others. Ideally, the heart may be transformed from selfishness into altruism. This is how "purity of heart" is typically portrayed in the Bahá'í writings.

HUMILITY AND TRUST

A praiseworthy character is comprised of a wide range of virtues, including humility. Generally, humility is the polar opposite of pride. Pride is generally frowned upon in the Bahá'í writings, with rare exceptions, such as this: "Take pride not in love for yourselves but in love for your fellow-creatures. Glory not in love for your country, but in love for all mankind" (Bahá'u'lláh, *Tablets*, BRL). Numerous Bahá'í texts discourage pride and vainglory, especially when one feels superior to others. Just as many Bahá'í texts encourage humility. Being humble is not the same thing as being ingratiating. Humility does not require self-deprecation. Rather, humility is its own nobility. The following passage, which is one of the most celebrated and often quoted of Bahá'u'lláh's writings, is his advice to one of his sons. Note how this advice ends with an exhortation to humility:

> Be generous in prosperity, and thankful in adversity. Be worthy of the trust of thy neighbor, and look upon him with a bright and friendly face. Be a treasure to the poor, an admonisher to the rich, an answerer of the cry of the needy, a preserver of the sanctity of thy pledge. Be fair in thy judgment, and guarded in thy speech. Be unjust to no man, and show all meekness to all men. Be as a lamp unto them that walk in darkness, a joy to the sorrowful, a sea for the thirsty, a haven for the distressed, an upholder and defender of the victim of oppression. Let integrity and uprightness distinguish all thine acts. Be a home for the stranger, a balm to the suffering, a tower of strength for the fugitive. Be eyes to the blind, and a guiding light unto the feet of the erring. Be an ornament to the countenance of truth, a crown to the brow of fidelity, a pillar of the temple of righteousness, a breath of life to the body of mankind, an ensign of the hosts of justice, a luminary above the horizon of virtue, a dew to the soil of the human heart, an ark on the ocean of knowledge, a sun in the heaven of bounty, a gem on the diadem of wisdom, a shining light in the firmament of thy generation, a fruit upon the tree of humility.
>
> (Bahá'u'lláh, *Gleanings*, BRL)

Trust in God is another Bahá'í virtue. Trust in God is the "source of all good." (See the very next passage below.) Trust is a universal virtue, as are all virtues. Trusting in God means to have faith that

God will provide the means when the way forward is uncertain, yet worthwhile. Trust in God attracts divine confirmations when efforts are good and worthy: "The source of all good is trust in God, submission unto His command, and contentment with His holy will and pleasure" (Bahá'u'lláh, "Words of Wisdom," *Tablets*, BRL). Trusting in God means going forward with a faith that inspires a measure of confidence and which, in and of itself, may prove to be a key factor in the successful outcome of any important undertaking, such as earning a living:

> Concerning the means of livelihood, thou shouldst, while placing thy whole trust in God, engage in some occupation. He will assuredly send down upon thee from the heaven of His favour that which is destined for thee. He is in truth the God of might and power.
>
> (Bahá'u'lláh, *Tablets*, BRL)

OTHER BAHÁ'Í SPIRITUAL TEACHINGS

The Bahá'í spiritual teachings presented in this chapter are basic to Bahá'í life and experience. Much more could be said about each of the Bahá'í beliefs outlined above. As an example of an advanced exposition of Bahá'í teachings, the late Bahá'í scholar, Dr. Udo Schaefer (d. 2019), wrote a two-volume treatise on Bahá'í ethics, which reflects a profound and thoroughgoing discussion of the topic (Schaefer 2007). Readers are therefore encouraged to read further, pursuant to any interest they may have. There are many other Bahá'í spiritual teachings as well. What has been presented in this chapter are just a few highlights.

Suffice it to say that the Bahá'í writings offer a wealth of profound insights and reliable guidance as to how best conduct one's life, for one's own good and especially for the good of others. This brief overview of Bahá'í spiritual teachings is not only meant to provide a useful introduction, but to spark interest in some readers to further investigate the Bahá'í teachings as well. In the next chapter, some basic Bahá'í social teachings will be presented. These Bahá'í social principles complement—i.e. complete—the Bahá'í spiritual teachings, as outlined above. These two sets of teachings are dynamically interrelated, as, for example, Bahá'í individual ethics and Bahá'í social ethics. Bahá'í spiritual teachings are universal in scope. They really do not distinguish between Bahá'ís and others, insofar as these teachings apply to everyone. They are meant to contribute to the betterment of all, and to serve as a practical and useful guide for individuals, families, communities, races, religions, and nations, from family relations to international relations.

SUMMARY

- One approach to the study of world religions is the disease/cure model.
- World religions are systems of salvation, liberation, or harmony.
- The salvation, liberation, or harmony that each world religion offers is in direct response to the "human predicament," as perceived by each particular religion.
- "Human predicament" means the fundamental problem—or grave social ill—facing humanity.
- Bahá'u'lláh wrote, "No two men can be found who may be said to be outwardly and inwardly united."
- The Bahá'í Faith is a monotheistic religion.
- God is the supreme mystery, with the greatest number of clues throughout the universe.
- Manifestations of God are sent at key turning points in history.
- Each Manifestation of God has a special mission, or emphasis.
- "Progressive revelation" is all about spiritual and social evolution.
- The soul is a profound mystery.
- The human soul is rational and immortal.
- The human soul, being spiritual, can manifest attributes of God, to varying degrees.
- Godly "attributes" can be transformed into goodly "virtues."
- Work, done in the spirit of service, is considered worship.
- Bahá'ís strive to develop good character by acquiring virtues, or positive moral qualities.
- Character and conduct are interrelated.
- A good character also involves following divine laws, including good morals and ethics.
- Bahá'í laws are meant to refine human character.
- There are many other Bahá'í spiritual and social teachings.

3

PRINCIPLES
BAHÁ'Í SOCIAL TEACHINGS

BAHÁ'Í PRINCIPLES—NEW AND RENEWED

The Bahá'í Faith, as noted earlier, is a new and independent world religion. This book, *Bahá'í Faith: The Basics*, is one introduction in a rich legacy of introductions to the Bahá'í Faith. So, it may be useful to consider how the Bahá'í Faith has been presented in the past, in order to appreciate some of its new and distinctive features in the present day. With the advent of the new religion, naturally, new religious teachings would be expected. This certainly holds true with the appearance of the Bahá'í Faith on the world's historical horizon, in the full glare of modernity.

As readers will recall, Bahá'u'lláh (1817–1892) had designated his eldest son, 'Abdu'l-Bahá (1844–1921), as the former's successor, interpreter, and exemplar. (See Chapter 4.) 'Abdu'l-Bahá's talks were many. His grandson and appointed successor, Shoghi Effendi (1897–1957), wrote that 'Abdu'l-Bahá

> had arisen not only to proclaim from pulpit and platform, in some of the chief capitals of Europe and in the leading cities of the North American continent, *the distinctive verities enshrined in His Father's Faith*, but to demonstrate as well the Divine origin of the Prophets gone before Him, and to disclose the nature of the tie binding them to that Faith.
>
> (Shoghi Effendi, *God Passes By*, BRL)(italics added)

DOI: 10.4324/9780429023088-3

This chapter will adopt a somewhat novel approach, based on an old one, by focusing on a couple of speeches by 'Abdu'l-Bahá, presented in America in 1912. What makes these two speeches important and relevant is that 'Abdu'l-Bahá focused on what he himself identified as "new" teachings brought by Bahá'u'lláh. Since the term "new" may be somewhat elastic and relative, perhaps a better descriptor would be the term, "distinctive," with respect to the Bahá'í teachings that will be surveyed in this chapter.

Of course, many of the Bahá'í spiritual, ethical, and moral teachings—and, to certain extent, some of its doctrinal teachings as well—resonate with similar teachings found in earlier religions. Those resonances create a kind of spiritual harmonics, worthy of appreciation. In that sense, the Bahá'í teachings effectively revoice and thereby "renew" the venerable teachings of prior religions. This fact, of course, is significant and important, in and of itself. But, for the purposes of this introduction, this chapter focuses on the relatively new Bahá'í teachings, as previously privileged and presented by 'Abdu'l-Bahá. In so doing, this will serve to highlight an aspect of Bahá'í history that has contemporary relevance today. In presenting these new teachings, no absolute claims to exclusivity are being made. Rather, such new Bahá'í teachings are important to consider in any basic overview of the Bahá'í Faith. These novel teachings primarily take the form of what may be considered to be modern-day social principles.

"New" is a relative term, as far as ideas go. In the history of ideas, many, if not most, important ideas may have their roots in past notions articulated centuries ago. Just about any idea may have its precursors. The legacy of any given concept therefore can be analyzed within a "history of ideas" approach, in which a "trajectory" of any given idea may be mapped out over time. Many major ideas, in their respective historical contexts, may be traced back to their roots, often to antiquity. However, this is not to say that any present-day idea can necessarily be fully explained and accounted for by reference to its ideological predecessors. Nor is it necessary, or even methodologically valid, to reduce any given idea to a "genetic" chain of origination. While some modern ideas may have been anticipated in the past, their current expression is properly regarded as new. Here, "new" will be used to refer to specific, noteworthy Bahá'í teachings that may be regarded as relatively original and recent within the history of religions.

These new Bahá'í teachings have received special emphasis in some of 'Abdu'l-Bahá's talks—especially in America in 1912—that specifically focus on Bahá'u'lláh's distinctive principles. For instance, on Sunday, 14 July 1912, 'Abdu'l-Bahá spoke in the All Souls Unitarian Church, Fourth Avenue (now Park Avenue South) and Twentieth Street, in West Englewood, New York. (15–17 November 2019 marks the bicentennial of the founding of the All Souls Church.) There, the pastor of the church, Rev. Leon A. Harvey, had advertised 'Abdu'l-Bahá's public appearance in the local newspapers and also posted announcements outside the church. After Rev. Harvey introduced his guest speaker, 'Abdu'l-Bahá addressed the congregation. "First," 'Abdu'l-Bahá explained, "He [Bahá'u'lláh] has proclaimed the oneness of mankind *and specialized religious teachings for existing human conditions*" ('Abdu'l-Bahá, *Promulgation*, BRL) (italics added). The other principles set forth during the rest of 'Abdu'l-Bahá's talk were also presented in the context of Bahá'u'lláh's "specialized religious teachings for existing human conditions" current in the 20th-century in 1912, the year that 'Abdu'l-Bahá spoke throughout the United States and Canada.

'Abdu'l-Bahá may have assumed that his audiences understood that Bahá'u'lláh's "specialized religious teachings," for the most part, were quite new. Probably some audience members did appreciate that fact. Such a perception may have been fairly obvious in the minds of many who attended these events, although it is impossible to know for certain. Yet we do know that there were others who openly questioned just how distinctive these new teachings of Bahá'u'lláh really were. It was only a matter of time before such questions were bound to arise. So, on Friday, 15 November 1912, also in New York, 'Abdu'l-Bahá was asked the following question: "What has Bahá'u'lláh brought that we have not heard before?" 'Abdu'l-Bahá himself refers to this very question—one that was posed directly to him, in fact:

I have spoken in the various Christian churches and in the synagogues, and in no assemblage has there been a dissenting voice. All have listened, and all have conceded that the teachings of Bahá'u'lláh are superlative in character, acknowledging that they constitute the very essence or spirit of this new age and that there is no better pathway to the attainment of its ideals. Not a single voice has been raised in objection. At most there have been some who have refused to acknowledge the mission of Bahá'u'lláh, although even these have admitted that He was a great teacher, a most powerful soul, a very great man. Some who could find no other pretext have said, "These teachings are not new;

they are old and familiar; we have heard them before." Therefore, I will speak to you upon the distinctive characteristics of the manifestation of Bahá'u'lláh and prove that from every standpoint His Cause is distinguished from all others. It is distinguished by its didactic character and method of exposition, by its practical effects and application to present world conditions, but especially distinguished from the standpoint of its spread and progress.

('Abdu'l-Bahá, Promulgation, BRL)

'Abdu'l-Bahá's opening statement, at this public meeting held in the home of Bahá'í artist, Julia Thompson, is quoted, in full, for the simple reason that few, if any, other such declarations by 'Abdu'l-Bahá, available in English, state the case so clearly, i.e. that Bahá'u'lláh's teachings are *sui generis* (Latin, literally "of its own kind")—that is, unique in the history of religions. This same question, in fact, came up again a little over two weeks later. On Monday, 2 December 1912, 'Abdu'l-Bahá gave a talk in New York on the "the special teachings of Bahá'u'lláh" in direct response to the question: "You have asked me what new principles have been revealed by Him" ('Abdu'l-Bahá, *Promulgation*, BRL). In answer to this excellent question, 'Abdu'l-Bahá had responded:

I will speak to you concerning *the special teachings of Bahá'u'lláh*. All the divine principles announced by the tongue of the Prophets of the past are to be found in the words of Bahá'u'lláh; *but in addition to these He has revealed certain new teachings which are not found in any of the sacred Books of former times.* I shall mention some of them; the others, which are many in number, may be found in the Books, Tablets and Epistles written by Bahá'u'lláh—such as the Hidden Words, the Glad Tidings, the Words of Paradise, Tajallíyát, Ṭarázát and others. Likewise, in the *Kitáb-i-Aqdas* there are *new teachings which cannot be found in any of the past Books or Epistles of the Prophets.* ...

1. A fundamental teaching of Bahá'u'lláh is the oneness of the world of humanity. ...
2. Another *new principle* revealed by Bahá'u'lláh is the injunction to investigate truth—that is to say, no man should blindly follow his ancestors and forefathers. ...
3. Bahá'u'lláh has announced that the foundation of all the religions of God is one, that oneness is truth and truth is oneness which does not admit of plurality. *This teaching is new and specialized to this Manifestation.*

4. He sets forth a *new principle* for this day in the announcement that religion must be the cause of unity, harmony and agreement among mankind. ...

5. Furthermore, He proclaims that religion must be in harmony with science and reason. ... *The harmony of religious belief with reason is a new vista which Bahá'u'lláh has opened for the soul of man.*

6. He establishes the equality of man and woman. *This is peculiar to the teachings of Bahá'u'lláh*, for all other religions have placed man above woman.

7. A *new religious principle* is that prejudice and fanaticism—whether sectarian, denominational, patriotic or political—are destructive to the foundation of human solidarity; therefore, man should release himself from such bonds in order that the oneness of the world of humanity may become manifest.

8. Universal peace is assured by Bahá'u'lláh as a fundamental accomplishment of the religion of God—that peace shall prevail among nations, governments and peoples, among religions, races and all conditions of mankind. *This is one of the special characteristics of the Word of God revealed in this Manifestation.*

9. Bahá'u'lláh declares that all mankind should attain knowledge and acquire an education. This is a necessary principle of religious belief and observance, *characteristically new in this dispensation.*

10. He has set forth the solution and provided the remedy for the economic question. *No religious Books of the past Prophets speak of this important human problem.*

11. He has ordained and established the House of Justice. ... Its rulings shall be in accordance with the commands and teachings of Bahá'u'lláh. ...

12. As to the most great characteristic of the revelation of Bahá'u'lláh, *a specific teaching not given by any of the Prophets of the past*: It is the ordination and appointment of the Center of the Covenant.

('Abdu'l-Bahá, *Promulgation*, BRL)
(italics and numbers added)

'Abdu'l-Bahá explicitly cites some of Bahá'u'lláh's most well-known "Tablets" (sacred writings)—"such as the Hidden Words, the Glad Tidings, the Words of Paradise, Tajallíyát, Ṭarázát and others" including the *Kitáb-i-Aqdas*—although these texts were not widely available in the West at that time. (These Bahá'í sacred writings will be discussed in Chapter Five: "Scripture and Authoritative Writings: Bahá'í Sacred Texts and Inspired Guidance.") After being asked which of Bahá'u'lláh's teachings were new, 'Abdu'l-Bahá gave some definite and explicit answers—this time, making sure that there could be no ambiguity as to the relative distinctiveness of Bahá'u'lláh's teachings. 'Abdu'l-Bahá's claims to the new and unique nature of Bahá'u'lláh's precepts should be understood and appreciated as relative, rather than absolute, in nature—since the roots of some of these teachings may be traced back, in various forms, in the history of ideas. In their fully developed and coherent form, these teachings, taken together, are certainly distinctive.

These two talks—i.e. of Friday, 15 November 1912 and Monday, 2 December 1912—are highly significant because the Bahá'í principles given were in direct response to questions, by Americans at that time, directly asking 'Abdu'l-Bahá to clearly identify what new teachings the Bahá'í Faith had to offer. Although these very same principles are set forth in later "Tablets" (writings) of 'Abdu'l-Bahá, they were not clearly characterized as new or otherwise distinctive Bahá'í teachings per se. Based primarily on these two talks, those principles of Bahá'u'lláh that are explicitly distinguished by 'Abdu'l-Bahá as "new," "specialized," or otherwise "distinctive" or "distinguished" have been selected for this chapter.

In the following presentation of each of these Bahá'í principles, selected quotes from 'Abdu'l-Bahá's 15 November 1912 and 2 December 1912 talks will be offered along with parallel statements from 'Abdu'l-Bahá's "Tablet to the Hague" (the first of two) for purposes of further corroboration. Dated 17 December 1919, the "Tablet to the Hague," according to Shoghi Effendi, is a "Tablet of far-reaching importance," noting that this was 'Abdu'l-Bahá's "reply to a communication addressed to Him by the Executive Committee of the 'Central Organization for a Durable Peace'" which was "dispatched to them at The Hague by the hands of a special delegation" (Shoghi Effendi, *God Passes By*, BRL). There is a good reason for this method: The translations that are available for 'Abdu'l-Bahá's 15 November 1912 and 2 December 1912 talks are simply contemporaneous notes transcribed, as in dictation, by Americans Bahá'ís, as 'Abdu'l-Bahá's translator would voice aloud English translations in real time. As for the "15 November 1912 Talk at Home of Miss Juliet Thompson, 48 West Tenth Street, New York," the available English translation consists of the "Notes by Hooper Harris" (*Promulgation of Universal Peace*, BRL). In the case of the "2 December 1912, Talk at Home of Mr. and Mrs. Edward B. Kinney, 780 West End Avenue, New York," the transcript of record are "Notes by Esther Foster" (*Promulgation of Universal Peace*, BRL).

These contemporaneous English translations—subsequently edited and later published—no doubt accurately convey the gist of what

'Abdu'l-Bahá actually said, and therefore have historical value. The reported English record, however, cannot be fully authenticated at present, and therefore may not represent exact translations of 'Abdu'l-Bahá's words verbatim. Doing so would require a retranslation from the original Persian texts, if extant. So, by citing parallel statements from 'Abdu'l-Bahá's first "Tablet to the Hague" (the second "Tablet to the Hague" was sent, after the First World War, on 1 July 1920), some measure of substantive authentication of the 15 November 1912 and 2 December 1912 talks themselves is achieved. (If no parallel statement in the Tablet to the Hague is available, then another parallel will be provided.)

The practice of presenting Bahá'í principles in numeric form began with Bahá'u'lláh himself and was later enlarged upon by 'Abdu'l-Bahá. Perhaps the most well known of these numbered lists of principles by Bahá'u'lláh is the "Tablet of Glad Tidings." (See Buck and Ioannesyan 2010.) Although the number, order, and substance of these principles would vary, depending on the audience and occasion, 'Abdu'l-Bahá was quite consistent in setting forth what may be regarded as Bahá'í social paradigms.

SEARCH FOR TRUTH

The order in which 'Abdu'l-Bahá presented Bahá'u'lláh's teachings would vary from time to time. The sequence in which Bahá'u'lláh's teachings were presented really made no difference, with one exception. Often, at the top of 'Abdu'l-Bahá's lists of Bahá'u'lláh's principles was the independent investigation of truth. For instance, prior to his visit to America and Canada in 1912, 'Abdu'l-Bahá stated, in Paris on 11 November 1911:

> I spoke yesterday of the first principle of the Teaching of Bahá'u'lláh, "The Search for Truth"; ... It is essential that he search for truth in all religions, and, if his seeking be in earnest, he will assuredly succeed. Now the first discovery which we make in our "Search after Truth", will lead us to the second principle, which is the "Unity of Mankind".
> ('Abdu'l-Bahá, *Paris Talks*, BRL)

This "Search for Truth" principle has foreseeable consequences, one of which is the "first discovery" of the "Unity of Mankind." This fundamental Bahá'í principle did enjoy a certain priority—and for good reason: Receptivity requires open-mindedness. Search for truth—that is, an open-minded willingness to investigate—is a necessary precondition to all inquiry, especially scientific investigation. 'Abdu'l-Bahá introduced this principle of Bahá'u'lláh—as a "new" religious teaching—as follows:

> First among the great principles revealed by Him [Bahá'u'lláh] is that of the investigation of reality. The meaning is that every individual member of humankind is exhorted and commanded to set aside superstitious beliefs, traditions and blind imitation of ancestral forms in religion and investigate reality for himself. Inasmuch as the fundamental reality is one, all religions and nations of the world will become one through investigation of reality. The announcement of this principle is not found in any of the sacred Books of the past.
>
> ('Abdu'l-Bahá, Promulgation, BRL) (italics added)

This statement, given at a public meeting at the home of Bahá'í artist, Juliet Thompson, on 15 November 1912, is remarkable not so much for the precept itself as for the prediction that "all religions and nations of the world will become one through investigation of reality." In other words, since truth is one, the truth simply remains to be discovered and, over time, attracts widespread assent, culminating in consensus. According to this prophecy—or foresight borne of profound insight— the eventual discrediting and invalidation of falsehoods will lead to general agreement as to universal spiritual and social principles, thereby gaining common ground in public opinion and social policy for the common good.

Although not a historian of religions in the academic sense, 'Abdu'l-Bahá takes a history-of-religions approach. His declaration that the "announcement of this principle is not found in any of the sacred Books of the past" certainly appears to be quite true when compared to the salient beliefs of previous world religions. This claim, if challenged, would not be invalidated if a prior religious text was produced that encouraged open-mindedness, for the simple reason that this Bahá'í "search for truth" mandate is given such great prominence in the Bahá'í social agenda. Such a religious text, if adduced as proof that the "search for truth" principle has precedent and is therefore not "new," can simply be seen as the proverbial "exception that proves the rule, in that the assertion that some Bahá'í teachings are "new" is best understood relatively, rather than absolutely.

This Bahá'í teaching of free inquiry has far-reaching consequences, since it optimizes the overarching goal of accelerating the process of bringing about world unity. This important Bahá'í principle was reiterated by 'Abdu'l-Bahá in a subsequent talk on 2 December 1912, at the home of Mr. and Mrs. Edward B. Kinney in New York, on the eve of his departure from North America on 5 December 1912:

> *Another new principle revealed by Bahá'u'lláh is the injunction to investigate truth*—that is to say, no man should blindly follow his ancestors and forefathers. Nay, each must see with his own eyes, hear with his own ears and investigate the truth himself in order that he may follow the truth instead of blind acquiescence and imitation of ancestral beliefs.
>
> ('Abdu'l-Bahá, *Promulgation*, BRL) (italics added)

So, another implication of the application of the Bahá'í "search for truth" principle is that it obviates (makes unnecessary) the central role of clergy in religious instruction and indoctrination. This is implied in the statement, "that he may follow the truth instead of blind acquiescence and imitation of ancestral beliefs." In keeping with this implication, the Bahá'í Faith has no clergy. As corroborated by his first "Tablet to the Hague," 'Abdu'l-Bahá ventures a broader prediction, or prophecy, of the ultimate outcome for the Bahá'í "search for truth" axiom:

> Among these teachings was the independent investigation of reality so that the world of humanity may be saved from the darkness of imitation and attain to the truth; may tear off and cast away this ragged and outgrown garment of a thousand years ago and may put on the robe woven in the utmost purity and holiness in the loom of reality. As reality is one and cannot admit of multiplicity, therefore different opinions must ultimately become fused into one.
>
> ('Abdu'l-Bahá, *Hague*, BRL)

Free inquiry allows for diversity of opinion. On matters of social importance, however, consensus facilitates the formulation and implementation of sound social policy. Perhaps the most ambitious Bahá'í-inspired predicate for enlightened social policy is the overarching vision and goal of "world unity."

SEE HUMANKIND AS ONE

Search after truth is a point of departure. It is a methodological principle, not a social principle *per se*. Also near the top of 'Abdu'l-Bahá's list of Bahá'u'lláh's major principles is the oneness of humankind: "In this wondrous Revelation, this glorious century, the foundation of the Faith of God and the distinguishing feature of His Law is the consciousness of the Oneness of Mankind" (quoted by Shoghi Effendi, *World Order*, BRL). This overarching principle is really a mission statement since the primary purpose of the Bahá'í Faith is to unify the world and to usher in a golden age of world civilization. 'Abdu'l-Bahá explains:

> *A second characteristic principle of the teachings of Bahá'u'lláh is that which commands recognition of the oneness of the world of humanity.* Addressing all mankind, He says, "Ye are all the leaves of one tree." There are no differences or distinctions of race among you in the sight of God. Nay, rather, all are the servants of God, and all are submerged in the ocean of His oneness. Not a single soul is bereft. On the contrary, all are the recipients of the bounties of God. Every human creature has a portion of His bestowals and a share of the effulgence of His reality. God is kind to all. Mankind are His sheep, and He is their real Shepherd. *No other scriptures contain such breadth and universality of statement; no other teachings proclaim this unequivocal principle of the solidarity of humanity.*
>
> ('Abdu'l-Bahá, *Promulgation*, BRL)

Throughout his ministry, 'Abdu'l-Bahá proclaimed the oneness of humanity time and again. What distinguishes the 15 November 1912 statement above is 'Abdu'l-Bahá's history-of-religions claim that "No other scriptures contain such breadth and universality of statement." What scholars call "universalisms" may be found in prior scriptures, yet the message of the oneness of humanity is paramount in the Bahá'í proclamation of its social principles, to which no other religion has accorded such prominence and given such priority. This is not a claim to superiority, but rather a teaching best suited for this day and age, as future peace and prosperity may well depend on acceptance of this foundational social outlook. On 2 December 1912, 'Abdu'l-Bahá again claimed that this was a special, or distinctive, Bahá'í principle:

> *A fundamental teaching of Bahá'u'lláh is the oneness of the world of humanity.* Addressing mankind, He says, "Ye are all leaves of one tree and the fruits of one branch." By this it is meant that the world of humanity is like a tree, the nations or peoples are the different limbs or branches of that tree, and the individual human creatures are as the fruits and blossoms thereof. In this way Bahá'u'lláh expressed the oneness of humankind, whereas in all religious teachings of the past the human world has been represented as divided into two parts: one known as the people of the Book of God, or the pure tree, and the other the people of infidelity and error, or the evil tree. ... *Bahá'u'lláh removed this by proclaiming the oneness of the world of humanity, and*

this principle is specialized in His teachings, for He has submerged all mankind in the sea of divine generosity.

('Abdu'l-Bahá, *Promulgation*, BRL) (italics added)

So, any and all religious notions of "saved" and "unsaved" are swept away as incompatible with the consciousness of the oneness of humankind. That this is a distinctive Bahá'í precept is indicated by 'Abdu'l-Bahá's claim that "this principle is specialized in His [Bahá'u'lláh's] teachings." This teaching, but not the claim, is restated in the Tablet to the Hague:

And among the teachings of Bahá'u'lláh is the oneness of the world of humanity; that all human beings are the sheep of God and He is the kind Shepherd.

('Abdu'l-Bahá, *Hague*, BRL)

What makes this Bahá'í principle so distinctive is that, according to 'Abdu'l-Bahá, Bahá'u'lláh removes all prejudices that are fundamentally divisive. Polarities are obliterated. In other words, the reason why this teaching is new is that it does away with all prior either/or religious notions of "saved" and "unsaved," "righteous" and "unrighteous," "believer" and "infidel," etc. Getting rid of such binary "us and them" dichotomies is a necessary prerequisite for world unity. Objectifying the "other" will be a thing of the past when the whole idea of the "other" becomes "brother." Although there may be some egalitarian teachings in past scriptures that may be cited here or there, according such paramount importance to human solidarity is comparatively unique in the history of religions, since no other world religion has promoted this teaching as a major tenet, at least to the superlative, self-defining way that the Bahá'í Faith has done. As a grand social experiment, time will tell how well this Bahá'í teaching will bear fruit in the course of human events. If humanity is one, then whatever causes of division remain are contrary and counterproductive to human unity. One such source of division is religious prejudice, which leads to the next Bahá'í principle.

SEE RELIGION AS ONE

On 19 May 1912, at the Church of the Divine Paternity in Central Park West, New York, 'Abdu'l-Bahá declared, "Religions are many, but the reality of *religion is one*" ('Abdu'l-Bahá, *Promulgation*, BRL) (italics added). "Religion is one" is therefore a short expression for the proposition that religions, although plural, are singular when it comes to pure spirituality.

That religions, at their heart and core, are fundamentally one is yet another major theme in the Bahá'í teachings. The "oneness of religions" is a principle that has the persuasive power and moral force needed to overcome religious prejudice, antagonism, and, in extreme cases, interreligious (and intra-religious) wars, which have plagued history with untold death and destruction, and continue to do so today. In his talk at the Kinney home, 'Abdu'l-Bahá explained this teaching as another distinctive Bahá'í principle:

> Bahá'u'lláh has announced that the foundation of all the religions of God is one, that oneness is truth and truth is oneness which does not admit of plurality. *This teaching is new and specialized to this Manifestation.*
> [Bahá'u'lláh]. ('Abdu'l-Bahá, *Promulgation*, BRL) (italics added)

This is verified by the Tablet to the Hague:

> But by religion is meant that which is ascertained by investigation and not that which is based on mere imitation, the foundations of Divine Religions and not human imitations.
> ('Abdu'l-Bahá, *Hague*, BRL)

Today, religions differ. They are not the same. Each is distinct. Religions, moreover, are typically split into different (and differing) sects. So, how is the "oneness of religions" best understood? Is this contrary to fact? Or is there a good explanation? Here, 'Abdu'l-Bahá distinguishes between "foundations" and "imitations." The former is divinely inspired; the latter is man-made. "Foundations" are true; "imitations" are false, insofar as they may become pretexts for disputes and conflicts. The "oneness of religions" therefore refers to whatever spiritual, moral, ethical, and social truths that religions have (or ideally should have) in common. These truths may be (and assuredly are) expressed in different ways. But these various expressions of the truth should be a source of mutual respect and even consensus—not a basis or pretext for friction and strife. "Truth is one" is an axiom that 'Abdu'l-Bahá often invoked. If the pristine teachings of each religion are approximations of pure truth, then the axiom, "religion is one," is a logical corollary of "truth is one."

Unity among religions can only happen when there is peace among religions, and whenever interreligious dialogue, mutual respect, reciprocity, and solidarity are cultivated, over time. Time will tell whether "oneness of religion" will ultimately lead to the emergence of "one religion" by general consensus, whereby the world's religions, over time, will grow to respect each other and, ideally, work together cooperatively and synergistically in making this world a better place.

RELIGIONS SHOULD UNIFY

Religion—boon or bane? Do religions help or harm the world? Or do they do both? Religions are supposed to benefit the world by promoting moral and ethical teachings. They exist for good. But religious sectarianism does just the opposite. Peace among religions is impossible so long as hostile sectarianism exists. The Bahá'í teachings address this issue with the proposition that, if any religion becomes the source of prejudice, hatred, or war, then its non-existence is preferable to its existence, as 'Abdu'l-Bahá explained in the public meeting at Juliet Thompson's home:

> Another fundamental announcement made by Bahá'u'lláh is that religion must be the source of unity and fellowship in the world. If it is productive of enmity, hatred and bigotry, the absence of religion would be preferable. *This is a new principle of revelation found only in the utterances of Bahá'u'lláh.*
>
> ('Abdu'l-Bahá, *Promulgation*, BRL) (italics added)

This teaching was briefly discussed in Chapter Two. (See the section, "The Purpose of Religion.") If religions cannot enjoy ecumenical and interfaith fellowship, at least they should get along with each other. That seems to be what 'Abdu'l-Bahá is implying here. Put another way, religions should unify, as 'Abdu'l-Bahá stated two weeks later in the Kinney meeting:

> He [Bahá'u'lláh] *sets forth a new principle for this day in the announcement that religion must be the cause of unity, harmony and agreement among mankind.* If it is the cause of discord and hostility, if it leads to separation and creates conflict, the absence of religion would be preferable in the world.
>
> ('Abdu'l-Bahá, *Promulgation*, BRL) (italics added)

So, the mission of religion is to promote "unity, harmony and agreement among mankind." If any religion fails to do so, then that is contrary to its purpose. This is reiterated in the Tablet to the Hague:

And among the teachings of Bahá'u'lláh is that religion must be the cause of fellowship and love. If it becomes the cause of estrangement then it is not needed, for religion is like a remedy; if it aggravates the disease then it becomes unnecessary.

('Abdu'l-Bahá, *Hague*, BRL)

This analysis accords with the metaphor of prophets as divine physician, as previously explained. A religion is good to the extent that it promotes good. This raises an inevitable question as to the relationship between science and religion, which is addressed in the next section.

RELIGION RESPECTS SCIENCE

Science studies nature. Religion focuses on human nature, with attention to spiritual realities and their practical applications. Science and religion, in the present writer's understanding of this important Bahá'í principle, each have their own respective domain and complementary sphere of influence, although reciprocal (and mutual) influence is possible in their ideal and socially progressive interactions, especially at the level of application, where ethical considerations may be at issue. The values that underpin the paradigms within which scientific activity can take place, moreover, can occur in meaningful conversations between science and religion. The large number of scientific questions on physical, social, and psychological issues—questions that religion also approaches—may present many areas that fall within the respective domains of both science and religion. Therefore, the dynamic interactions between science and religion can and should reflect the organic and interlinked nature of their relationship as described in the Bahá'í writings. (See Buck 2013b.) The interchange between reason and faith can be understood in much the same way.

This has not always been so. Prior to the Bahá'í Faith, there has been a long and sad history of scientists being persecuted in the name of religion. Galileo, the famed astronomer, is a case in point. Historical conflicts between religion and science had much to do with a presumed dichotomy (i.e. differences) between the two. If science disagreed with religion, then science was wrong, when religion was the exclusive standard of all truth. In the Juliet Thompson event, 'Abdu'l-Bahá taught:

Bahá'u'lláh teaches that religion must be in conformity with science and reason. If belief and teaching are opposed to the analysis of reason and principles of science, they are not worthy of acceptance. *This principle has not been revealed in any of the former Books of divine teaching.*

('Abdu'l-Bahá, *Promulgation*, BRL) (italics added)

'Abdu'l-Bahá's declaration that the Bahá'í principle of the harmony of science and religion "has not been revealed in any of the former Books of divine teaching" makes perfect sense when considering that this really is a modern-day question. Many people today, across all faiths, believe that science and religion can be, or should be, compatible and not at odds with one another. This is how it should be. The whole idea of promoting and putting this important principle into practice is so that the world will benefit thereby. This principle, moreover, will serve to reduce superstitions—which are unworthy as they are contrary to reason—as 'Abdul-Bahá indicated in the Kinney meeting:

> *Furthermore, He* [Bahá'u'lláh] *proclaims that religion must be in harmony with science and reason.* If it does not conform to science and reconcile with reason, it is superstition. Down to the present day it has been customary for man to accept a religious teaching, even though it was not in accord with human reason and judgment. *The harmony of religious belief with reason is a new vista which Bahá'u'lláh has opened for the soul of man.*
>
> ('Abdu'l-Bahá, *Promulgation*, BRL) (*italics added*)

Religion should respect science. And science should respect religion. As stated, each has its own primary domain and sphere of influence (in the present writer's understanding of this key Bahá'í concept). That said, elevated discussions of social ethics and values, and also the role of the spiritual dimension of our world—what has been referred to in Bahá'í sources as "God and the universe"—can take place between science and religion as well. Religion should promote science, not oppose it. 'Abdu'l-Bahá's reported statements at the Thompson and Kinney events are confirmed and validated by this statement in the Tablet to the Hague:

> And among the teachings of Bahá'u'lláh is that religion must be in conformity with science and reason, so that it may influence the hearts of men. The foundation must be solid and must not consist of imitations.
>
> ('Abdu'l-Bahá, *Hague*, BRL)

The harmony of science and religion is a social teaching that has an individual counterpart as well: The harmony of reason and faith. Reason is as to the individual as science is to society, whereas faith is to the individual as religion is to society. By harmonizing reason and faith, the harmony of science and religion is thereby strengthened. In this way, superstition will vanish, over time, as a function of the harmony of science and religion at a societal level, as put into practical application by the harmony of reason and faith at an individual level. According to 'Abdu'l-Bahá at the Kinney event, this Bahá'í teaching opens up a "new vista" for soul and society alike. This principle, in turn, implicates the gender imbalance in scientific research which, fortunately, is receiving the attention it deserves thanks, in large part, to the next principle.

WOMEN AND MEN ARE EQUAL

Spiritually, women and men are equal, but, not socially—yet. "Another [new] teaching," 'Abdu'l-Bahá announced at the Thompson event, "is that *there shall be perfect equality between men and women*" ('Abdu'l-Bahá, *Promulgation*, BRL) (italics added). This is both a mandate and prophecy. For 'Abdu'l-Bahá, this issue had great social importance, and is a distinctive feature of the Bahá'í social agenda. Bahá'u'lláh "establishes the equality of man and woman," 'Abdu'l-Bahá declared at the Kinney event, hastening to add: "*This is peculiar to the teachings of Bahá'u'lláh, for all other religions have placed man above woman*" ('Abdu'l-Bahá, *Promulgation*, BRL) (italics added).

In a historical context, the claim that this is a distinctive Bahá'í principle makes perfect sense, considering that gender equality is a modern issue. In 1848, at the Seneca Falls Convention in Seneca Falls, New York, the "Declaration of Sentiments" boldly proclaimed, "We hold these truths to be self-evident, that all men and women are created equal, that they are endowed by their creator with certain inalienable rights, that among these are life, liberty, and the pursuit of happiness." This, of course, is a deliberative and clever restatement—as applied to women's right to vote—of the celebrated preamble to the US Declaration of Independence.

To the extent that any Bahá'í teaching has been preceded by *secular* events in which the same, or similar, principle was promulgated, then the Bahá'í teaching serves to render that same principle *sacred*—thereby adding more weight and force to the secular conviction, in a process that the present writer has previously characterized as "sacralizing the secular."

Since half of the human race consists of women (and girls), this issue is of paramount importance, at least in terms of the sheer scale and sweep of the issue itself. 'Abdu'l-Bahá, throughout his talks and writings, has compared humanity to a bird, which needs equal strength in both wings in order to fly. This Bahá'í teaching of gender equality is corroborated in the Tablet to the Hague, with an added explanation:

> And among the teachings of Bahá'u'lláh is the equality of women and men. The world of humanity has two wings—one is women and the other men. Not until both wings are equally developed can the bird fly. Should one wing remain weak, flight is impossible. Not until the world of women becomes equal to the world of men in the acquisition of virtues and perfections, can success and prosperity be attained as they ought to be.
>
> ('Abdu'l-Bahá, *Hague*, BRL)

Gender equality, moreover, is a peace issue: "The sixth principle or teaching of Bahá'u'lláh concerns the equality of man and woman," 'Abdu'l-Bahá proclaimed on 7 May 1912, at the Hotel Schenley (or "Schenley Park Hotel") in Pittsburgh, Pennsylvania. "Assuredly, woman will abolish warfare among mankind" ('Abdu'l-Bahá, *Promulgation*, BRL) (italics added).

To set things right, the advancement of equality of women and men is high on the current Bahá'í agenda, especially at the international level. The Bahá'í International Community (BIC), established as a nongovernmental organization (NGO) with the United Nations in 1948, has promoted implementation of this principle with the highest priority. (More information on this effort will be provided in Chapter Nine.) Any secular issue, such as women's rights, will receive added impetus when the support is intensified by a religious commitment as well. Thus, the equality of women and men is an important Bahá'í contribution, and will continue to be so, especially as the Bahá'ís themselves learn how best to implement this key principle in Bahá'í community life, at both personal and institutional levels.

ABOLISH EVERY PREJUDICE

Prejudice is a global problem in societies across the world and may be the single most challenging barrier to human unity. The Bahá'í Faith has long recognized this social problem, which is of world-historical importance. Obviously, prejudices take different forms. Prejudice is a broad term that encompasses such negative, socially harmful biases as racial, ethnic, religious, national, political, class-based, and gender-referenced biases (including both bigoted attitudes and antisocial actions), as 'Abdu'l-Bahá has explained, in brief at the Thompson event:

> *Again, Bahá'u'lláh declares that all forms of prejudice among mankind must be abandoned* and that until existing prejudices are entirely removed, the world of humanity will not and cannot attain peace, prosperity and composure. *This principle cannot be found in any other sacred volume than the teachings of Bahá'u'lláh.*
>
> ('Abdu'l-Bahá, *Promulgation*, BRL) (italics added)

The claim that this principle is relatively "new" in the history of religion is clearly announced at the Kinney event, in which 'Abdu'l-Bahá elaborated on what is meant by "all forms of prejudice," as stated above:

> A *new religious principle is that prejudice and fanaticism—whether sectarian, denominational, patriotic or political—are destructive to the foundation of human solidarity*; therefore, man should release himself from such bonds in order that the oneness of the world of humanity may become manifest.
>
> ('Abdu'l-Bahá, *Promulgation*, BRL) (italics added)

Eradicating prejudice is no easy task. But it must be done. The future of the human race depends upon it. One way to eradicate prejudice, which is a negative attitude that takes various forms, is to promote the positive principle of the "oneness of humankind." These two initiatives complement one another. Prejudices may be gross or subtle. Some gross prejudices were singled out by 'Abdu'l-Bahá in "Tablet to the Hague": "And among the teachings of Bahá'u'lláh is that religious, racial, political, economic and patriotic prejudices destroy the edifice of humanity" ('Abdu'l-Bahá, *Hague*, BRL). One example of a subtle prejudice is what, in Canada and the United Kingdom, is often described as "polite racism." Subtle prejudices—often deeply ingrained culturally and religiously—may be more difficult to root out, but the major prejudices obviously take priority and command immediate and sustained attention in order to reduce, and eventually eliminate altogether, this long-standing social problem, which is a major barrier to peace, both world peace and domestic tranquility.

PROMOTE WORLD PEACE

The foregoing Bahá'í principles are part and parcel of a broad-based Bahá'í peace paradigm. The following statement by 'Abdu'l-Bahá is brief, and is a topic that he devoted considerable attention to in other public discourses as well, as 'Abdu'l-Bahá proclaimed at the Kinney event:

> *Universal peace is assured by Bahá'u'lláh as a fundamental accomplishment of the religion of God*—that peace shall prevail among nations, governments and peoples, among religions, races and all conditions of mankind. *This is one of the special characteristics of the Word of God revealed in this Manifestation.*
>
> ('Abdu'l-Bahá, *Promulgation*, BRL) (italics added)

Here, "special characteristics" means "new"—and therefore a distinctive Bahá'í teaching. Each and every one of the foregoing Bahá'í social principles, moreover, is attributed to Bahá'u'lláh—and rightly so— but without recounting how a given principle was first promulgated in Bahá'í history. On the issue of world peace, however, 'Abdu'l-Bahá gives this brief historical account:

> Therefore Bahá'u'lláh, fifty years ago, expounded this question of universal peace at a time when He was confined in the fortress of 'Akká and was wronged and imprisoned. He wrote about this important matter of universal peace to all the great sovereigns of the world, and established it among His friends in the orient. ... Among His teachings was the declaration of universal peace.
>
> ('Abdu'l-Bahá, *Promulgation*, BRL)

World peace requires an organic change in international relations, whereby mechanisms for the equitable and efficient maintenance of world order must be established, including institutions and procedures for resolving international disputes. The Bahá'í writings clearly envision such an institution for international conflict-resolution, referred to as the "Supreme Tribunal," the adjudicating role of which 'Abdu'l-Bahá explains as follows:

For example, the question of universal peace, about which Bahá'u'lláh says that the Supreme Tribunal must be established: although the League of Nations has been brought into existence, yet it is incapable of establishing universal peace. But the Supreme Tribunal which Bahá'u'lláh has described will fulfil this sacred task with the utmost might and power.

('Abdu'l-Bahá, *Hague*, BRL)

Again, secular commitments to such global issues as world peace are strengthened when intensified by religious commitments. For instance, in Chapter Four, "History: Bahá'u'lláh and His Covenant," Bahá'u'lláh's public proclamation to the rulers and religious leaders of the world may be described as the world's "first international peace mission."

PROVIDE EDUCATION FOR ALL

Although most nations around the world have adopted compulsory education of children as a social policy, the fact remains that illiteracy still persists as an intractable problem, especially in developing nations. Universal education of children is a basic Bahá'í principle, the importance and necessity of which 'Abdu'l-Bahá emphasized, time and time again. "He has also proclaimed the principle that all mankind shall be educated and that no illiteracy be allowed to remain," 'Abdu'l-Bahá declared by adding: *"This practical remedy for the need of the world cannot be found in the text of any other sacred Books"* ('Abdu'l-Bahá, *Promulgation*, BRL) (italics added).

Education for all is not set forth as a human right as such, but as a collective responsibility which is as important to society at large as it is to the individual, for illiteracy retards human progress, and ultimately creates a social deficit and cost. "Bahá'u'lláh declares that all mankind should attain knowledge and acquire an education," 'Abdu'l-Bahá declares, adding: *"This is a necessary principle of religious belief and observance, characteristically new in this dispensation"* ('Abdu'l-Bahá, *Promulgation*, BRL) (italics added). "And among the teachings of Bahá'u'lláh is the promotion of education," 'Abdu'l-Bahá affirms in the "Tablet to the Hague," adding, "Every child must be instructed in sciences as much as is necessary. If the parents are able to provide the expenses of this education, it is well, otherwise the community must provide the means for the teaching of that child" ('Abdu'l-Bahá, *Hague*, BRL). Bahá'u'lláh's solutions to world problems are "new" to the extent that they are established as important religious priorities.

Every means at a society's disposal must be dedicated to eradicating illiteracy. But literacy, in and of itself, is not the sum total of children's education, which should be well-rounded and comprehensive. Besides reading, writing, math, and science (not to mention the arts and humanities), moral and spiritual education are also needed. Bahá'í teachings strongly advocate the moral education of children and youth, which is a major emphasis worldwide and within the global Bahá'í community today. (See Chapter Seven: "Building Community: What Bahá'ís Do.")

ECONOMIC PROBLEMS REQUIRE SPIRITUAL SOLUTIONS

Bahá'í teachings are fairly comprehensive at the level of principle. This includes consideration of the economy. One well-known Bahá'í teaching is the elimination of extremes of wealth and poverty. In brief, 'Abdu'l-Bahá, at the Kinney meeting in New York, introduced the idea that Bahá'u'lláh's teachings offer spiritual solutions to economic problems as follows, "He [Bahá'u'lláh] has set forth the solution and provided the remedy for the economic question. *No religious Books of the past Prophets speak of this important human problem*" ('Abdu'l-Bahá, *Promulgation*, BRL) (italics added). This is a simple and clear way of saying that past religions have typically not addressed economic concerns on a systemic, global scale.

Economic policy, moreover, is a major concern of societies worldwide, whether capitalist or communist. "With regard to the party of 'equality' which seeks the solution of the economic problems," 'Abdu'l-Bahá commented, likely referring to socialist ideology, adding that "until now all proposed solutions have proved impracticable except the economic proposals in the teachings of Bahá'u'lláh which are practicable and cause no distress to society" ('Abdu'l-Bahá, *Hague*, BRL). "And among the teachings of Bahá'u'lláh is voluntary sharing of one's property with others among mankind," 'Abdu'l-Bahá further explained in the "Tablet to the Hague," adding, "This voluntary sharing is greater than equality, and consists in this, that man should not prefer himself to others, but rather should sacrifice his life and property for others" ('Abdu'l-Bahá, *Hague*, BRL). To their credit, the Bahá'í writings set forth various economic teachings, although not systematically developed (a task for economists). Bahá'í teachings do so largely by anchoring *economic* values in *human* values. The two are, or should be, dynamically interrelated. Generally speaking, economic systems should be just and equitable.

THE UNIVERSAL HOUSE OF JUSTICE IS UNIQUE

There is an implied principle here, namely that religion can benefit from a divinely ordained institution of authority—something that, in secular terms, German philosopher Max Weber had famously referred to as the "routinization of charisma." This "principle" is actually an institutional principal, i.e. the Universal House of Justice, which is a unique religious institution. Ordained by Bahá'u'lláh in his *Most Holy Book*, the *Kitáb-i-Aqdas* (1873), the Universal House of Justice was established in 1963. This august institution is the democratically elected council that oversees the affairs of the global Bahá'í community today and has no real precedent or parallel in prior religious history. Bahá'u'lláh "has ordained and established the House of Justice. ... A universal, or international, House of Justice shall also be organized," 'Abdu'l-Bahá proclaimed at the Kinney event. "Its rulings shall be in accordance with the commands and teachings of Bahá'u'lláh, and that which the Universal House of Justice ordains shall be obeyed by all mankind," that this "international House of Justice shall be appointed and organized from the Houses of Justice of the whole world" ('Abdu'l-Bahá, *Promulgation*, BRL). Analogous to "exceptions to the general rule" in the practice of law, 'Abdu'l-Bahá explains that "women are exempt from military engagements" and are also exempt from serving on the Universal House of Justice ('Abdu'l-Bahá, Paris Talks, BRL) "for a wisdom of the Lord God's, which will erelong be made manifest as clearly as the sun at high noon" ('Abdu'l-Bahá, Selections, BRL). For more information on the Universal House of Justice, see Chapter Five, "History: Bahá'u'lláh and His Covenant."

THE SPECIAL BAHÁ'Í "COVENANT" PROTECTS BAHÁ'Í UNITY

Another implicit "principle" is that there should be a way to keep religion unified, and not to succumb to fissiparous (i.e. schismatic

and divisive) forces that would otherwise fragment and factional-
ize religion. Applying this implied principle to the Bahá'í religion,
'Abdu'l-Bahá introduces a specialized Bahá'í teaching known as the
"Covenant," which is actually an institution of Bahá'í successorship
and is of paramount importance. This primarily refers to the fact that
Bahá'u'lláh designated 'Abdu'l-Bahá as successor, interpreter, and
exemplar of Bahá'u'lláh himself and his teachings. As such, 'Abdu'l-
Bahá is referred to as the "Center of the Covenant." At the Kinney
meeting, Abdul-Bahá briefly introduced this key Bahá'í institution.
*"As to the most great characteristic of the revelation of Bahá'u'lláh, a
specific teaching not given by any of the Prophets of the past: It is the
ordination and appointment of the Center of the Covenant,"* 'Abdu'l-
Bahá declared, adding, "By this appointment and provision He has
safeguarded and protected the religion of God against differences and
schisms, making it impossible for anyone to create a new sect or fac-
tion of belief" ('Abdu'l-Bahá, *Promulgation*, BRL) (italics added).

The Covenant is the lynchpin that keeps the Bahá'í community unified. The Covenant is intended to ensure and preserve Bahá'í unity
and continuity and safeguard the Bahá'í Faith from schism, thereby
preserving its integrity and viability as a religion whose purpose it is
to unify the world. "Today the dynamic power of the world of existence is the power of the Covenant which like unto an artery pulsa-
teth in the body of the contingent world and protecteth Bahá'í unity,"
'Abdu'l-Bahá elsewhere proclaimed, adding that Bahá'u'lláh "hath,
therefore, commanded that whatever emanateth from the Centre of
the Covenant is right and is under His protection and favour, while all
else is error" ('Abdu'l-Bahá, *Selections*, BRL).

ADOPT A UNIVERSAL AUXILIARY LANGUAGE

Another new religious teaching of Bahá'u'lláh, which 'Abdu'l-Bahá
often spoke about, is the adoption of a universal auxiliary language:
"Bahá'u'lláh has announced the necessity for a universal language
which shall serve as a means of international communication and thus
remove misunderstandings and difficulties," 'Abdu'l-Bahá declared at
the Thompson meeting. "This [new] teaching is set forth in the *Kitáb-
i-Aqdas* (*Most Holy Book*) published fifty years ago" ('Abdu'l-Bahá,
Promulgation, BRL) (italics added). This is why: "And among the
teachings of Bahá'u'lláh is the origination of one language that may

be spread universally among the people," 'Abdu'l-Bahá stated in the "Tablet to the Hague," further explaining: "This teaching was revealed from the pen of Bahá'u'lláh in order that this universal language may eliminate misunderstandings from among mankind" ('Abdu'l-Bahá, *Selections*, BRL). This is a compelling reason. The adoption of a universal auxiliary language will greatly facilitate communication and thereby promote peace and prosperity worldwide.

WORK IS WORSHIP

The following principle was also presented by 'Abdu'l-Bahá in the context of the "new" teachings given by Bahá'u'lláh. At the Kinney event, 'Abdu'l-Bahá emphasized that Bahá'u'lláh "teaches that it is incumbent upon all mankind to become fitted for some useful trade, craft, or profession by which subsistence may be assured, and this efficiency is to be considered as an act of worship" ('Abdu'l-Bahá, *Promulgation*, BRL). "If a man engageth with all his power in the acquisition of a science or in the perfection of an art, it is as if he has been worshipping God in churches and temples," 'Abdu'l-Bahá, elsewhere states, adding, "In this universal dispensation man's wondrous craftsmanship is reckoned as worship of the Resplendent Beauty" ('Abdu'l-Bahá, *Selections*, BRL). This Bahá'í principle was previously discussed in Chapter Two. (See the "Work and Service" Section.)

THE BAHÁ'Í FAITH OFFERS OTHER "NEW PRINCIPLES"

Each of the foregoing precepts can also be located in the writings of Bahá'u'lláh. The above statements by 'Abdu'l-Bahá have been privileged primarily because they present Bahá'u'lláh's teachings as "new principles" that represent the spirit of the new age and offer the best and surest remedy for the world's problems today. In the "Tablet to the Hague," 'Abdu'l-Bahá refers to Bahá'u'lláh's "numerous" teachings and "manifold principles" which "constitute the greatest basis for the felicity of mankind" and which "must be added to the matter of universal peace and combined with it, so that results may accrue" ('Abdu'l-Bahá, *Hague*, BRL). At the end of his discourse at the Kinney event on 2 December 1912, 'Abdu'l-Bahá concluded, "The teachings of Bahá'u'lláh are boundless and illimitable. *You have asked me what new principles have been revealed by Him*. I have mentioned a few only. There are many others, but time does not permit their mention tonight" ('Abdu'l-Bahá, *Promulgation*, BRL) (italics added). As corroboration of this reported statement, 'Abdu'l-Bahá, in a Tablet, likens Bahá'u'lláh's "new principles" to a "new garment" for the new age":

> Out of this pitch blackness there dawned the morning splendour of the Teachings of Bahá'u'lláh. He hath dressed the world with a garment new and fair, and that new garment is the principles which have come down from God.
>
> Now the new age is here and creation is reborn. Humanity hath taken on new life. The autumn hath gone by, and the reviving spring is here. All things are now made new. Arts and industries have been reborn, there are new discoveries in science, and there are new inventions; even the details of human affairs, such as dress and personal effects—even weapons—all these have likewise been renewed. The laws and procedures of every government have been revised. Renewal is the order of the day.
>
> And all this newness hath its source in the fresh outpourings of wondrous grace and favour from the Lord of the Kingdom [Bahá'u'lláh], which have renewed the world. The people, therefore, must be set completely free from their old patterns of thought, *that all their attention may be focused upon these new principles, for these are the light of this time and the very spirit of this age*.
>
> ('Abdu'l-Bahá, *Selections*, BRL) (italics added)

Readers may consider, and judge for themselves, the relevance and importance of Bahá'u'lláh's teachings, which are presented here by way of introduction, in keeping with the purpose of this book. Further reading is encouraged.

"FIFTY BAHÁ'Í PRINCIPLES OF UNITY" AS A PARADIGM OF "SOCIAL SALVATION"

The writings of Bahá'u'lláh comprise an estimated equivalent of one hundred volumes. To these may be added the writings and public discourses of 'Abdu'l-Bahá, which are considerable (not to mention the writings of the Báb, Bahá'u'lláh's forerunner and herald). Further guidance in the writings of Shoghi Effendi and the Universal House of Justice is also included within the wide range of authoritative Bahá'í texts. Thus, there is an enormous corpus (i.e. "body") of Bahá'í teachings and principles. On a scale so large, obviously the Bahá'í teachings cannot be reduced to a simple list, except in the most simplified and basic way. That said, most of the major Bahá'í social principles (with a special emphasis on those principles that have been characterized as "new") have been presented in this chapter. Bahá'u'lláh has written:

> We have already in the foregoing pages assigned two stations unto each of the Luminaries arising from the Daysprings of eternal holiness. One of these stations, the station of essential unity .... The other is the station of distinction, and pertaineth to the world of creation and to the limitations thereof. In this respect, each Manifestation of God hath a distinct individuality, a definitely prescribed mission, a predestined Revelation, and specially designated limitations. Each one of them is known by a different name, is characterized by a special attribute, fulfils a definite Mission, and is entrusted with a particular Revelation.
>
> (Bahá'u'lláh, *Kitáb-i-Íqán*, BRL)

As shown in this chapter, Bahá'u'lláh—as the "Manifestation of God" for this day and age according to Bahá'í belief—had "a distinct individuality" and a "definite Mission." Bahá'u'lláh's mission was to "quicken" and "unify" and "unite" the world, as proclaimed in open epistles, or public letters, addressed to the most powerful political and religious rulers of Bahá'u'lláh's day and age in the 19th century, as shown in the passages below:

- Consider these days in which He Who is the Ancient Beauty hath come in the Most Great Name, that He may quicken the world and unite its peoples. (Bahá'u'lláh, *Summons*, BRL)
- Say: ... This is your Lord, the Almighty, the All-Knowing, Who hath come to quicken the world and unite all who dwell on earth. (Bahá'u'lláh, *Summons*, BRL)
- Say: He Who is the Unconstrained is come, in the clouds of light, that He may quicken the world with the breezes of His name, the Most Merciful, and unify its peoples, and gather all men around this Table which hath been sent down from heaven. (Bahá'u'lláh, *Summons*, BRL)
- Say: This Youth hath come to quicken the world and unite all its peoples.

  (Bahá'u'lláh, *Summons*, BRL)

As one indication of the breadth and depth of Bahá'í principles, the present writer has researched, for well over two decades, the Bahá'í paradigm of unity. Based on an extensive and intensive study of the original Bahá'í writings in Persian and Arabic (to the best of his ability), and on Bahá'í texts available in English as well, this author has identified "Fifty Bahá'í Principles of Unity," which were identified and selected using a particular method:

> As a preliminary investigation into the Bahá'í illness/cure soteriology, with its paradigm of unity, the methodology pursued in the present study is simply to inventory those Bahá'í principles that are directly presented as "unity of" or "oneness of" formulations, as indicated by selected genitive constructions, or "of-constructions" (i.e. the Persian/Arabic *'iḍáfa*) involving the Persian/Arabic terms of *ittiḥád, ittifáq, yigánigí, vaḥdat, ulfat,* etc.
>
> (Buck 2015b, 10)

In other words, each of these "Fifty Bahá'í Principles of Unity" was selected whenever a Bahá'í teaching was presented with such expressions as "unity of" or "oneness of." This list is exemplary, not exhaustive. With this explanation of the research and selection method (and with this disclaimer also in mind), the "Fifty Bahá'í Principles of Unity" are enumerated below, as follows:

FIFTY BAHÁ'Í PRINCIPLES OF UNITY

INDIVIDUAL RELATIONSHIP WITH GOD: (1) Mystic Feeling which Unites Man with God; II. FAMILY RELATIONS: (2) Unity of Husband and Wife; (3) Unity of the Family; III. INTERPERSONAL RELATIONS: (4) Oneness of Emotions; (5) Spiritual Oneness; IV. GENDER RELATIONS: (6) Unity of the Rights of Men and Women; (7) Unity in Education; V. ECONOMIC RELATIONS: (8) Economic Unity; (9) Unity of People and Wealth; VI. RACE RELATIONS: (10) Unity in Diversity; (11) Unity of Races; VII. ENVIRONMENTAL RELATIONS: (12) Unity of Existence (Oneness of Being and Manifestation; (13) Unity of Species; (14) Unity with the Environment; VIII. INTERFAITH RELATIONS: (15) Unity of God; (16) Mystic Unity of God and His Manifestations; (17) Unity of the

Manifestations of God; (18) Unity of Truth; (19) Unity Among Religions; (20) Peace Among Religions; IX. SCIENTIFIC RELATIONS: (21) Unity of Science and Religion; (22) Methodological Coherence; (23) Unity of Thought in World Undertakings; X. LINGUISTIC RELATIONS: (24) Unity of Language; XI. INTERNATIONAL RELATIONS: (25) Unity of Conscience; (26) Unity in Freedom; (27) Evolving Social Unities; (28) Unity in the Political Realm; (29) Unity of Nations; (30) Unity of All Mankind/World Unity; (31) Unity of the World Commonwealth; (32) Unity of the Free; XII. BAHÁ'Í RELATIONS: (33) Unity of the Bahá'í Revelation; (34) All-Unifying Power; (35) Unity of Doctrine; (36) Unity of Meaning; (37) Bahá'í Unity; (38) Unity among Bahá'í Women; (39) Unity in Religion; (40) Unity of Station; (41) Unity of Souls; (42) Unity in Speech; (43) Unity in [Ritual] Acts; (44) Unity of Bahá'í Administration; (45) Unity of Purpose; (46) Unity of Means; (47) Unity of Vision; (48) Unity of Action; (49) Unity of the Spiritual Assembly; (50) Unity of Houses of Justice and Governments.

(Buck 2015a, 329.)

This research finding was published as an academic journal article, and presented at Princeton University in an invited lecture on 21 February 2014. By way of a disclaimer, this research is an individual contribution by an independent Bahá'í scholar, and does not represent an official Bahá'í position. These research results, furthermore, are tentative and subject to revision. That said, these "Fifty Bahá'í Principles of Unity" are impressive, and give pause for thought, considering that the world today stands to greatly benefit from these powerful Bahá'í principles of unity, which represent new teachings by a relatively new world religion, the Bahá'í Faith. Although they have intrinsic merit, independent of how others view them, suffice it to say that, pursuant to the Bahá'í principle of independent "search for truth," it is up to the readers of this book, *Bahá'í Faith: The Basics*, to judge for themselves.

SUMMARY

- The Bahá'í Faith is a new, independent world religion.
- The purpose of the Bahá'í Faith is to unify the world.

- Bahá'u'lláh, according to 'Abdu'l-Bahá, brought new and renewed spiritual teachings.
- Bahá'u'lláh's new teachings are not found in previous religions.
- "Search for truth" is a first principle.
- The "oneness of humankind" is the pivotal Bahá'í principle, which encompasses all other Bahá'í principles.
- The Bahá'í "Covenant" protects the Bahá'í Faith from schism.
- Work performed in the spirit of service is considered an act of worship.
- There are many other "new principles" that Bahá'u'lláh has brought.
- The Bahá'í teachings constitute a new "paradigm" of unity.
- There are at least 50 Bahá'í principles of unity that have been identified so far.

4

HISTORY
BAHÁ'U'LLÁH AND HIS COVENANT

Originating in Persia (now Iran), the Bahá'í Faith is a world religion born in the full light of history, starting from the mid-19th century down to the present day. Today, in Haifa, Israel, the Bahá'í World Centre is established on the majestic slopes of Mount Carmel and attracts thousands of visitors and Bahá'í pilgrims each year. So impressive are its splendid gardens, shrines, and the architecture of its other edifices that, in 2008, the "Bahá'í Holy Places in Haifa and the Western Galilee" were declared a United Nations World Heritage Site. (See UNESCO 2019.) Attracting more than half a million visitors a year, this dignified site—known locally in Haifa and Akko as the "Bahá'í Gardens"—is one of the most popular destinations in the Middle East, visited not just by members of the Bahá'í Faith, but also by tourists, newlyweds for wedding pictures, and students on field trips from surrounding schools. Much Bahá'í history is enshrined in these "Bahá'í Holy Places in Haifa and the Western Galilee."

This chapter briefly introduces the co-founders, central figures, and highest institution of the Bahá'í Faith: The Báb (1819–1850); Bahá'u'lláh (1817–1892); 'Abdu'l-Bahá (1844–1921); Shoghi Effendi (1897–1957); and the Universal House of Justice (established in 1963). The Bahá'í Faith was founded by two messengers of God: the Báb and Bahá'u'lláh. Although the Báb preceded Bahá'u'lláh historically, the latter was born two years before the former. According to the Islamic

DOI: 10.4324/9780429023088-4

lunar calendar, Bahá'u'lláh was born one day after the Báb. That is why, today, Bahá'ís observe these two historic events together, in two-day commemorations. On 22 October 2017, Bahá'ís around the world celebrated the Bicentenary of the Birth of Bahá'u'lláh (and the Birth of the Báb the day before). Similarly, on 29 October 2019, Bahá'ís commemorated the Bicentenary of the Birth of the Báb (and the Birth of Bahá'u'lláh the day after).

Today, the distinctive unity and integrity of the Bahá'í Faith are preserved and protected by the explicit instructions—given by the "Central Figures" of the Bahá'í Faith (i.e. the Báb, Bahá'u'lláh, and 'Abdu'l- Bahá), as well as by Shoghi Effendi, and the Universal House of Justice—regarding the line of succession, referred to as "the Covenant." A covenant is a promise—a mutual compact, or contract, of reciprocal obligation—a binding agreement between two or more parties, who agree to honor and abide by the terms of the covenant for the benefit of all involved.

The Bahá'í writings distinguish between the "Greater Covenant" and the "Lesser Covenant." The Greater Covenant is one which every prophet of God makes with his followers, promising that, when the time is ripe, a new prophet will be sent, whom people should follow when this occurs. The Lesser Covenant that a prophet of God makes with his followers is that they should accept his designated successor. If they do so, that religion can remain unified and free of schism. It is this latter type of covenant that Bahá'u'lláh made with Bahá'ís regarding 'Abdu'l-Bahá, and that 'Abdu'l-Bahá perpetuated by appointing Shoghi Effendi as the former's successor. The Bahá'í Administrative Order today is in place thanks to further provisions of the Bahá'í Covenant.

Thus, in the Bahá'í Covenant, ongoing divine guidance and blessings are assured by an explicitly designated line of succession, or continuity of leadership, which extends from the Báb to Bahá'u'lláh, then from Bahá'u'lláh to his eldest son, 'Abdu'l-Bahá, then from 'Abdu'l-Bahá to his grandson, Shoghi Effendi, and then to the Universal House of Justice—an institution that was ordained by Bahá'u'lláh in 1873, even though the House of Justice was not established until 1963, after a lapse of some 90 years, when the conditions for its election were ripe and a uniquely spiritual and purely democratic electoral process was put in place. Therefore, a Bahá'í accepts the divine authority of the Báb and Bahá'u'lláh and of their explicitly designated successors and institutions. The Bahá'í Covenant safeguards the Bahá'í Faith from schisms and divisions—especially in withstanding challenges during transitions in Bahá'í leadership, during which the remarkable power of the Covenant became quite evident.

Prior to 1948, when present-day Israel was formerly known as Palestine, much Bahá'í history took place, especially in the fortress-prison city of Acre (Akko, Akká), across the Bay of Haifa from Mt. Carmel. The prison of Acre/Akká is where Bahá'u'lláh, the second of the "Twin Founders" of the Bahá'í Faith, and his eldest son, 'Abdu'l-Bahá, lived in exile as prisoners of the Ottoman Empire, together with around 75 other Bahá'ís. In 1948, much of former Palestine became present-day Israel. That, in brief, is how the Bahá'í World Centre was established in Israel.

Bahá'í history begins with the Báb, as follows:

THE BÁB (1819–1850)

HISTORICAL SIGNIFICANCE

Born in Shiraz on 20 October 1819, Sayyid 'Alí-Muḥammad Shírází—later known by his spiritual title, the Báb (the "Gate")—founded the Bábí religion, which eventually evolved into the Bahá'í Faith. The Báb's primary mission was to announce the imminent advent of an even greater messenger of God, whom most Bábís (followers of the Báb) accepted as Bahá'u'lláh. In other words, the Báb was the herald of Bahá'u'lláh. The Báb, moreover, is also considered the "Co-Founder" of the Bahá'í Faith. Like John the Baptist, the Báb foretold the imminent advent of Bahá'u'lláh—but did far more. The Báb set forth laws in the Persian Bayán (c. 1848) and in the Arabic Bayán (c. 1848)—a number of which laws were later adopted and modified by Bahá'u'lláh in the Bahá'í book of laws, known as the Kitáb-i-Aqdas (c. 1873), or *Most Holy Book*. This noteworthy fact—along with the profound doctrinal influence of the Báb—as seen in *Selections from the Writings of the Báb*—fully authenticates and demonstrates the truth behind Shoghi Effendi's designation of the Báb as the co-founder of the Bahá'í Faith, noted in such statements as the following: "the Founders of the Bahá'í Faith" (Shoghi Effendi, *The Promised Day is Come*, BRL), and parallels. Shoghi Effendi honored and acclaimed the Báb, not only as the precursor, herald, and harbinger of Bahá'u'lláh—as John the Baptist was for Jesus Christ—but as an independent messenger of God whose writings have been enshrined in the Bahá'í scriptures, and whose laws, doctrines, and principles form part and parcel of the Bahá'í Faith and Bahá'í life today.

KEY LIFE EVENTS

The founders of the Bahá'í Faith—the Báb and Bahá'u'lláh—were born and raised as faithful Muslims in Persia (now Iran), as were the majority of their first followers. The sum and substance of the teachings of the Báb were predominantly "Islamicate" in outward appearance— wherein post-Islamic ideas were astutely expressed as quintessentially Islamic ideas and ideals. Yet a profound paradigm-shift—a transformation of worldview—took place, mediated by a clear break from Islam, while still respecting Islamic origins. Fundamentally, no matter how outwardly "Islamic" in character the Báb's discourse (especially in the earliest texts) formally appeared to be, a profound transformation of great moment was taking place. From the chrysalis of Islamic origins, the butterfly emerged. A new world religion was born, the Bábí religion which, in due course, evolved into the Bahá'í Faith.

On the evening of 22 May 1844, at the youthful age of 24 "while your Redeemer [the Báb] was raised up by God at the age of twenty-four" (the Báb, *Selections*, BRL), the Báb privately proclaimed his prophetic mission to a young religious scholar, Mullá Ḥusayn Bushrú'í (d. 1848), in Shiraz, Persia (now Iran). This signal event marks the beginning of Bahá'í history. On this historic occasion, the Báb wrote the opening chapter of his *Commentary on the Sura of Joseph* (also known as the *Qayyúmu'l-Asmá'*), which he completed in 40 consecutive days. The "Sura of Joseph" itself is Chapter 12 (of 114 chapters, called "suras") of the Qur'an, the holy book of Islam. A highly original and unusual work, the *Commentary on the Sura of Joseph* "purports to be at once a commentary on the Qur'an, the 'True Qur'an', and a new Qur'an" (Lawson 2011, 21–22).

The Qur'an is universally regarded by Muslims as the latest and greatest revelation from God. According to Islamic doctrine, the Qur'an cannot be superseded by any other holy book. Similarly, the prophet Muhammad is the last and final prophet—the "Seal of the Prophets" (Qur'an 33:40)—such that will be no other prophet after him, except on the Day of Judgment. This is a central doctrine in Islam. Therefore, for the Báb to announce and reveal his *Qayyúmu'l-Asmá'* as a "new

Qur'an"—and even more boldly, the "true Qur'an"—was, in theory, an impossible, unimaginable event. In the following passage, the Báb declares that he has revealed "the same Qur'án which was sent down in the past":

> O ye concourse of the believers! Utter not words of denial against Me once the Truth is made manifest, for indeed the mandate of the Báb hath befittingly been proclaimed unto you in the Qur'án aforetime. I swear by your Lord, this Book is verily the same Qur'án which was sent down in the past.

> (the Báb, *Selections*, BRL)

The manuscript of the *Qayyúmu'l-Asmá'* (which was not formally published at this time) was copied far and wide—and deeply impressed many who read it. The Báb presented new teachings in the form of the old by paraphrasing the Qur'an in a style that closely resembles the Qur'an in form and content, and by adding commentary and new teachings. The very act of putting forward a further holy text after the Qur'an, as a new source of religious authority, was revolutionary. By doing so—and by later revealing other holy books as well—ultimately cost the Báb his life, with his public execution on 9 July 1850 in Tabriz (see below). What the Báb "revealed" to Mullá Ḥusayn on that historic night is the first chapter of the *Qayyúmu'l-Asmá,'* i.e. the "Sura of Dominion," of which the following passage is an excerpt:

> O concourse of kings! Deliver with truth and in all haste the verses sent down by Us to the peoples of Turkey and of India, and beyond them, with power and with truth, to lands in both the East and the West. ... And know that if ye aid God, He will, on the Day of Resurrection, graciously aid you, upon the Bridge, through Him Who is His Most Great Remembrance. ...
>
> O people of the earth! Whoso obeyeth the Remembrance of God and His Book hath in truth obeyed God and His chosen ones and he will, in the life to come, be reckoned in the presence of God among the inmates of the Paradise of His good-pleasure.

> (the Báb, *Selections*, BRL)

In 1848, the Báb, in a work known as the *Persian Bayán*, announced a new set of religious and social laws. These new laws were meant to replace the laws of traditional Islam. The Báb, in setting forth his new code of laws, had three main purposes in mind: (1) to prepare the way for the appearance of a greater messianic figure, known as "He Whom God shall manifest" (later understood by the majority of his followers as Bahá'u'lláh); (2) to declare the Báb's own prophetic mission; and (3) to demonstrate the complete independence of the Báb's religion from Islam (Eschraghi 2011). Since the practice of Islam is based squarely on obeying Islamic laws, therefore, the Báb, by revealing a completely new set of laws, made a clear break from Islam—as dramatic as it was definitive—yet declaring this as a fulfillment and continuation of the prophecies of Islam and previous religions.

Between 1845 and 1850, the Báb was held in various prisons. Around July 1847, the Báb was imprisoned in Mákú, Azerbaijan. In early May 1848, the Báb was transferred to Chihríq, near Urmia, where he was incarcerated. There, the Báb was placed under strict confinement. This restriction was intended to isolate the Báb, by preventing him from having any direct contact with any of his followers. Yet, despite official disapproval, a surprising number of Bábís succeeded in visiting the Báb in prison. Meanwhile, the Báb's writings were copied and spread, far and wide, throughout Persia. This greatly increased the Báb's fame and influence—a fact that inflamed the wrath of religious and political leaders. To put an end to the Báb's growing influence, the "final solution," so to speak, was to execute the Báb, by a joint decree issued by political and clerical authorities.

So, on 9 July 1850, the Báb was condemned to death at the order of Mírzá Taqí Khán ("Amír Kabír," the grand vizier of the Qájár monarch, Náṣer al-Dīn Sháh, r. 1848–1896) and by the death warrant jointly signed by several Muslim clerics. Sentenced to be executed by a firing squad in Tabriz, Persia, the Báb was suspended, by ropes, from a wall in an army barracks square. Also suspended was a Bábí youth—Mírzá Muḥammad-'Alíy-i-Zunúzí ("Anís")—who had asked for the honor of being martyred along with the Báb. What followed was as dramatic as it was extraordinary.

The firing squad was a regiment of 750 soldiers, positioned in three files of 250 of infantrymen each. One at a time, each of the three groups of riflemen (who, at that time, were using muskets) in turn, was ordered to open fire upon the Báb. After the clouds of smoke from the muskets had cleared away, the crowd of onlookers gazed in amazement. By all accounts, the Báb had vanished from sight. Only the ropes that had held the Báb in suspension, remained. The ropes had been severed by the volley of bullets. After a frenzied search, the Báb was found back in his prison cell, giving his final instructions to his secretary. The commander of the regiment, a Christian, refused to fire again. So, another firing squad (this time, of Muslim soldiers), was ordered to carry out the execution. The Báb was just 30 years old when he was martyred.

Eventually, some 25 followers of the Báb (called "Bábís") each claimed to be the messianic figure foretold by the Báb. The one whose claim the majority of the Bábís accepted was Bahá'u'lláh, who announced his prophetic mission on 22 April 1863 (nearly 19 years after the Báb declaration), in Baghdad. Bahá'u'lláh subsequently adopted many of the Báb's laws and teachings, thereby rendering the Báb a co-founder of the Bahá'í Faith.

A WESTERNER'S FIRST IMPRESSION

The only Westerner to have met the Báb was Dr. William Cormick (1822–1877), an Irish physician in Tabriz, Persia (present-day Iran). Born in Tabriz as the son of an Irish physician and an Armenian woman, Dr. McCormick studied medicine at University College, London, where he became a licensed doctor, and returned to Persia in 1845 as second physician to the British mission. He later served as a physician for the family of the crown prince, Náṣiri'd-Dín Mírzá, who, in 1848, became Náṣiri'd-Dín Sháh, or King, of Iran. In July 1848, after the Báb was tried before a religious and civil tribunal in Tabriz and convicted of heresy, Dr. Cormick, along with two Persian physicians, was sent by the Shah to examine the Báb in order to certify his insanity, apparently since there was some reluctance to carry out the death sentence.

The Báb was bastinadoed instead. While the soles of his feet were being caned (to inflict punishment by this torture), the Báb was struck severely across the face and injured. Afterward, the Báb asked to be treated by Dr. Cormick, who thus saw the Báb several times before the latter was sent back to prison. Dr. Cormick wrote the following account of these meetings, in a letter to Rev. Benjamin Labaree, D.D., a Presbyterian missionary in Persia, found in the papers of his fellow American missionary, John H. Shedd, D.D.

> You ask me for some particulars of my interview with the founder of the sect known as Bábís. Nothing of any importance transpired in

this interview, as the Báb was aware of my having been sent with two other Persian doctors to see whether he was of sane mind or merely a madman, to decide the question whether to put him to death or not. With this knowledge he was loth to answer any questions put to him. To all enquiries he merely regarded us with a mild look. ... He only once deigned to answer me, on my saying that I was not a Musulmán [Muslim] and was willing to know something about his religion, as I might perhaps be inclined to adopt it. He regarded me very intently on my saying this, and replied that he had no doubt of all Europeans coming over to his religion.

Our report to the Sháh at that time was of a nature to spare his life. He was put to death some time after by the order of the Amír-i-Nizám Mírzá Taqí Khán. On our report he merely got the bastinado, in which operation a farrásh, whether intentionally or not, struck him across the face with the stick destined for his feet, which produced a great wound and swelling of the face. On being asked whether a Persian surgeon should be brought to treat him, he expressed a desire that I should be sent for, and I accordingly treated him for a few days, but in the interviews consequent on this I could never get him to have a confidential chat with me, as some Government people were always present, he being a prisoner.

He was very thankful for my attentions to him. He was a very mild and delicate-looking man, rather small in stature and very fair for a Persian, with a melodious soft voice, which struck me much. Being a Sayyid, he was dressed in the habits of that sect, as were also his two companions. In fact his whole look and deportment went far to dispose one in his favour. Of his doctrine I heard nothing from his own lips, although the idea was that there existed in his religion a certain approach to Christianity. He was seen by some Armenian carpenters, who were sent to make some repairs in his prison, reading the Bible, and he took no pains to conceal it, but on the contrary told them of it. Most assuredly the Musulmán fanaticism does not exist in his religion, as applied to Christians, nor is there that restraint of females that now exists.

> (Dr. William Cormick, cited in E. G. Browne's *Materials for the Study of the Bábí Religion*, pp. 260–62, 264)

MAJOR WORKS

For more information on the writings of the Báb, along with selected excerpts, see Chapter Five, "Scripture and Authoritative Writings: Bahá'í Sacred Texts and Inspired Guidance."

BAHÁ'U'LLÁH (1817–1892):

HISTORICAL SIGNIFICANCE

Mystic, prophet, and lawgiver, Bahá'u'lláh (1817–1892) is most well known as the founder of the Bahá'í Faith. As an independent world religion, the Bahá'í Faith embodies the spiritual teachings, mystical insights, human values, moral foundations, ethical precepts, social principles, and the religious and civil laws promulgated by Bahá'u'lláh—later interpreted and elaborated upon by his eldest son and designated successor, 'Abdu'l-Bahá, followed by Shoghi Effendi, and now by the Universal House of Justice.

Beyond this, Bahá'u'lláh is historically significant, in part, for having declared his mission and principles of world peace to the most powerful rulers and religious leaders in the world. This audacious "proclamation" by Bahá'u'lláh, from his prison cell in Akká, Palestine (now Israel), may be considered among the world's first international peace missions of modern times. In or around 1868, in his open letter to Queen Victoria (r. 1837–1901), Bahá'u'lláh collectively addresses the reigning monarchs and religious leaders of the world as follows:

> Now that ye have refused the Most Great Peace, hold ye fast unto this, the Lesser Peace, that haply ye may in some degree better your own condition and that of your dependents.
>
> O rulers of the earth! Be reconciled among yourselves, that ye may need no more armaments save in a measure to safeguard your territories and dominions. Beware lest ye disregard the counsel of the All-Knowing, the Faithful.
>
> Be united, O kings of the earth, for thereby will the tempest of discord be stilled amongst you, and your peoples find rest, if ye be of them that comprehend. Should any one among you take up arms against another, rise ye all against him, for this is naught but manifest justice. Thus did We exhort you in the Tablet sent down aforetime, and We admonish you once again to follow that which hath been revealed by Him Who is the Almighty, the All-Wise. Should anyone seek refuge with you, extend unto him your protection and betray him not. Thus doth the Pen of the Most High counsel you, as bidden by Him Who is the All-Knowing, the All-Informed.
>
> (Bahá'u'lláh, *Summons*, BRL)

Beyond this historical legacy, Bahá'u'lláh's influence continues to the present day. The global Bahá'í community, after all, is the product and living legacy of Bahá'u'lláh's teachings and enduring spirit.

Formative Years, Iran, 1817–1843

Born on 12 November 1817 in Tehran, Persia (present-day Iran), Bahá'u'lláh was known as Mírzá Ḥusayn-'Alí Núrí. His father, Mírzá 'Abbás Núrí (d. 1839)—also known as Mírzá Buzurg—served as an official in the court of the reigning king of Iran (or "Persia"), Fatḥ-'Alí Sháh Qájár (1797–1834). So, the young Mírzá Ḥusayn-'Alí grew up in the lap of luxury. Small in stature, the young boy stood tall in wisdom. He was precocious, spiritually inclined, remarkably outspoken and audacious, as several historical accounts attest, and as 'Abdu'l-Bahá, on 18 April 1912 in New York, further recounted:

> The Blessed Perfection, Bahá'u'lláh, belonged to the nobility of Persia. From earliest childhood He was distinguished among His relatives and friends. They said, "This child has extraordinary power." In wisdom, intelligence and as a source of new knowledge, He was advanced beyond His age and superior to His surroundings. All who knew Him were astonished at His precocity. It was usual for them to say, "Such a child will not live," for it is commonly believed that precocious children do not reach maturity. During the period of youth the Blessed Perfection did not enter school. He was not willing to be taught. This fact is well established among the Persians of Ṭihrán. Nevertheless, He was capable of solving the difficult problems of all who came to Him. In whatever meeting, scientific assembly or theological discussion He was found, He became the authority of explanation upon intricate and abstruse questions presented.
>
> ('Abdu'l-Bahá, *Promulgation*, BRL)

His family's ancestral home was the village of Takur, in the province of Mazandaran, where Bahá'u'lláh often spent his childhood summers. The name, Bahá'u'lláh—which means the "Glory of God" or "Splendor of God"—is a spiritual title that Bahá'u'lláh adopted later in life. As a youth, Bahá'u'lláh was profoundly disheartened and saddened after reading an account of a Jewish tribe, punished severely for treason in betraying Muhammad's army in war. In that memorable turning point, Bahá'u'lláh resolved to dedicate his life to promoting peace and unity. While no date can be ascertained for this signal event, it must have occurred well before 1844.

Bábí Religion, Imprisonment, First Revelation, 1844–1852

Around three months after the Báb declared his mission on the evening of 22 May 1844, Bahá'u'lláh, as a young man of 26, became a dedicated and ardent follower of the Báb, and soon rose to prominence as one of the leaders of the Bábí movement, for which Bahá'u'lláh suffered imprisonment and eventual exile. The Qajar Dynasty (1794–1925) that ruled Iran at the time and the Islamic clergy felt threatened by the Bábí religion and relentlessly persecuted the Báb and his followers.

In the fall of 1852—soon after August 1852, when three young followers of the Báb made a misguided and failed attempt on the life of the Shah of Iran—Bahá'u'lláh, who had no part in the assassination plot, was arrested, as were many other Bábís, and was imprisoned, with around 150 fellow Bábís, in an underground dungeon infamously known as the "Black Pit" (Síyáh-Chál) in Tehran. As a result, Bahá'u'lláh's home was plundered and ransacked, stripped of all of its wealthy furnishings, forcing his family to seek shelter elsewhere in a rented home in a back alley. Other children thereafter would taunt and ridicule young 'Abbás Effendi (later known as 'Abdu'l-Bahá), Bahá'u'lláh's first-born son (and Bahá'u'lláh's future successor, interpreter, and exemplar of his teachings), and, in one episode, threw stones at 'Abbás Effendi, who was only eight years old at that time. Bahá'u'lláh himself was yoked to very heavy chains (notoriously known as the "Qará-Guhar" chains, the heaviest weighing approximately 51 kilograms). During the four months of his incarceration in the notorious "Black Pit", Bahá'u'lláh experienced a series of profound, transformative visions that further awakened him to his prophetic destiny. Bahá'u'lláh recounts the following:

> One night, in a dream, these exalted words were heard on every side: "Verily, We shall render Thee victorious by Thyself and by Thy Pen. Grieve Thou not for that which hath befallen Thee, neither be Thou afraid, for Thou art in safety. Erelong will God raise up the treasures of the earth—men who will aid Thee through Thyself and through Thy Name, wherewith God hath revived the hearts of such as have recognized Him." ...
>
> During the days I lay in the prison of Ṭihrán, though the galling weight of the chains and the stench-filled air allowed Me but little sleep, still in those infrequent moments of slumber I felt as if something flowed from the crown of My head over My breast, even as a mighty torrent that

precipitateth itself upon the earth from the summit of a lofty mountain. Every limb of My body would, as a result, be set afire. At such moments My tongue recited what no man could bear to hear.

(Bahá'u'lláh, *Epistle*, BRL)

Exile in Baghdad, Private Declaration, 1853–1863

After four months of intense suffering—under such cruel and harrowing conditions that reportedly turned his hair white—Bahá'u'lláh was released in January 1853, but was permanently banished from Iran, doomed to live life as an exile, never to return. Bahá'u'lláh chose to go to Baghdad in Iraq, then a province of the Ottoman Empire, where he remained until 1863, with a short interval of two years, from 1854 to 1856, when he retreated to the mountains in Kurdistan in relative seclusion. At the end of this period—beginning on Wednesday, 22 April 1863, and lasting for 12 days—Bahá'u'lláh privately declared that he was "He whom God shall manifest," the divine messenger foretold by Báb. Bahá'u'lláh made his declaration in a garden near Baghdad, later called the Garden of Riḍván or Garden of Paradise, where he spent 12 days with close companions before continuing into exile in Constantinople (now Istanbul). The declaration took place either on the first day or on the eighth day of his stay in Riḍván, according to two different accounts.

According to Bahá'í history, Bahá'u'lláh and his companions arrived in the Garden of Najibiyyih at around 3:00 p.m. on 22 April 1863. The garden was located on the east bank of the Tigris River in Baghdad. Muhammad Najib Pasha (Mehmed Necib, d. 1851), the governor of Baghdad (r. 1842–1847), had built a palace there and surrounded the garden with a wall; today, it is the site of Baghdad Medical City (formerly known as Saddam Medical City), a large modern teaching hospital. On this day, Bahá'u'lláh, left his house in Baghdad, and, after being bidden farewell by an emotional throng of admirers, crossed the fast-moving Tigris River by boat. Bahá'u'lláh took with him his three sons—'Abdu'l-Bahá (18), Mírzá Mihdí (the "Purest Branch," aged 14), and Mírzá Muḥammád-'Alí (aged 10)—along with Mírzá Aqá Ján, his secretary, and perhaps others. The heavy river flow during the spring season prevented the rest of Bahá'u'lláh's family from joining Bahá'u'lláh until the ninth day of Riḍván.

The details of Bahá'u'lláh's declaration are shrouded in obscurity. However, according to 'Abdu'l-Bahá (in a talk given at Bahjí on 29 April 1916), Bahá'u'lláh, on the first day of Riḍván, declared his prophetic mission to a select few of his close companions (Taherzadeh 1987, 260). Prior to this day, Bahá'u'lláh had kept his mission a secret. Bahá'u'lláh himself designated this ten-year period (1853–1863) leading up to the declaration the "Days of Concealment."

Although the exact words of what Bahá'u'lláh declared on that historic occasion are not known, on the first day of Riḍván Bahá'u'lláh wrote the "Tablet of Job," also known as the "Sura of Patience" or the "City of Patience." From later autobiographical texts, it is clear that Bahá'u'lláh's statements during the Riḍván declaration event included: (1) abolishing all "holy war" henceforth; (2) announcing that another messenger of God would not appear for at least 1,000 years; and (3) abrogating all religious notions of ritual uncleanness after "all created things were immersed in the sea of purification ... on that first day of Riḍván." Ten years later, Bahá'u'lláh would enshrine these three laws in his *Kitáb-i-Aqdas* (Bahá'u'lláh, *Kitáb-i-Aqdas*, BRL).

On 30 April 1863, the ninth day of Riḍván, Bahá'u'lláh's remaining family ferried across the Tigris River, after the floodwaters had subsided, and rejoined Bahá'u'lláh. On the 12th day of Riḍván (3 May 1863), Bahá'u'lláh departed from the Garden of Riḍván to begin his journey to the remote location of Constantinople, where he had been sent by the Persian authorities who feared his influence in Baghdad.

Exiles in Istanbul, Edirne, Public Proclamation, 1863–1868

Immediately after this prophetic announcement, Bahá'u'lláh was exiled again, this time to Constantinople (now Istanbul), from there to Adrianople (now Edirne, in Turkey, 1863–1868), and finally to the prison-city of Acre (now Akko/Akká, Israel, 1868–1892), a notorious penal colony of the Ottoman Empire.

In September 1867, while still in Edirne, Bahá'u'lláh began his public proclamation through series of open letters addressed to political and religious leaders. Alarmed by his growing influence, Ottoman authorities, in 1868, banished Bahá'u'lláh to the fortress-city of Acre in Palestine.

Exile in Acre, Further Proclamation, Laws, Passing, 1868–1892

From his prison cell in Acre, Bahá'u'lláh continued to send open epistles to the leaders of the "Great Powers" in Europe and America including Queen Victoria, Napoleon III, Czar Nicolaevitch Alexander II, Násiri'd-Dín Sháh—stigmatized by Bahá'u'lláh as the "Prince of Oppressors" (Shoghi Effendi, *God Passes By*, BRL), Sultán Abdu'l-'Azíz, and Pope Pius IX. Bahá'u'lláh also publicly proclaimed his mission to Francis Joseph, Emperor of Austria and Hungary, Kaiser Wilhelm I, King of Prussia and, collectively, to the "Presidents of the Republics of the Americas" (Buck 2004). Bahá'u'lláh's public proclamation may be considered to be an early, if not the first, international peace mission, as previously stated. That proclamation was largely unheeded by the kings and ecclesiastics whom Bahá'u'lláh openly addressed. That proclamation would have a delayed impact, a century later in 1968, when His Highness Malietoa Tanumafili II, the King of Samoa—Head of State, or *O le Ao o le Malo* ("the First Warrior"), embraced the Bahá'í Faith, thereby becoming the first reigning sovereign to accept the message of Bahá'u'lláh.

In 1873, Bahá'u'lláh completed his book of laws, known as the *Kitáb-i-Aqdas* (the *Most Holy Book*). As with the Báb's book of laws, the Persian *Bayán*, the *Aqdas* was much more than a code of laws, and functions, as a whole, much like a Constitution, with an abundance and wide array of principles and precepts.

On 29 May 1892, Bahá'u'lláh passed away in Bahjí, near Akká. In his last will and testament, known as the *Kitáb-i-Ahd*, "Book of the Covenant" (or, alternatively, the *Kitáb-i-Ahdí*, the "Book of My Covenant"), Bahá'u'lláh explicitly designated his eldest son, 'Abdu'l-Bahá, as his successor, interpreter, and exemplar of Bahá'u'lláh's teachings, confirming a previous statement to the same effect in the *Kitáb-i-Aqdas*. 'Abdu'l-Bahá's appointment as Bahá'u'lláh's successor was known to Russian scholars, who published the original Persian/Arabic text of the "Book of the Covenant," along with a Russian translation, in 1893, in a leading academic journal. (See Buck and Ioannesyan 2010.)

A WESTERNER'S FIRST IMPRESSION

What was it like to be in the presence of Bahá'u'lláh, to behold his face, to listen to his words, and to be captivated by his charisma? To give an impression, one particular "pen portrait" stands out. It is the account by Cambridge Orientalist, Edward Granville Browne

(1862–1926), who was one of the leading scholars of the late 19th and early 20th centuries in researching and publishing on the Bábí and Bahá'í religions. On Wednesday, 16 April 1890, Professor Browne was granted an audience with Bahá'u'lláh in Acre (aka Acco, or Akká) in Ottoman Palestine (present-day Israel). Browne's initial impressions vividly describe his meeting with Bahá'u'lláh as follows:

> Though I dimly suspected whither I was going and whom I was to behold ..., a second or two elapsed ere, with a throb of wonder and awe, I became definitely conscious that the room was not untenanted. In the corner where the divan met the wall sat a wondrous and venerable figure, crowned with a felt head-dress of the kind called *táj* ["crown"] by dervishes (but of unusual height and make), round the base of which was wound a small white turban. The face of him on whom I gazed I can never forget, though I cannot describe it. Those piercing eyes seemed to read one's very soul; power and authority sat on that ample brow; while the deep lines on the forehead and face implied an age which the jet-black hair and beard flowing down in indistinguishable luxuriance almost to the waist seemed to belie. No need to ask in whose presence I stood, as I bowed myself before one who is the object of a devotion and love which kings might envy and emperors sigh for in vain! ...
>
> A mild dignified voice bade me be seated, and then continued:— "Praise be to God that thou hast attained! ... Thou hast come to see a prisoner and an exile. ... We desire but the good of the world and the happiness of the nations; yet they deem us a stirrer up of strife and sedition worthy of bondage and banishment. ... That all nations should become one in faith and all men as brothers; that the bonds of affection and unity between the sons of men should be strengthened; that diversity of religion should cease, and differences of race be annulled— what harm is there in this? ... Yet so it shall be; these fruitless strifes, these ruinous wars shall pass away, and the 'Most Great Peace' shall come. ... Do not you in Europe need this also? Is not this that which Christ foretold? ... Yet do we see your kings and rulers lavishing their treasures more freely on means for the destruction of the human race than on that which would conduce to the happiness of mankind. ... These strifes and this bloodshed and discord must cease, and all men be as one kindred and one family. ... Let not a man glory in this, that he loves his country; let him rather glory in this, that he loves his kind.".
> ... Such, so far as I can recall them, were the words which, besides many others, I heard from Beha. Let those who read them consider

> well with themselves whether such doctrines merit death and bonds,
> and whether the world is more likely to gain or lose by their diffusion.
>
> (Browne 1891/2012, xxxix–xl)

These memorable words, left to posterity, convey a real sense of the force and magnetism of Bahá'u'lláh's personality. (For further details of this historic encounter, see Buck and Ioannesyan, "Scholar Meets Prophet," 2018.) This extraordinary power of personal influence, as previously stated, is referred to by scholars as "charisma." Bahá'u'lláh's charisma, to say the least, was—by all accounts—quite remarkable. Yet it is not only the quality of this unique and outstanding individual that matters, but what that individual stands for. One can say that what Bahá'u'lláh proclaimed, promulgated, preached, and promoted is equally, if not more, important than the impression he made on Professor Browne and countless others. The body of Bahá'u'lláh's teachings, as well as the community of followers, that he established, are part and parcel of the rich legacy that Bahá'u'lláh left for future generations—indeed, for centuries to come, Bahá'ís firmly believe—which is the subject matter of the present book.

MAJOR WORKS

Bahá'u'lláh's legacy is as prolific as it is profound, with the equivalent of around 100 volumes of his writings now extant. Official translations of this enormous body of work are ongoing. For the most part, the most important works of Bahá'u'lláh had already been translated into English.

In 1873, Bahá'u'lláh revealed the *Kitáb-i-Aqdas* (*The Most Holy Book*), the most significant and outstanding Bahá'í scripture overall. Other major works by Bahá'u'lláh include his preeminent doctrinal text, the *Kitáb-i-Iqan* (*The Book of Certitude*, composed in the course of two days and two nights in January 1861); his foremost ethical work, *Kalimát-i-Maknúnih* (*The Hidden Words*, 1858), a collection of pithy aphorisms said to contain the essence of all religions; and his most celebrated mystical work, *Haft Vádí* (*The Seven Valleys*, 1856). For further details and selected excerpts, see Chapter Five, "Scripture and Authoritative Writings: Bahá'í Sacred Texts and Inspired Guidance."

Since this book, *Bahá'í Faith: The Basics*, is an introductory text, space does not permit a full account of Bahá'u'lláh's life and significance. Readers are encouraged to consult the references, at the end of this book, for further reading.

'ABDU'L-BAHÁ (1844–1921):

HISTORICAL SIGNIFICANCE

Born 'Abbás Effendi on 23 May 1844 in Tehran, Persia (now Iran), 'Abdu'l-Bahá ("Servant of Bahá") was the eldest son of Bahá'u'lláh, the founder (along with his predecessor, the Báb) of the Bahá'í Faith. Briefly, 'Abdu'l-Bahá was Bahá'u'lláh's designated successor, interpreter, and "Perfect Exemplar" of Bahá'u'lláh's teachings. 'Abdu'l-Bahá, the "Centre of the Covenant of Bahá'u'lláh," led the fledgling Bahá'í community from Bahá'u'lláh's passing on 29 May 1892 until his own departure from this mortal world, at the age of 77, on 28 November 1921. 'Abdu'l-Bahá's historical significance is primarily seen in terms of Bahá'í history, especially in light of the public proclamation and exposition of Bahá'í teachings, the international expansion of the Bahá'í community, and its institutional development. Time will tell as to what wider historical significance 'Abdu'l-Bahá will have in a broader context, depending on the future development and influence of the Bahá'í community itself.

The late historian and Yale Professor Emeritus, Firuz Kazemzadeh, has periodized 'Abdu'l-Bahá's life as follows: Life with Bahá'u'lláh, 1844–1892; Iran, 1844–1853; Exile and Imprisonment, 1853–1892; Ministry, 1892–1921 (Acre Period, 1892–1908; Freedom, 1908–1921; International Travels, 1910–1913; War Years, 1914–1918; Final Years, 1919–1921). It is difficult to encompass the life, achievements, and full historical significance of this unique individual. Therefore, a few highlights will be offered as a sketch, falling short of a suitable portrait of this notable Bahá'í leader.

KEY LIFE EVENTS

LIFE WITH BAHÁ'U'LLAH, 1844–1892

Childhood, Iran, 1844–1852

'Abdu'l-Bahá (whose given name was 'Abbás Effendi) was born on the very same day that the Báb declared his prophetic mission in Shiraz, Persia, an event that is considered the beginning of Bahá'í history. The Báb announced that a greater prophet would come soon. Since most of the Báb's followers, called "Bábís," recognized Bahá'u'lláh as the one whom the Báb foretold, the Báb has come to be regarded as Bahá'u'lláh's herald. Having been born in a well-to-do and distinguished family, the young boy lived in the lap of luxury, but only for a few years, after which a life of privation, exile, and imprisonment would follow.

'Abbás Effendi's father was Bahá'u'lláh (whose life is briefly surveyed in the previous section of this chapter). 'Abbás Effendi's mother, Asíyih Khánum, was also from a noble family in the province of Mazandaran. She was known as Navváb, whom Bahá'u'lláh honored with the title, "Most Exalted Leaf." In 1835, she and Bahá'u'lláh married. Together, Bahá'u'lláh and Navváb had seven children, with 'Abbás Effendi being the oldest. Bahíyyih, his younger sister (known as Bahíyyih Khánum as an adult), was later honored by Bahá'u'lláh with the title, the "Greatest Holy Leaf." Mihdí, his younger brother (known as Mírzá Mihdí as an adult) was later honored by Bahá'u'lláh by the title, the "Purest Branch," and tragically died on 23 June 1870, after falling through an open sky-light on the rooftop of the prison in 'Akká, Palestine, where 'Abbás Effendi and his family would be incarcerated, with Bahá'u'lláh, under strict confinement (from 1868–1870). For the first several years of his life, 'Abbás Effendi's childhood was idyllic. That situation dramatically changed soon after Bahá'u'lláh, in the fall of 1852, was put in the subter-ranean dungeon known as the Síyáh-Chál (the Black Pit) under the cruel and harrowing circumstances briefly described in the preceding section.

Exile and Imprisonment, 1853–1892

On 12 January 1853, after his release from the Síyáh-Chál, Bahá'u'lláh and his family, including young 'Abbás Effendi (who was eight years old at the time), began the arduous journey over mountains under severe winter conditions, a result of which he reportedly suffered frostbite, with lifelong effects. On arrival in Baghdad in April 1853, 'Abbás Effendi witnessed firsthand how the small enclave of Bábí exiles was profoundly demoralized, in utter disarray, their commu-nity riven by bitter rivalry, whereupon Bahá'u'lláh chose to live in seclusion as a wandering dervish in the mountains of Kurdistan from 1854 to 1856 where he gained a reputation as a notable Sufi mystic. Separation from his beloved father was anguishing for the young boy. During his sojourn in Baghdad, he had no formal schooling, but was encouraged by Bahá'u'lláh to study the works of the Báb.

At some point in his life, 'Abbás Effendi became known as 'Abdu'l-Bahá ("Servant of the Glory [of God]," referring to Bahá'u'lláh). As a youth in his teens, 'Abdu'l-Bahá took on increasing responsibilities on behalf of his father, serving as Bahá'u'lláh's ambassador, amanuensis (personal secretary), and administrator of his father's affairs. In 1863, Bahá'u'lláh was exiled to Constantinople (Istanbul) for four months (arriving on 16 August 1863); then to Adrianople (Edirne) for over four years (arriving on 12 December 1863); and finally, on 31 August 1868, to the prison city of Acre in Palestine (modern Akko in northern Israel), where, by Ottoman decree, 'Abdu'l-Bahá's status as an Ottoman prisoner continued thereafter for 40 years (ending in 1908). On arrival, Bahá'u'lláh and his entourage were imprisoned in the army barracks, under harsh conditions, for over two years.

Prior to that, in 1867 while still in Adrianople, Bahá'u'lláh, after publicly proclaiming his prophetic mission in open epistles to the world's most powerful political and religious leaders, withdrew from the general public, whereupon 'Abdu'l-Bahá became Bahá'u'lláh's representative in all external matters except those affecting the community of exiled Bahá'ís (as they came to be known) internally. In 1872, at the urging of Bahá'u'lláh, 'Abdu'l-Bahá married Munírih Khánum, from a distinguished Bábí/Bahá'í family. They had nine children—seven daughters and two sons, of which four daughters survived to adulthood.

MINISTRY, 1892–1921

Ministry, Acre Period, 1892–1908

After Bahá'u'lláh passed away on 9 May 1892, 'Abdu'l-Bahá led the Bahá'í community for the next 29 years (1892–1921). Bahá'u'lláh's had explicitly designated 'Abdu'l-Bahá as the Bahá'í community's officially appointed successor, authorized interpreter, and moral exemplar. 'Abdu'l-Bahá's subsequent role as the Center of the Covenant is pivotal in Bahá'í history, for it was the lynchpin of Bahá'í solidarity as a faith-community, safeguarding it from schism. This was not without great difficulty, as 'Abdu'l-Bahá's rightful position was challenged, ultimately unsuccessfully, by one of his half-brothers, causing great pain, turmoil, and division within Bahá'u'lláh's surviving family and, to some extent, within the wider Bahá'í community itself, for a period of time.

In 1907, 'Abdu'l-Bahá began relocating his family to Haifa, where he had built a house at the foot of Mount Carmel, one of the most sacred places in the Holy Land. On the majestic slopes of Carmel, 'Abdu'l-Bahá also constructed a shrine in honor of the Báb. In March 1909, he tearfully placed the Báb's mortal remains in the Shrine of the Báb, thereby establishing it as a holy pilgrimage site for Bahá'ís, second in importance only to the Shrine of Bahá'u'lláh in Bahjí. Soon after, 'Abdu'l-Bahá took up residence in the house in Haifa, thereafter, serving as the administrative center of the Bahá'í Faith which, over time, evolved into what is now known as the "Baha'i World Centre," which is permanently established on Mount Carmel, in Haifa, Israel.

Ministry, Freedom, 1908

In the early 19th-century, the world was rocked by a series of revolutions, which included, notably, the Russian Revolution of 1905, the Persian Revolution of 1906, the Ottoman Revolution in 1908, the Portuguese Revolution of 1910, and the Chinese Revolution of 1911. In July 1908, the Ottoman "Young Turk" Revolution took place (when Sulṭán Abdülhamid was divested of his autocratic powers), with amnesty for all political prisoners following in its wake. As a direct result, 'Abdu'l-Bahá was liberated. Thus freed, he could now travel abroad to spread Bahá'u'lláh's message of world unity, far and wide.

Ministry, International Travels, 1910–1913

'Abdu'l-Bahá's travels abroad first began at the advice of his treating physicians. After suffering several bouts of serious illness, 'Abdu'l-Bahá was urged by his doctors to change his environment for the betterment of his health. So, in August 1910, 'Abdu'l-Bahá sailed to Egypt, where he spent the next year. There he associated with leading intellectuals, prominent religious leaders, influential journalists and editors, as well as notable political officials. Then, in August 1911, 'Abdu'l-Bahá—his health having improved—traveled to Europe, eventually reaching London where, on 10 September 1911, he gave his first public address, from the pulpit of the City Temple. His one-month stay in England was filled with public talks, interviews with the press, and private meetings with a number of prominent intellectual and religious leaders, along with a host of other individuals, thereby setting a pattern for his future travels abroad. In December, 'Abdu'l-Bahá returned to Egypt for the winter, thus concluding his first journey to the West. 'Abdu'l-Bahá's second journey to the West (25 March 1912–17 June 1913) was much more extensive, most notably in America, where he spent 239 days, from 11 April 1912 to 5 December 1912. Earlier in this chapter, significant attention was given to 'Abdu'l-Bahá's talk, published as "2 December 1912: Talk at Home of Mr. and Mrs. Edward B. Kinney, 780 West End Avenue, New York" ('Abdu'l-Bahá, *Promulgation*, BRL), about which historian Robert Stockman, in the concluding chapter of *'Abdu'l-Bahá in America*, commented:

> His talk at the Kinney residence on December 2, 1912—three days before his departure—perhaps summarized the Bahá'í approach to race, religion, and the progress of humanity most fully. That day, he offered "certain new teachings which are not found in any of the religious books of the past." The list of twelve distinctive Bahá'í teachings began with the oneness of humanity, followed by independent investigation of truth, the oneness of the religions of the world, the need for religion to be a cause of unity and harmony, the principle that religion must be in accord with science and reason, the equality of men and women, the principle that human beings must free themselves from religious and patriotic prejudices, the need to establish universal peace, the importance of universal education, the solution to economic questions, the need for the organization of the Universal House of Justice to explain and implement the commands of Bahá'u'lláh, and Bahá'u'lláh's establishment of a Covenant. All this will be possible, he asserted, through obedience to the Center of the Covenant. The talk blended together the "themes he often presented to the public with those he emphasized to the Bahá'í audience. It made clear an important Bahá'í teaching: that the principles of social reform could accomplish only so much without the spiritual impetus provided by Bahá'u'lláh's establishment of a system to embody the principles and direct their implementation in the world."
>
> (Stockman 2012)

After departing New York, 'Abdu'l-Bahá embarked on the rest of his itinerary to England, France, Germany, and Austria-Hungary. This was a highly successful mission, whereby 'Abdu'l-Bahá effectively proclaimed Bahá'u'lláh's teachings, expounded his major principles, applied them to the most pressing contemporary issues of the day, and consolidated the fledgling Bahá'í communities throughout North America.

Ministry, War Years, 1914–1918

During the First World War, 'Abdu'l-Bahá's contacts with the outside world were drastically curtailed. Notwithstanding, he penned a series of 14 important letters—known as the "Tablets of the Divine Plan" (in March–April 1916 and February–March 1917)—which served as a charter and mandate for greatly expanding the Bahá'í Faith internationally. The "Tablets of the Divine Plan" were addressed primarily to the Bahá'ís of the United States and Canada, whom he charged with the task of leading this global mission. Meanwhile, 'Abdu'l-Bahá encouraged the Bahá'í farmers (who were of Zoroastrian background) throughout the Jordan River valley and on the shores of the Sea of Galilee to produce an abundance of wheat, which 'Abdu'l-Bahá then distributed to the people of Haifa, saving them from starvation, since food supply chains were cut off. The British—who had occupied Haifa at the end of September 1918—witnessed firsthand this extraordinary humanitarian service of famine relief.

Ministry, Final Years

On 27 April 1920, the British government, in a formal recognition of his humanitarian service, knighted 'Abdu'l-Bahá (investing him with the insignia of the Knighthood of the British Empire, which title he accepted but never used). On 28 November 1921, 'Abdu'l-Bahá, at the age of 77, passed away in Haifa, British Palestine (now Israel). His funeral was held the very next day. On short notice, an estimated 10,000 mourners assembled to pay their respects, in spontaneous tribute, to 'Abdu'l-Bahá. Throngs of ethnic Arabs, Jews, Kurds, Turks, and Europeans and Americans were also in attendance. The procession was led by the British High Commissioner for Palestine, who was accompanied by the governors of Jerusalem and Phoenicia along with other officials, including religious leaders from among the local Muslim, Catholic, Orthodox, Anglican, Jewish, and Druze faith-communities. The coffin was solemnly carried up the slopes of Mount Carmel, where 'Abdu'l-Bahá's mortal remains were laid to rest in one of the chambers of the Shrine of the Báb.

Cambridge Orientalist, Edward Granville Browne—in "Sir 'Abdu'l-Bahá Abbás: Died 28th November, 1921," an obituary published in 1922 in the *Journal of the Royal Asiatic Society*—claimed that 'Abdu'l-Bahá "has probably exercised a greater influence not only in the Orient but in the Occident than any Asiatic thinker and teacher of recent times" (Browne 1922). Browne's eulogy of 'Abdu'l-Bahá as likely the most influential Asiatic thinker of his day may be controversial, yet there is no question of the historical importance of this remarkable individual. Professor Browne, in that significant tribute, recognized 'Abdu'l-Bahá as a great man.

A WESTERNER'S FIRST IMPRESSION

In April 1890, Cambridge Orientalist, Edward Granville Browne, conveyed his first impressions of 'Abdu'l-Bahá as follows:

> Seldom have I seen one whose appearance impressed me more. A tall strongly-built man holding himself straight as an arrow, with white turban and raiment, long black locks reaching almost to the shoulder, broad powerful forehead indicating a strong intellect combined with an unswerving will, eyes keen as a hawk's, and strongly-marked but pleasing features—such was my first impression of 'Abbás Efendí ['Abdu'l-Bahá], "the master" (Aká) as he *par excellence* is called by the Bábís. Subsequent conversation with him served only to heighten the respect with which his appearance had from the first inspired me. One more eloquent of speech, more ready of argument, more apt of illustration, more intimately acquainted with the sacred books of the Jews, the Christians, and the Muhammadans, could, I should think, scarcely be found even amongst the eloquent, ready, and subtle race to which he belongs. These qualities, combined with a bearing at once majestic and genial, made me cease to wonder at the influence and esteem which he enjoyed even beyond the circle of his father's [Bahá'u'lláh's] followers. About the greatness of this man and his power no one who had seen him could entertain a doubt.
>
> (Browne 1891/2012, vii–liii)

MAJOR WORKS

'Abdu'l-Bahá also left a literary—and, for Bahá'ís, a scriptural—legacy. Among his writings are three books: (1) *The Secret Divine Civilization* (written in 1875, first published in Bombay, 1882); (2) *A Traveler's Narrative* (c. 1886, published by Cambridge University Press in 1891 in the original Persian and in an English translation by

Cambridge scholar, Edward G. Browne); (3) *A Treatise on Politics* (1892), an authorized translation of which is not yet available. Among the published collections of 'Abdu'l-Bahá's that have been translated into English are the following works: (4) *Some Answered Questions* (1908; new translation, 2014); (5) *Memorials of the Faithful*; (6) *The Promulgation of Universal Peace: Talks Delivered by 'Abdu'l-Bahá during His Visit to the United States and Canada in 1912*; (7) *'Abdu'l-Bahá in London*; (8) *'Abdu'l-Bahá in Canada*; (9) *Paris Talks*; and (10) *Selections From the Writings of 'Abdu'l-Bahá*. These works effectively explain and expound the teachings of Bahá'u'lláh, often with reference to contemporary issues in the West and to Christian topics as well.

Addressed to the rulers and people of Persia (present-day Iran), *The Secret Divine Civilization*, published anonymously, applied Bahá'u'lláh's social principles (without mentioning Bahá'u'lláh as the source) to the modernization of a specific country. As a response to modernity, 'Abdu'l-Bahá proposed reforms in all spheres of Persian state and society, thereby setting an ambitious and enlightened agenda for the regeneration and social progress of Persia as a nation. In so doing, 'Abdu'l-Bahá championed the adoption of modern science and technology, advocated the establishment of a parliament, encouraged diplomacy and effective statecraft, condemned militarism, called for a codification of laws to establish and safeguard individual rights and liberties, urged equitable distribution of resources for the benefit of the nation, and promoted ethical and secular education. For further details, including elected excerpts, see Chapter Five, "Scripture and Authoritative Writings: Bahá'í Sacred Texts and Inspired Guidance."

SHOGHI EFFENDI (1897–1957):

HISTORICAL SIGNIFICANCE

Appointed as the "Guardian" of the Bahá'í Faith (from 1921–1957), Shoghi Effendi was the grandson of 'Abdu'l-Bahá and great-grandson of Bahá'u'lláh, the prophet-founder of the Bahá'í Faith. Shoghi Effendi served as 'Abdu'l-Bahá's designated successor and Guardian of the Bahá'í Faith for 35 years. The greatest accomplishments of Shoghi Effendi are said to be four: (1) his translations of writings of Bahá'u'lláh, the Báb, 'Abdu'l-Bahá, and *Nabíl's Narrative* (a history); (2) his own works and correspondence; (3) completion, construction, and/or beautification of Bahá'í Shrines, Houses of Worship, and acquisition of national and local headquarters and endowments in various countries around the world; and (4) doctrinal exposition of Bahá'í teachings (Rabbani 1969, 226–227). These achievements are some of the hallmarks of Shoghi Effendi's significance in Bahá'í history itself. As for his wider impact on future history, time will tell, depending on the foreseeable spiritual and social influence of the Bahá'í institutions which Shoghi Effendi played so key a role in developing and through the Bahá'í community itself, on which Shoghi Effendi had such a formative and far-ranging impact.

KEY LIFE EVENTS

On 1 March 1897, Shoghi Effendi (given name: Shoghi Rabbani) was born in Acre, Palestine (now Akko/Akká, Israel). Prior to assuming his responsibilities as the Guardian of the Bahá'í Faith, Shoghi Effendi studied at the Collège des Frères in Haifa, Syrian Protestant College (American University of Beirut), and finally at Balliol College (1920–1921), University of Oxford. Shoghi Effendi was still at Oxford at the time that 'Abdu'l-Bahá passed away on 28 November 1921. In his last Will and Testament, 'Abdu'l-Bahá explicitly appointed Shoghi Effendi as successor, interpreter, and chief administrator of the Bahá'í community. But it was not until 3 January 1922, that the provisions of 'Abdu'l-Bahá's last Will and Testament were officially read and first made known to Shoghi Effendi. Both the death of 'Abdu'l-Bahá and Shoghi Effendi's appointment, by 'Abdu'l-Bahá, as Guardian of the Bahá'í Faith came as a complete shock and surprise, which took some time for Shoghi Effendi, who was deeply grieved by the passing of his beloved grandfather, to fully absorb. After all, assuming the position of Guardian was a tremendous responsibility and burden, which Shoghi Effendi came to accept, and executed brilliantly, with total dedication.

As part of his enduring legacy, Shoghi Effendi effectively established the Bahá'í administrative order as it exists today. These Bahá'í institutions were ordained by Bahá'u'lláh and further elucidated by 'Abdu'l-Bahá. Shoghi Effendi instituted local and national consultative bodies (known as "spiritual assemblies") and clearly defined electoral and administrative procedures for their annual elections and successful functioning. The Bahá'í community became effectively globalized under Shoghi Effendi's leadership. By distancing it from the Islamic matrix in which it originated, the Guardian achieved widespread recognition of the independent character of the Bahá'í Faith. After laying the foundations of the Bahá'í administrative order, Shoghi Effendi then launched a series of expansion plans that succeeded in establishing Bahá'í communities throughout the world.

Shoghi Effendi, in his further efforts to gain official recognition of the Bahá'í Faith, encouraged local and national spiritual assemblies to incorporate, thereby acquiring another layer of rights and protections as legal entities. He also urged Bahá'ís to obtain state recognition of Bahá'í marriage, as well as holy days, so that Bahá'í students would be excused from school for religious observances. In addition, his role in establishing these elected Bahá'í administrative bodies, Shoghi Effendi expanded Bahá'u'lláh's institution of specially designated leaders called the Hands of the Cause of God. This elite and distinguished leadership group consisted of outstanding Bahá'ís who, assisted by their auxiliary boards, were charged with the propagation and defense of the Bahá'í Faith. Prior to Shoghi Effendi's death in 1957, some 27 Hands of the Cause had been appointed.

On 4 November 1957, Shoghi Effendi passed away in London. His premature death, at a relatively young age, was completely unexpected, and came as a great shock to the entire Bahá'í world. Although the institution of the Guardianship was a hereditary office, Shoghi Effendi had no son to succeed him. So, after Shoghi Effendi's death, a council of distinguished Bahá'ís, previously appointed as Hands of the Cause of God, served as the "custodians" of the Bahá'í Faith until the election of the Universal House of Justice in Haifa in April 1963.

A WESTERNER'S FIRST IMPRESSION

Alain Leroy Locke (1885–1954) became the first African American Rhodes Scholar in 1907. He later went on to become the "Dean" of the Harlem Renaissance, during which time he edited an anthology entitled, *The New Negro: an Interpretation* (1925), acclaimed by one scholar as "our first national book" (referring to African Americans). In 1918, Alain Locke embraced the Bahá'í Faith in the very same year that he was awarded his PhD in philosophy from Harvard University. In 1923, Alain Locke went on his first Bahá'í pilgrimage to Haifa,

Palestine (now Israel), where he first met Shoghi Effendi. These, in part, are Locke's brief, but vivid impressions:

IMPRESSIONS OF HAIFA

Alain Locke, Ph.D. (1924/1930)

It was a privilege to see and experience these things. But it was still more of a privilege to stand there with the Guardian of the Cause [Shoghi Effendi], and to feel that, accessible and inspiring as it was to all who can come and will come, there was available there for him a constant source of inspiration and vision from which to draw, in the accomplishment of his heavy burdens and responsibilities. That thought of communion with ideas and ideals without the mediation of symbols, seemed to me the most reassuring and novel feature. For after all the only enlightened symbol of a religious or moral principle is the figure of a personality endowed to perfection with its qualities and necessary attributes. Earnestly renewing this inheritance seemed the constant concern of this gifted personality, and the quiet but insistent lesson of his temperament.

Refreshingly human after this intense experience, was the relaxation of our walk and talk in the gardens. Here the evidences of love, devotion and service were as concrete and as practical and as human as inside the shrines they had been mystical and abstract and super-human. Shoghi Effendi is a master of detail as well as of principle, of executive foresight as well as of projective vision. But I have never heard details so redeemed of their natural triviality as when talking to him of the plans for the beautifying and laying out of the terraces and gardens. They were important because they all were meant to dramatize the emotion of the place and quicken the soul even through the senses. It was night in the quick twilight of the East before we had finished the details of inspecting the gardens, and then by the lantern light, the faithful gardener showed us to the austere retreat of the great Expounder of the teaching. It taught me with what purely simple and meager elements a master workman works. It is after all in Himself that He finds His message and it is Himself that He gives with it to the world.

(Locke, "Impressions of Haifa")

MAJOR WORKS

Despite the heavy administration responsibilities that he bore as Guardian of the Bahá'í Faith, Shoghi Effendi produced his prodigious and impressive translation work in his spare time. (As a result, Shoghi Effendi is said to have slept, on average, a mere four hours per night.) In the course of his important and exacting translation projects, Shoghi Effendi translated several works of Bahá'u'lláh into English, such as *The Hidden Words of Bahá'u'lláh* (London, 1923, rev. ed. London, 1929), *The Book of Certitude* (New York, 1931), a selected anthology, *Gleanings from the Writings of Bahá'u'lláh* (New York, 1935), another compendium of Bahá'u'lláh's writings, entitled *Prayers and Meditations of Bahá'u'lláh* (New York, 1938), and *The Epistle to the Son of the Wolf* (Wilmette, 1941).

Shoghi Effendi's translations have taken on a special status of their own. So much so that subsequent translations of these very same works into other European languages have been modeled on Shoghi Effendi's original English translations (rather than translating the same words directly from their Arabic and Persian originals). The Guardian's translations of Bahá'í scriptures—considered not only to be superb, but also inspired and inerrant in terms of accurately conveying the purport of these sacred texts—set a standard for generations to come, and are relied upon as an authoritative model for future translations, since there is a wealth of Bahá'í texts that are as yet untranslated. So profoundly accurate are the Guardian's translations that those Bahá'ís whose native language is Arabic often consult Shoghi Effendi's translations whenever the original Arabic text is ambiguous.

As one of his first major literary accomplishments, Shoghi Effendi edited and translated a historical chronicle of the Bábí origins of the Bahá'í Faith by Nabíl-i-Zarandí (aka Nabíl-i-A'ẓam), which he entitled, *The Dawn-Breakers* (New York, 1932), a lengthy volume with copious footnotes. Other works followed. *The Dispensation of Bahá'u'lláh* (New York, 1934) highlights and sets forth, in detail, the distinct stations and respective roles of the central figures of the Bahá'í Faith, i.e. the Báb, Bahá'u'lláh, and 'Abdu'l-Bahá. Two of Shoghi Effendi's letters were of such length that they were published as individual volumes: *The Advent of Divine Justice* (New York, 1939) and *The Promised Day Is Come* (Wilmette, 1941). Shoghi Effendi also authored a history of the first century of the Bahá'í religion, *God Passes By*

(Wilmette, 1944), which exists in a slightly shorter version in Persian, *Lawḥ-i Qarn* (Tehran, 1944).

As part of his strategic efforts to gain recognition of the Bahá'í Faith as an independent world religion, Shoghi Effendi oversaw the publication of successive volumes of *The Bahá'í World*, which he considered to be the most important Bahá'í publications next to translations of the Bahá'í scriptures. These volumes, which serve as sourcebooks full of documentation of the nature and character of the Bahá'í religion, were typically presented to civic leaders and other dignitaries by representatives of local Bahá'í communities.

Shoghi Effendi wrote thousands of letters in English, Persian, and Arabic. Although not regarded as Bahá'í scripture, these writings are considered authoritative and thus are an invaluable source of guidance for the development of Bahá'í institutions and for the ideal conduct of Bahá'ís as individuals. Many of these letters have been collected and published in more than 15 volumes in English and ten volumes in Persian (which have not yet been translated into English).

For further details, see Chapter Five, "Scripture and Authoritative Writings: Bahá'í Sacred Texts and Inspired Guidance."

THE UNIVERSAL HOUSE OF JUSTICE (ESTABLISHED 1963):

HISTORICAL SIGNIFICANCE

The Universal House of Justice, based at the Bahá'í World Centre in Haifa, Israel, oversees the affairs of the worldwide Bahá'í community. Ordained by Bahá'u'lláh in 1873, the House was established in 1963. Bahá'u'lláh conferred the necessary authority on the Universal House of Justice to supplement, as well as gradually apply, Bahá'u'lláh's laws and ordinances. The House, consisting of nine members, is elected once every five years by all members of national Bahá'í councils, each called a "National Spiritual Assembly," from around the world. The Universal House of Justice, as the supreme Bahá'í institution, exerts direct influence on Bahá'í affairs the world over. Its mandate, vision, and vista, moreover, extend far beyond the horizons of the Bahá'í community itself, in seeking to contribute to the unity, peace, and prosperity of the world at large. The extent to which the Universal House of Justice may succeed in doing so depends on the course of future events, especially in terms of the growth, expansion, and positive influence which the Bahá'í community, under the auspices and oversight of the House itself, may have in terms of its prospective, future impact on society, and, in due course, on world affairs.

KEY ADMINISTRATIVE EVENTS

As stated, the Universal House of Justice is the international governing body of the Bahá'í Faith, and its supreme administrative institution. Bahá'ís see the House of Justice as a sacred institution, invested with spiritual and administrative authority, and it is therefore considered to be divinely inspired and guided in the process of its decision-making. This is because the House was ordained by Bahá'u'lláh in the Kitáb-i-Aqdas (*The Most Holy Book*). The permanent Seat of the Universal House of Justice is established on the slopes of Mount Carmel, in Haifa, Israel, near the Shrine of the Báb and the resting places of members of Bahá'u'lláh's family. Thus, this is a sacred institution situated in a sacred place.

The Universal House of Justice is elected once every five years, at an international convention of Bahá'í delegates from around the world, as the culmination of a three-stage electoral process. First, Bahá'ís, in their local "Unit Convention," annually elect a delegate (or delegates, depending on the number of Bahá'ís in an electoral district) to their respective national convention. This is an annual election. Next, these locally elected delegates meet at a national convention, in order to elect the National Spiritual Assembly of a given country. This election also takes place annually. Finally, members of all National Spiritual Assemblies throughout the Bahá'í world gather together, once every five years, at the International Bahá'í Convention at the Bahá'í World Centre in Haifa, Israel, to elect the nine members of the Universal House of Justice by confidential, plurality vote—with no nominations or campaigning allowed. This electoral process is considered to be purely democratic and divinely inspired in nature.

On 21 April 1963, the first Universal House of Justice was elected at the home of 'Abdu'l-Bahá, on 7 Haparsim Street, in Haifa, Israel. Ballots were received from all 56 existing National Spiritual Assemblies, with 288 members of 51 National Spiritual Assemblies present at the election. (As of 2019, there are more than 180 National Spiritual Assemblies.) These elections—characterized as "a democratic global electoral process"—are entirely free of nomination, fund-raising, and campaigning. On 26 November 1972, "The Constitution of the Universal House of Justice" was adopted and signed, with a mission statement that reads, in part:

Among the powers and duties with which the Universal House of Justice has been invested are:

> To ensure the preservation of the Sacred Texts and to safeguard their inviolability; to analyse, classify, and coordinate the Writings; and to defend and protect the Cause of God and emancipate it from the fetters of repression and persecution;
>
> To advance the interests of the Faith of God; to proclaim, propagate and teach its Message; to expand and consolidate the institutions of its Administrative Order; to usher in the World Order of Bahá'u'lláh; to promote the attainment of those spiritual qualities which should characterize Bahá'í life individually and collectively; to do its utmost for the realization of greater cordiality and comity amongst the nations and for the attainment of universal peace; and to foster that which is conducive to the enlightenment and illumination of the souls of men and the advancement and betterment of the world;
>
> To enact laws and ordinances not expressly recorded in the Sacred Texts; to abrogate, according to the changes and requirements of the time, its own enactments; to deliberate and decide upon all problems which have caused difference; to elucidate questions that are obscure; to safeguard the personal rights, freedom and initiative of individuals; and to give attention to the preservation of human honour, to the development of countries and the stability of states;
>
> To promulgate and apply the laws and principles of the Faith; to safeguard and enforce that rectitude of conduct which the Law of God enjoins; to preserve and develop the Spiritual and Administrative Centre of the Bahá'í Faith, permanently fixed in the twin cities of 'Akká and Haifa; to administer the affairs of the Bahá'í community throughout the world; to guide, organize, coordinate and unify its activities; to found institutions; to be responsible for ensuring that no body or institution within the Cause abuse its privileges or decline in the exercise of its rights and prerogatives; and to provide for the receipt, disposition, administration and safeguarding of the funds, endowments and other properties that are entrusted to its care;
>
> To adjudicate disputes falling within its purview; to give judgement in cases of violation of the laws of the Faith and to pronounce sanctions for such violations; to provide for the enforcement of its decisions; to provide for the arbitration and settlement of disputes arising between

peoples; and to be the exponent and guardian of that Divine Justice which can alone ensure the security of, and establish the reign of law and order in, the world.

(Universal House of Justice, *Constitution*)

The House's avowed mission "to do its utmost for the realization of greater cordiality and comity amongst the nations and for the attainment of universal peace; and to foster that which is conducive to the enlightenment and illumination of the souls of men and the advancement and betterment of the world" is universal in scope, such that the House is not exclusively a Bahá'í institution within the purview of its purpose and undertakings.

MAJOR WORKS

From time to time, the Universal House of Justice releases messages addressed to the world at large. Examples of this are "The Promise of World Peace" (October 1985)—the first official public statement issued by the Universal House of Justice since its inception in 1963—and "Letter to the World's Religious Leaders" (April 2002). For excerpts of these two global letters, see Chapter Five, "Scripture and Authoritative Writings: Bahá'í Sacred Texts and Inspired Guidance."

SUMMARY

- The Bahá'í Faith originated in Persia (now Iran) in the 19th century, in the full light of history.
- The Bahá'í Shrines in Haifa, Israel, were declared a UNESCO World Heritage Site in 2008.
- The co-founders, central figures, and highest institution of the Bahá'í Faith are the Báb (1819–1850); Bahá'u'lláh (1817–1892); 'Abdu'l-Bahá (1844–1921); Shoghi Effendi (1897–1957); and the Universal House of Justice (established 1963).
- Today, the distinctive unity and integrity of the Bahá'í Faith is preserved and protected by the explicit line of succession, referred to as "the Covenant."

5

SCRIPTURES AND AUTHORITATIVE WRITINGS
BAHÁ'Í SACRED TEXTS AND INSPIRED GUIDANCE

Presenting information about the Bahá'í Faith would be insufficient without giving readers some direct access to the Bahá'í scriptures, which are at the heart of Bahá'í life. Providing a representative sampling of these sacred texts will go far in acquainting readers with those very scriptures that inspire and guide Bahá'ís worldwide today.

The Bahá'í Faith, as previously stated, was co-founded by the Báb in 1844 and by Bahá'u'lláh in 1863. Bahá'ís see the writings of the Báb and Bahá'u'lláh as direct revelations from God. Therefore, these sacred texts are considered the "Word of God," just as Christians typically regard the Bible. The sacred writings of the Báb and Bahá'u'lláh are considered universal. Their intended audience includes all the peoples of the world. That said, the immediate cultural matrix of Baha'i origins was Islamic in nature. This important fact will help readers better understand the context and content of the writings of the Báb, which are transitional in nature, serving as a bridge from the Islamic social world from which the Bahá'í religion originated, to the cosmopolitan Bahá'í message of world peace through world unity and justice, the bedrock foundations of which Bahá'ís are endeavoring to establish and bring into reality today.

Other Bahá'í texts have a special status by virtue of their "conferred infallibility," meaning that they are also considered divinely guided, and therefore provide unerring directives and guidance—in principle, for the world at large, and, in practice, for Bahá'ís themselves.

DOI: 10.4324/9780429023088-5

These include the writings of 'Abdu'l-Bahá, Shoghi Effendi, and the Universal House of Justice. In order to give readers a fair impression of the general nature and salient themes of Bahá'í texts, this chapter presents selections from the writings of Bahá'u'lláh, the Báb, and 'Abdu'l-Bahá, whose works constitute Bahá'í scriptures—along with excerpts from the authoritative guidance by Shoghi Effendi and the Universal House of Justice as well.

WRITINGS OF THE BÁB

In order to best represent a sampling of the Báb's writings, adopting the Báb's own way of viewing them is a good way to present them to the readers of this book. The Báb classified his own writings and divided them into five groups, or "modes of revelation." This classification offers a key insight into the Báb's own works. The five modes are as follows: (1) divine verses (revelation); (2) prayers; (3) commentaries/sermons; (4) rational discourse (or "educational forms"); and (5) the "Persian mode" (Saiedi 2008, 44). The first four modes are essentially "Islamic" in nature, which makes perfect sense, given the Báb's immediate background and audience. The Báb's writings in these first four (of five) modes are primarily in Arabic, which Muslims believe to be a sacred language, since the Qur'an is the first book in Arabic and was revealed in Arabic by God to the prophet Muhammad, through the Archangel Gabriel, according to Islamic tradition. The "Persian mode" is innovative, however. Of these five "modes of revelation," the primary mode is that of divine revelation, which is the source of the other four modes (Saiedi 2008, 48). Again, the best way to present a representative selection of the Báb's writings is to adopt the Báb's own view of them, especially considering his immediate audience, as will be explained in the next section below.

DIVINE VERSES

The Bahá'í calendar—and Bahá'í history itself—began two hours and 11 minutes after sunset on 22 May 1844, when the Báb announced his prophetic mission to his first disciple, Mullá Ḥusayn Bushrú'í, and, in so doing, revealed the first chapter of the Báb's first scripture. So, perhaps the single best example of the Báb's writing in this mode of "divine verses" are the very words that launched the Báb's prophetic mission—the first chapter of the *Qayyúmu'l-Asmá'*. This sacred scripture represents the founding of the Bábi religion, which evolved into the Bahá'í Faith.

To his predominantly Muslim audience at that time, "divine verses" were understood as the verses of the Qur'an, held by all Muslims to be divinely revealed, as well as being as the latest and greatest—and the last—of all divine scriptures revealed by God. With this context in mind, what the Báb wrote that historic night was the first chapter of his commentary on the 12th chapter of the Qur'an, known as the "Sura of Joseph." Interestingly and ironically, the Báb also represented the *Qayyúmu'l-Asmá'* as a new Qur'an—an audacious, controversial (and perhaps Islamically unimaginable) claim that eventually led to the Báb's eventual imprisonment and execution. That is why Bahá'í scholar Nader Saiedi notes a "fundamental paradox" in the *Qayyúmu'l-Asmá'*: "Although the text is a commentary—an interpretive work—it is written in the mode of divine verses" (Saiedi 2008, 132). In 1844, the Báb revealed the *Qayyúmu'l-Asmá'* (over a period of 40 days) at the age of 24, and, on 9 July 1850, was executed at the age of 30.

Even the word "commentary" should be understood in a broad and somewhat unconventional way, since the Báb does not follow the standard interpretive techniques that prevailed in the vast majority of Qur'an commentaries current at that time. By contrast, the Báb's expository style and exegetical style were highly original and thus represented a radical departure from conventional works in that genre. The first chapter of the *Qayyúmu'l-Asmá'*, revealed during that momentous encounter between the Báb and Mullá Husayn on the evening of 22 May 1844, was titled, the "Sura of *Mulk*" ("Chapter of Dominion"). This opening chapter is not a commentary as such, but rather serves as "an introductory chapter which does not interpret any of the verses of the Súrih of Joseph" (Saiedi 2008, 132). Yet Saiedi goes on to say that "the first chapter is a general commentary on the entire Súrih of Joseph" (Saiedi 2008, 142). This paradox can best be resolved by noting that, although the "Chapter of Dominion" is not a commentary in form and structure (unlike the 110 chapters that follow), this opening chapter is a general commentary in that the "title and the message of the introductory chapter of the *Qayyúmu'l-Asmá'* allude to verse 101" (Saiedi 2008, 124) of the Sura of Joseph in the Qur'an, which reads, in part: "O my Lord! Thou hast indeed bestowed on me some power, and taught me something of the interpretation of dreams and events" (Q.

12:101, trans. Yusuf Ali). "Dominion" (or "sovereignty" or "power") refers to the kingdoms of this world, and to the sovereignty of the monarchs and other rulers who exercise their authority over their own realms. However, there is a higher authority, which is the spiritual sovereignty of the Báb, who refers to himself throughout the following passages as the "Remembrance of God." In order to give readers a full and fair sampling of the very words that launched Bahá'í history, the following will be an extended quote (the last two paragraphs of which were previously quoted in Chapter 4):

> All praise be to God Who hath, through the power of Truth, sent down this Book unto His servant, that it may serve as a shining light for all mankind. ... Verily this is the true Faith of God, and sufficient witness are God and such as are endowed with the knowledge of the Book. This is indeed the eternal Truth which God, the Ancient of Days, hath revealed unto His omnipotent Word—He Who hath been raised up from the midst of the Burning Bush. This is the Mystery which hath been hidden from all that are in heaven and on earth, and in this wondrous Revelation it hath, in very truth, been set forth in the Mother Book by the hand of God, the Exalted. ...
>
> O concourse of kings! Deliver with truth and in all haste the verses sent down by Us to the peoples of Turkey and of India, and beyond them, with power and with truth, to lands in both the East and the West. ... And know that if ye aid God, He will, on the Day of Resurrection, graciously aid you, upon the Bridge, through Him Who is His Most Great Remembrance. ...
>
> O people of the earth! Whoso obeyeth the Remembrance of God and His Book hath in truth obeyed God and His chosen ones and he will, in the life to come, be reckoned in the presence of God among the inmates of the Paradise of His good-pleasure.
>
> (the Báb, *Selections*, BRL)

This passage pulses with power, and is directed to the "concourse of kings" and the "people of the earth." There could be no more audacious message imaginable than one such as this. In this passage, the Báb speaks with divine authority. Whether or not the Báb was directly inspired by God to convey this message to the kings and peoples of the earth is, of course, a matter of faith. Yet this text is clear in its apparent meaning, and speaks for itself.

What is also remarkable in this opening chapter of the *Qayyúmu'l-Asmá'* is its "startlingly new definition of Islam" (Saiedi 2008, 142). Islam is traditionally defined as "submission" to God. So, a Muslim is one who submits to the will of God. As Saiedi points out, the Báb's mission is declared by the direct assertion of divine sovereignty, in which Islam is redefined as belief in the Báb and submission to his commandments. Later on in his ministry, the Báb makes a definitive break from Islam, in which it is clear and manifest that the Báb is going way beyond the orbit of Islam in order to establish a new, independent religion.

PRAYERS

The mode of "prayers" takes on a different voice and orientation. This mode is essentially the inverse of divine verses (Saiedi 2008, 42), since, in prayers, people address God, rather than in "divine verses," where God, through a prophet, addresses the peoples of the world. In other words, in the mode of "divine verses," the Báb speaks *from* God and on behalf of God, with the voice of divine authority. By contrast, in the mode of prayers and supplications, the Báb speaks *to* God, in the voice of servitude (Saiedi 2008, 46). One example of the mode of prayers is the following prayer:

> Glory be unto Thee, O Lord, Thou Who hast brought into being all created things, through the power of Thy behest.
>
> O Lord! Assist those who have renounced all else but Thee, and grant them a mighty victory. Send down upon them, O Lord, the concourse of the angels in heaven and earth and all that is between, to aid Thy servants, to succor and strengthen them, to enable them to achieve success, to sustain them, to invest them with glory, to confer upon them honor and exaltation, to enrich them and to make them triumphant with a wondrous triumph.
>
> Thou art their Lord, the Lord of the heavens and the earth, the Lord of all the worlds. Strengthen this Faith, O Lord, through the power of these servants and cause them to prevail over all the peoples of the world; for they, of a truth, are Thy servants who have detached themselves from aught else but Thee, and Thou verily art the protector of true believers.
>
> Grant Thou, O Lord, that their hearts may, through allegiance to this, Thine inviolable Faith, grow stronger than anything else in the heavens and on earth and in whatsoever is between them; and strengthen, O Lord, their hands with the tokens of Thy wondrous power that they may manifest Thy power before the gaze of all mankind.
>
> (the Báb, *Selections*, BRL)

This prayer is for the future triumph of the Báb's religion—not by wars or by force—but during the time of "the exaltation of the Cause of God in the Day of Him Whom God shall make manifest [Bahá'u'lláh]" (Saiedi 2008, 364). This request for empowerment in the path of God inspires confidence and assurance of eventual triumph, by virtue of its implied promise of divine assistance. This prayer is found in the standard Bahá'í prayer books of today, and thus is part of the living legacy of the Báb in Bahá'í life today. (See Buck, "The Báb's Living Legacy.")

COMMENTARIES/SERMONS

In the predominantly Christian West, readers are quite familiar with the practice of sermons being preached to congregations every Sunday. So, the following text is easily recognizable as a "sermon" when the Báb addresses his followers so: "O congregation of the Bayán." The Báb's "congregation" is his immediate audience, although his audience was not immediately available, since most likely the Báb was writing from prison. The topic of this sermon is "the Day of the appearance of Him Whom God shall manifest," which was coming soon. The Báb's primary mission was to prepare his followers for the imminent advent of "Him Whom God shall manifest," whom the majority of the Bábis later came to recognize and accept as Bahá'u'lláh. The Báb's sermon is as follows:

> It behooveth you to await the Day of the appearance of Him Whom God shall manifest. Indeed My aim in planting the Tree of the Bayán hath been none other than to enable you to recognize Me. In truth I Myself am the first to bow down before God and to believe in Him. Therefore let not your recognition become fruitless, inasmuch as the Bayán, notwithstanding the sublimity of its station, beareth fealty to Him Whom God shall make manifest, and it is He Who beseemeth most to be acclaimed as the Seat of divine Reality, though indeed He is I and I am He. ...
>
> Suffer not yourselves to be shut out as by a veil from God after He hath revealed Himself. For all that hath been exalted in the Bayán is but as a ring upon My hand, and I Myself am, verily, but a ring upon the hand of Him Whom God shall make manifest—glorified be His mention! He turneth it as He pleaseth, for whatsoever He pleaseth, and through whatsoever He pleaseth. He, verily, is the Help in Peril, the Most High.
>
> (the Báb, *Selections*, BRL)

In this sermon, the Báb makes clear that his primary mission is to prepare the way for the advent of "Him Whom God shall make manifest," whom the vast majority of the Báb's followers, as previously stated, accepted as Bahá'u'lláh. That being the case, all of the Báb's laws and ordinances were conditioned upon Bahá'u'lláh's acceptance. Many of the Báb's laws, ethics, morals, devotions, and principles were selectively adopted and adapted by Bahá'u'lláh, such that they may be said to constitute the Báb's "living legacy" in Bahá'í life today. (See Buck, "The Báb's Living Legacy.")

RATIONAL DISCOURSE

The Báb's "Seven Proofs" (*Dalá'il-i-Sab'ih*) is acclaimed by Shoghi Effendi as "the most important of the polemical works of the Báb" (Shoghi Effendi, *God Passes By*, BRL). This work was written while the Báb was incarcerated in the prison of Mákú (West Azarbaijan Province, Iran). In the following passage, the Báb sets forth "rational arguments" to demonstrate that the very same proof of the truth of the Qur'an applies to the "Bayán" (used here to refer to all of the Báb's writings) with equal persuasive force:

Let Me set forth some rational arguments for thee. ...

Now consider the Revelation of the Bayán. If the followers of the Qur'án had applied to themselves proofs similar to those which they advance for the nonbelievers in Islám, not a single soul would have remained deprived of the Truth, and on the Day of Resurrection everyone would have attained salvation. ...

"By what proof hast thou embraced the Religion of Islám? Is it the Prophet on whom thou hast never set eyes? Is it the miracles which thou hast never witnessed? If thou hast accepted Islám unwittingly, wherefore hast thou done so? But if thou hast embraced the Faith by recognizing the Qur'án as the testimony, because thou hast heard the learned and the faithful express their powerlessness before it, or if thou hast, upon hearing the divine verses and by virtue of thy spontaneous love for the True Word of God, responded in a spirit of utter humility and lowliness—a spirit which is one of the mightiest signs of true love and understanding—then such proofs have been and will ever be regarded as sound."

(the Báb, *Selections*, BRL)

In this passage, the Báb states that, just as the Qur'an is the real proof of the essential truth of Islam (in its pure form), so also is the Bayán the real proof of the truth of the religion of the Báb.

THE "PERSIAN MODE"

The *Persian Bayán* is generally considered to be the single most important work of the Báb. Outwardly, it is a book of laws. On closer reading, there is much exposition of doctrine as well. Therefore Shoghi Effendi acclaimed the *Persian Bayán* as "peerless among the doctrinal works of the Founder of the Bábí Dispensation" (Shoghi Effendi, *God Passes By*, BRL). In the following representative passage, the Báb explains what the Qur'an refers to as the "Day of Resurrection":

> The substance of this chapter is this, that what is intended by the Day of Resurrection is the Day of the appearance of the Tree of divine Reality, but it is not seen that anyone of the followers of Shí'ih Islám hath understood the meaning of the Day of Resurrection; rather have they fancifully imagined a thing which with God hath no reality. In the estimation of God and according to the usage of such as are initiated into divine mysteries, what is meant by the Day of Resurrection is this, that from the time of the appearance of Him Who is the Tree of divine Reality, at whatever period and under whatever name, until the moment of His disappearance, is the Day of Resurrection. ...
>
> The stage of perfection of everything is reached when its resurrection occurreth. The perfection of the religion of Islám was consummated at the beginning of this Revelation; and from the rise of this Revelation until its setting, the fruits of the Tree of Islám, whatever they are, will become apparent. The Resurrection of the Bayán will occur at the time of the appearance of Him Whom God shall make manifest. ...
>
> At the present time, however, only adverse effects have resulted; for although He hath appeared in the midmost heart of Islám, and all people profess it by reason of their relationship to Him [the Qá'im], yet unjustly have they consigned Him to the Mountain of Máh-Kú, and this notwithstanding that in the Qur'án the advent of the Day of Resurrection hath been promised unto all by God. For on that Day all men will be brought before God and will attain His Presence; which meaneth appearance before Him Who is the Tree of divine Reality and attainment unto His presence; inasmuch as it is not possible to appear before the Most Holy Essence of God, nor is it conceivable to seek

reunion with Him. That which is feasible in the matter of appearance before Him and of meeting Him is attainment unto the Primal Tree.

(the Báb, *Selections*, BRL)

In this doctrinally important passage, the Báb defines "perfection" as the culmination of one prophetic Dispensation and the rise of the next prophet of God, which is the real meaning of "Resurrection": "The stage of perfection of everything is reached when its resurrection occurreth." Each prophet points forward to the next prophet in a series of successive religious dispensations (eras of primary influence).

WRITINGS OF BAHÁ'U'LLÁH

The writings of Bahá'u'lláh are huge and vast. They comprise an estimated equivalent of one hundred book-length volumes. The scriptural resources of the Bahá'í Faith are therefore rich and deep. Much remains to be explored. An estimated 10% of Bahá'u'lláh's writings have been translated into English. This section will feature a few selections, which are also provided throughout the rest of this book. As in the previous section on the writings of the Báb, a classification of Bahá'u'lláh's writings is offered here, based upon Bahá'u'lláh's own statement, to wit:

Say: We have revealed Our verses in nine different modes. Each one of them bespeaketh the sovereignty of God, the Help in Peril, the Self-Subsisting. A single one of them sufficeth for a proof unto all who are in the heavens and on the earth; yet the people, for the most part, persist in their heedlessness. Should it be Our wish, We would reveal them in countless other modes.

(Bahá'u'lláh, *Summons*, BRL)

The present writer, based on some relevant statements by Shoghi Effendi, has developed the following proposed classification of Bahá'u'lláh's "nine modes" (or styles of discourse):

1. "Mystical Compositions" (Shoghi Effendi, *God Passes By*, BRL) Bahá'u'lláh's mystical discourses and allegorical writings.
2. "Doctrinal Writings" (Shoghi Effendi, *God Passes By*, BRL). Bahá'u'lláh's explanations of past scriptures (usually symbolic interpretations of apocalyptic prophecies), along with the exposition of related doctrines of theology, theophany, and revelation.

3. "Ethical Writings" (Shoghi Effendi, *God Passes By*, BRL). Bahá'u'lláh's exhortations regarding acquiring godly virtues and goodly character (i.e. "unnumbered exhortations").

4. "Proclamation" (Shoghi Effendi, *God Passes By*, BRL). Bahá'u'lláh's public announcement, by open epistles to "kings and ecclesiastics," to statesmen and other world leaders, of his prophetic mission (i.e. "addresses or references to kings, to emperors and to ministers, of both the East and the West, to ecclesiastics of divers denominations, and to leaders in the intellectual, political, literary, mystical, commercial and humanitarian spheres of human activity."

5. "Laws and Ordinances" (Shoghi Effendi, *God Passes By*, BRL). Bahá'u'lláh's laws and ordinances, as set forth in the *Kitab-i-Aqdas (The Most Holy Book), and supplemental texts.*

6. "Fundamental Tenets and Principles" (Shoghi Effendi, *God Passes By*, BRL). Bahá'u'lláh's statements regarding various social teachings, including matters of good governance and world order (i.e. "revolutionizing principles").

7. "Prophecies" (Shoghi Effendi, *God Passes By*, BRL) (i.e. "dire warnings and portentous prophecies").

8. "Discourses" (Shoghi Effendi, *God Passes By*, BRL). Bahá'u'lláh's expositions on a wide range of topics and themes (i.e. "illuminating commentaries and interpretations, impassioned discourses and homilies").

9. "Prayers and Meditations" (Shoghi Effendi, *God Passes By*, BRL). Bahá'u'lláh's prayers and contemplative meditations (i.e. "soul-uplifting prayers and meditations").

This proposed classification is not meant to be comprehensive or exhaustive. It does not classify Bahá'u'lláh's writings according to literary style. For instance, this typology does not include the classification of Bahá'u'lláh's poetry, writings in "pure Persian," etc. That said, what follows will provide a good overview of Bahá'u'lláh's work, which constitutes a major part of Bahá'í scripture.

MYSTICAL COMPOSITIONS

The category of "Mystical Compositions" encompasses Bahá'u'lláh's mystical discourses and allegorical writings. Of these, Shoghi Effendi distinguishes the "Seven Valleys" as Bahá'u'lláh's "greatest mystical composition" (Shoghi Effendi, *God Passes By*, BRL).

Mystical writings are found in just about every religious tradition. They are typically about quests for profound experiences, and how to progress along the mystic path. In most mystical literature, the goal is union with God. A mystic's "peak experience" is typically achieved through "beatific vision" (seeing God) or "divine audition" (hearing God). In Bahá'í thought, however, this cannot be done directly. Union with God, in Bahá'í terms, is possible only through the Manifestation of God (who, in this day and age, is Bahá'u'lláh, according to Bahá'í belief). Keeping this in mind, it now becomes clear how and why Bahá'u'lláh's mystic writings are a form of "proclamation," with Bahá'u'lláh as the teacher—or Sufi master (Persian: *pīr*)—progressively unveiling his revelation, station, and mission through hints and cryptic self-references. This idea is based on Bahá'u'lláh's own statements. Bahá'u'lláh progressively proclaimed His mission to mystics, divines, and rulers:

> "Behold and observe! This is the finger of might by which the heaven of vain imaginings was indeed cleft asunder. Incline thine ear and Hear! This is the call of My Pen which was raised among mystics, then divines, and then kings and rulers."
>
> (Bahá'u'lláh 1893, 260) Provisional translation by Nader Saiedi.
> (Saiedi 2000, 241.)

So, generally speaking, Bahá'u'lláh outwardly wrote as a mystic (1852–1863), prophet (1863–1867), and lawgiver (1867–1892). "Sufis" are the mystics of Islam, formally speaking, with a wide array of organizations, often referred to as Sufi "orders." But Bahá'u'lláh was not writing strictly as a "Sufi master." Rather, he was proclaiming his mission, in a very subtle way to mystics, who were seeking union with God, which is really quite impossible, except in the mystic's imagination. So, there is a dynamic relationship between mysticism and messianism in Bahá'u'lláh's early writings. In other words, Bahá'u'lláh appears to allude to his impending revelation throughout his mystical works. Perceptive readers would pick up on these messianic "hints"— i.e. on Bahá'u'lláh's "messianic secret"—a mystery with an abundance of clues (i.e. implied self-references, a covert messianic disclosure, in advance of an impending overt messianic declaration and public proclamation).

In this respect, Bahá'u'lláh's approach to mysticism is effectively "historicized" (Saiedi 2000, 62–66). As an analogy, those who were seeking God at the time of Christ could experience the divine presence of God in Jesus Christ himself: "He that hath seen me hath seen the Father" (John 14:9, KJV). Hence, the mystical quest—often described as a "path" or a "journey"—is as "horizontal" (i.e. experiencing the presence of God in history) in nature as it is "vertical" (i.e. experiencing the presence of God in prayer and contemplation). In the "horizontal" or historical sense, the opportunity to experience the "presence of God" was not far off, in that the "Manifestation of God" (Bahá'u'lláh) was historically present in Baghdad, at that particular time and place in history.

The mystical journey is a salient *leitmotif* in Sufi literature. This journey has a destination, i.e. a goal. In the mystical journey, the "wayfarer" has a path and ultimate destination. The traveler will encounter difficulties and obstacles along the way. The mystic will also reach certain milestones. These milestones are referred to variously as "valleys," "cities," "stations," etc. These represent progress in the mystic quest, and typically indicate increased knowledge and heightened awareness as a result of deepened spirituality. Whatever the metaphors that are used, and whichever the various "stations" that are described, these are not required formulas or strict requirements as much as they are intended to be fuller explanations of mystical experience which, in the final analysis, is "ineffable" (beyond words).

The most famous example of the mystic journey in Sufi literature is Attar's *The Conference of the Birds* (*Manṭiq al-ṭayr*)—an epic poem of over 4,500 lines. In this work, there is a section called the "Seven Valleys." This is the model for Bahá'u'lláh's preeminent mystical work, *The Seven Valleys*. In the following passage, Bahá'u'lláh outlines various stages in the mystical journey:

> By My life, O friend! Wert thou to taste the fruits of these verdant trees that spring from the soil of true understanding, once the effulgent light of His Essence hath been reflected in the Mirrors of His names and attributes yearning would seize the reins of patience and restraint from out thy hand and stir thy spirit into commotion with the splendours of His light. It would draw thee from this abode of dust unto thy true and heavenly habitation in the midmost heart of mystic knowledge, and raise thee to a station wherein thou wilt soar in the air even as thou

treadest upon the earth, and wilt walk upon the water even as thou movest over the land. ...

And further: the stages that mark the wayfarers' journey from their mortal abode to the heavenly homeland are said to be seven. Some have referred to them as seven valleys, and others, as seven cities. And it is said that until the wayfarer taketh leave of self and traverseth these stages, he shall never attain the ocean of nearness and reunion nor taste of the matchless wine.

(Bahá'u'lláh, *Call*, BRL)

In this passage, Bahá'u'lláh entices and engages the reader with the prospect experiencing a peak mystical experience, which would mystically transport the seeker's spirit "to a station wherein thou wilt soar in the air even as thou treadest upon the earth, and wilt walk upon the water even as thou movest over the land." The idea here is that the physical world is not the only realm of experience. There are, in fact, spiritual worlds. These are nonphysical, imaginal (as distinct from "imaginary") realms of intensely psychological experience. This passage, moreover, introduces the "Seven Valleys" of the mystical quest, as the mystic embarks on a spiritual journey. Each of the mileposts in the *Seven Valleys* (composed by Bahá'u'lláh in Baghdad circa 1858) are as set forth as follows: (1) the Valley of Search; (2) the Valley of Love; (3) the Valley of Knowledge; (4) the Valley of Unity; (5) the Valley of Contentment; (6) the Valley of Wonderment; and (7) the Valley of True Poverty and Absolute Nothingness. In the seventh Valley, the reader is told that this leads to four more Valleys:

They who soar in the heaven of Divine Unity and attain the depths of the sea of detachment reckon this city—which is the station of life in God—as the loftiest state of the mystic knowers and the furthermost homeland of the faithful lovers. But to this evanescent One of the mystic ocean, this station is the first gate of the heart's citadel, that is, man's first entrance to the city of the heart; and the heart is endowed with four stages, which would be recounted should a kindred soul be found.

(Bahá'u'lláh, *Call*, BRL)

Mysticism is typically individual in nature, and will always remain so. But Bahá'u'lláh has effected a revolution in mysticism by adding a collective dimension as well. The traditional Sufi goal was a mystical "peak experience"—i.e. "beatific vision" ("seeing" God) or "divine audition" ("hearing" God). In contrast to this, Bahá'u'lláh encouraged the mystical seeker to search for divine revelation, rather than divine audition, because the real "divine audition" inheres in revelation itself. While mystics sought God through direct experience, Bahá'u'lláh connects the mystic quest with prophetic "revelation." What greater "peak experience" than to directly encounter and experience God in person, through the "person of God," i.e. the "Manifestation of God" (a Bahá'í term of art), who is God by proxy (i.e. the theophany, or "appearance" of God, insofar as Bahá'u'lláh, Bahá'ís believe, is "God in nature," even though Bahá'u'lláh is not "God in essence"? Such is the sum and substance of Bahá'u'lláh's mystical writings, the primary purpose of which is to subtly redirect the attention of mystics from the realm of imagination to the present reality of God's self-revelation in human history.

DOCTRINAL WRITINGS

Since Bahá'í doctrines, as in other religions, are wide-ranging in scope, this section will present one major Bahá'í belief that may best represent the essence of how the Bahá'í Faith sees its place in the world today, from a historical perspective. The Bahá'í doctrine selected for this section is known as "progressive revelation." By "progressive" it is meant that when a new religion is born, that religion renews time-less spiritual truths—yet more fully, in keeping with the increased capacity of the people—and new laws suited for that day and age. This process occurs, time and again, throughout human history. As such, the Bahá'í doctrine of progressive revelation is a general theory of religious relativity, whereby the appearances of the world's religions throughout history are understood and explained in a unified theory of successive religious dispensations, i.e. prophetic eras.

This key idea is of paramount importance in Bahá'í belief, self-iden-tity, and sense of purpose. It holds that each religion has its own sphere of influence, over a span (or "cycle") of time—much like seasons of the year. According to this "seasonal" analogy, when a religion first appears on the historical horizon, that is its "spiritual springtime." As spring is followed by summer, that religion will then reach the zenith of its influence, after which its fortunes will eventually decline—that is, over the course of its fall and winter. Then it is time for religion to be renewed.

So, at key junctures in human history, God has sent prophets and messengers to reveal new and fuller teachings, from age to age. This Bahá'í view of the history of religions culminates with the appearance of the Báb and Bahá'u'lláh, who are the latest, although not the last, of this series of divine educators and lawgivers. The following passage is an excerpt from Bahá'u'lláh's writings that sets forth the Bahá'í doctrine of progressive revelation:

> Contemplate with thine inward eye the chain of successive Revelations that hath linked the Manifestation of Adam with that of the Báb. I testify before God that each one of these Manifestations hath been sent down through the operation of the Divine Will and Purpose, that each hath been the bearer of a specific Message, that each hath been entrusted with a divinely-revealed Book and been commissioned to unravel the mysteries of a mighty Tablet. ...
>
> And when this process of progressive Revelation culminated in the stage at which His peerless, His most sacred, and exalted Countenance was to be unveiled to men's eyes, He chose to hide His own Self behind a thousand veils, lest profane and mortal eyes discover His glory. This He did at a time when the signs and tokens of a divinely-appointed Revelation were being showered upon Him—signs and tokens which none can reckon except the Lord, your God, the Lord of all worlds. And when the set time of concealment was fulfilled, We sent forth, whilst still wrapt within a myriad veils, an infinitesimal glimmer of the effulgent Glory enveloping the Face of the Youth, and lo, the entire company of the dwellers of the Realms above were seized with violent commotion and the favored of God fell down in adoration before Him. He hath, verily, manifested a glory such as none in the whole creation hath witnessed, inasmuch as He hath arisen to proclaim in person His Cause unto all who are in the heavens and all who are on the earth.
>
> (Bahá'u'lláh, *Gleanings*, BRL)

In the course of the world's spiritual and social evolution, the requirements of each succeeding age in human history necessarily differ from previous eras. Simply put, the needs and exigencies of modern times differ profoundly from those of antiquity. Another analogy used in the Bahá'í writings is that human history can be compared to the process of individual maturation. A human being starts off as a baby, progresses through childhood and youth, and, eventually, matures into adulthood. This process occurs collectively as well as individually. In other words, humankind has gone through similar developmental stages, and has reached the end of its adolescence, and is now at the threshold of human maturity. At this stage in human history, God's will for humanity is that the world can, and should, achieve its own unity. This, of course, represents a significant milestone in human consciousness and world affairs. According to the Bahá'í view, Bahá'u'lláh therefore was sent to guide and accelerate this process. In other words, Bahá'u'lláh was commissioned by God to usher in an era of world peace and prosperity, through the power and influence of his spiritual and social principles.

ETHICAL WRITINGS

Social progress cannot be made without a solid foundation based on moral and ethical individual conduct. Individuals impact society. The collective health of a given society is a reflection of the sum total of individual human actions—with their cumulative moral and ethical outcomes and consequences—taken together. Bahá'í ethical teachings are therefore fundamental components of social well-being. The preeminent Bahá'í ethical text is "The Hidden Words of Bahá'u'lláh"—a collection of pithy aphorisms (i.e. short words of advice or pearls of wisdom)—which opens as follows:

HE IS THE GLORY OF GLORIES

This is that which hath descended from the realm of glory, uttered by the tongue of power and might, and revealed unto the Prophets of old. We have taken the inner essence thereof and clothed it in the garment of brevity, as a token of grace unto the righteous, that they may stand faithful unto the Covenant of God, may fulfill in their lives His trust, and in the realm of spirit obtain the gem of divine virtue.

O Son of Spirit! My first counsel is this: Possess a pure, kindly and radiant heart, that thine may be a sovereignty ancient, imperishable and everlasting.

> O Son of Spirit! The best beloved of all things in My sight is Justice;
> turn not away therefrom if thou desirest Me, and neglect it not that I may
> confide in thee. By its aid thou shalt see with thine own eyes and not
> through the eyes of others, and shalt know of thine own knowledge and
> not through the knowledge of thy neighbor. Ponder this in thy heart; how
> it behooveth thee to be. Verily justice is My gift to thee and the sign of My
> loving-kindness. Set it then before thine eyes.
>
> (Bahá'u'lláh, *Hidden Words*, BRL)

Bahá'u'lláh's claim that *The Hidden Words* contains the essence of the
world's religions is profound and far-reaching. The truth of this claim
cannot be objectively determined, but is a matter of faith. Bahá'ís, of
course, accept this claim as true. If true, then *The Hidden Words* can
be seen as a valuable resource for moral and ethical conduct. That,
after all, is the purpose and intention of this sacred text.

PROCLAMATION

Each religion has its own "truth-claims." Bahá'u'lláh claimed to be the
"Promised One" of all world religions. Generally speaking, each world
religion has its own prophecies of the future. This includes the coming,
at a future time, of a world-messiah. This is more or less an accepted fact,
as evidenced by the prophecies themselves. Where faith comes into play
is to see these prophecies as part of a convergent vision—and one that
Bahá'u'lláh fulfills. Such is a basic component of Bahá'í faith and belief.

For a period of several years, from 1867 to 1873, Bahá'u'lláh proclaimed his mission as a messenger of God, sent for this day and age,
to unify the world, as mentioned earlier. Bahá'u'lláh sent open letters
to kings and rulers of the world, including its religious leaders as well,
announcing his prophetic role in world affairs. The following is an
example of one of these proclamatory declarations, which is an epistle
to Queen Victoria:

> O Queen in London! Incline thine ear unto the voice of thy Lord, the
> Lord of all mankind, calling from the Divine Lote-Tree: Verily, no God is
> there but Me, the Almighty, the All-Wise! Cast away all that is on earth,

and attire the head of thy kingdom with the crown of the remembrance of thy Lord, the All-Glorious. He, in truth, hath come unto the world in His most great glory, and all that hath been mentioned in the Gospel hath been fulfilled. ...

We have been informed that thou hast forbidden the trading in slaves, both men and women. This, verily, is what God hath enjoined in this wondrous Revelation. God hath, truly, destined a reward for thee, because of this. ...

We have also heard that thou hast entrusted the reins of counsel into the hands of the representatives of the people. Thou, indeed, hast done well, for thereby the foundations of the edifice of thine affairs will be strengthened, and the hearts of all that are beneath thy shadow, whether high or low, will be tranquillized. ...

O ye the elected representatives of the people in every land! Take ye counsel together, and let your concern be only for that which profiteth mankind and bettereth the condition thereof, if ye be of them that scan heedfully. ...

That which the Lord hath ordained as the sovereign remedy and mightiest instrument for the healing of all the world is the union of all its peoples in one universal Cause, one common Faith. This can in no wise be achieved except through the power of a skilled, an all-powerful and inspired Physician. ...

Consider these days in which He Who is the Ancient Beauty hath come in the Most Great Name, that He may quicken the world and unite its peoples. They, however, rose up against Him with sharpened swords, and committed that which caused the Faithful Spirit to lament, until in the end they imprisoned Him in the most desolate of cities, and broke the grasp of the faithful upon the hem of His robe. ...

O ye rulers of the earth! ... Hearken unto the counsel given you by the Pen of the Most High, that haply both ye and the poor may attain unto tranquillity and peace. We beseech God to assist the kings of the earth to establish peace on earth. ...

Now that ye have refused the Most Great Peace, hold ye fast unto this, the Lesser Peace, that haply ye may in some degree better your own condition and that of your dependents.

(Bahá'u'lláh, *Summons*, BRL)

In this passage, Bahá'u'lláh endorses certain signal developments under Queen Victoria's watch, such as the abolition of slavery and parliamentary democracy as well. As previously stated, this is a process that the present writer has elsewhere described as "sacralizing the secular."

So, in the course of proclaiming His prophetic mission, Bahá'u'lláh addresses key social teachings as well. In 1873, in fact, Bahá'u'lláh formally abolished slavery in his book of laws, the *Kitáb-i-Aqdas* (*The Most Holy Book*). This, of course, was not the first time in history that slavery had been abolished. This had already been done in the secular world, and was still in the process, depending on time and place, country by country. Therefore, the significance of Bahá'u'lláh's abolition of slavery is that this is the first time in religious history that slavery had been abrogated as a fundamental religious law. Christianity permitted slavery. So did Islam. Although there are teachings that encouraged manumission (i.e. liberation) of individual slaves by their owners, this was entirely up to the slave masters themselves. Otherwise, there was no binding religious obligation to do so. Thus, there was no hard-and-fast religious prohibition of slavery until Bahá'u'lláh's pronouncement in 1873.

This is important because abolition, historically speaking, was driven by sincere religious individuals who were convinced, on moral grounds, that slavery was ethically reprehensible and therefore utterly wrong. In Christianity itself, slaveowners would try to justify slavery by appealing to certain key passages in the Bible. By contrast, Christian abolitionists would appeal to other scriptural passages in support of their view that slavery was fundamentally evil. This debate would have been totally unnecessary had Christianity adopted a clear and unequivocal stand against slavery. The spiritual and social effect of Bahá'u'lláh's religious abrogation of slavery is that, when legislated as a religious law, that prohibition, in and of itself, added a powerful dimension of moral force to the question of slavery. The time had come for the abolition of slavery to take place not only as a secular development, but as an emphatic and absolute religious requirement as well.

LAWS AND ORDINANCES

In the previous section, the example of Bahá'u'lláh's abolition of slavery, as a definitive and unequivocal religious law, illustrates the general nature of Bahá'í laws as a whole. The single most important Bahá'í scripture, in fact, is the *Kitáb-i-Aqdas* (*The Most Holy Book*), also previously mentioned. The following laws are quoted below in order to further illustrate the scope and nature of Bahá'u'lláh's religious laws, which are "secular" in their application as well:

The Lord hath ordained that in every city a House of Justice be established wherein shall gather counsellors to the number of Bahá, and
should it exceed this number it doth not matter. They should consider
themselves as entering the Court of the presence of God, the Exalted,
the Most High, and as beholding Him Who is the Unseen. It behoveth
them to be the trusted ones of the Merciful among men and to regard
themselves as the guardians appointed of God for all that dwell on earth.
It is incumbent upon them to take counsel together and to have regard
for the interests of the servants of God, for His sake, even as they regard
their own interests, and to choose that which is meet and seemly. Thus
hath the Lord your God commanded you. Beware lest ye put away that
which is clearly revealed in His Tablet. Fear God, O ye that perceive.

O people of the world! Build ye houses of worship throughout the
lands in the name of Him Who is the Lord of all religions. Make them
as perfect as is possible in the world of being, and adorn them with
that which befitteth them, not with images and effigies. Then, with
radiance and joy, celebrate therein the praise of your Lord, the Most
Compassionate. Verily, by His remembrance the eye is cheered and the
heart is filled with light.

(Bahá'u'lláh, *Kitáb-i-Aqdas*, BRL)

In this passage, Bahá'u'lláh sets forth two laws, requiring that a house of
worship and a House of Justice be created in every city throughout the
world. By "House of Justice" is meant an assembly of nine or more members (women and men, elected by prayerful, and private, plurality vote)
who will consult together on the affairs of the community. Although
there is provision for these assemblies to be more than nine people, they
are currently limited to nine.) However, Bahá'u'lláh, for certain reasons
that will become apparent in the future, restricted the membership of the
Universal House of Justice to men—an "exception that proves the rule"
of the key Bahá'í principle of the equality of women and men, as encouraged and implemented in Bahá'í life today, individually and socially.

Also central to Bahá'í community planning is the creation of a
"house of worship" as well, open to people of all religions. Open to
people of all religions, races, and nations, Bahá'í houses of worship
are distinctive buildings with a purpose far beyond a place for prayer
and meditation. Bahá'í temples—known in Arabic as *Mashriqu'l-
Adhkár* (literally the "Dawning Place of the Praise [of God]")—link
worship with service to humanity. Every Bahá'í house of worship will,
in due course and resources permitting, establish satellite institutions

("dependencies") dedicated to medical, charitable, educational, and scientific pursuits, and thus over time develop into a complex of institutions that contributes to the advancement of civilization.

These two laws of Bahá'u'lláh are far-reaching and significant, and they will be coextensive with the growth and development of the worldwide Bahá'í community, as time and circumstances permit.

FUNDAMENTAL TENETS AND PRINCIPLES

Readers are no doubt familiar with the term, "Gospel," which means "good news" or "glad-tidings." By analogy, the Bahá'í message is its own "gospel" as well. Bahá'u'lláh, in fact, revealed a set of principles—characterized as a series of "glad-tidings"—which is quoted, in part, below:

O PEOPLE OF THE EARTH!

The first Glad-Tidings

which the Mother Book hath, in this Most Great Revelation, imparted unto all the peoples of the world is that the law of holy war hath been blotted out from the Book. Glorified be the All-Merciful, the Lord of grace abounding, through Whom the door of heavenly bounty hath been flung open in the face of all that are in heaven and on earth.

The second Glad-Tidings

It is permitted that the peoples and kindreds of the world associate with one another with joy and radiance. O people! Consort with the followers of all religions in a spirit of friendliness and fellowship. Thus hath the daystar of His sanction and authority shone forth above the horizon of the decree of God, the Lord of the worlds.

The third Glad-Tidings

concerneth the study of divers languages. This decree hath formerly streamed forth from the Pen of the Most High: It behooveth the sovereigns

---

of the world—may God assist them—or the ministers of the earth to take counsel together and to adopt one of the existing languages or a new one to be taught to children in schools throughout the world, and likewise one script. Thus the whole earth will come to be regarded as one country. Well is it with him who hearkeneth unto His Call and observeth that whereunto he is bidden by God, the Lord of the Mighty Throne. …

The fifteenth Glad-Tidings

Although a republican form of government profiteth all the peoples of the world, yet the majesty of kingship is one of the signs of God. We do not wish that the countries of the world should remain deprived thereof. If the sagacious combine the two forms into one, great will be their reward in the presence of God.

(Bahá'u'lláh, *Tablets*, BRL)

Space does not permit a detailed exposition of each of these "glad-tidings." The present writer has co-authored a paper on this particular Tablet, to which the reader is referred (see Buck and Ioannesyan 2010). Suffice it to say that these laws and precepts, presented in the form of numbered principles, are representative both of Bahá'u'lláh's messianic proclamation as well as religious legislation.

PROPHECIES

The Greek word, *prophētēs* (προφήτης), means "forthteller," as well as "foreteller." Thus, a prophet declares things as they are, as well as things that shall be—i.e. the present and the future. Bahá'u'lláh, of course, did both. His prophecies are both general and specific in nature. See, for instance, "A Westerner's First Impression" in Chapter Four for Bahá'u'lláh's prophecies on the future of the world, as recounted by Cambridge Orientalist, Edward Granville Browne, in his historic audience with Bahá'u'lláh on Wednesday, April 16, 1890, in Acre, Ottoman Palestine (now in northern Israel). Here are more prophecies of Bahá'u'lláh regarding the future of the world, i.e. its present course and ultimate destiny:

God's purpose is none other than to usher in, in ways He alone can bring about, and the full significance of which He alone can fathom, the Great, the Golden Age of a long-divided, a long-afflicted humanity. Its present state, indeed even its immediate future, is dark, distressingly dark. Its distant future, however, is radiant, gloriously radiant—so radiant that no eye can visualize it.

"The winds of despair," writes Bahá'u'lláh, as He surveys the immediate destinies of mankind, "are, alas, blowing from every direction, and the strife that divides and afflicts the human race is daily increasing. The signs of impending convulsions and chaos can now be discerned, inasmuch as the prevailing order appears to be lamentably defective." "Such shall be its plight," He, in another connection, has declared, "that to disclose it now would not be meet and seemly." "These fruitless strifes," He, on the other hand, contemplating the future of mankind, has emphatically prophesied, in the course of His memorable interview with the Persian orientalist, Edward G. Browne, "these ruinous wars shall pass away, and the 'Most Great Peace' shall come. ... These strifes and this bloodshed and discord must cease, and all men be as one kindred and one family." "Soon," He predicts, "will the present-day order be rolled up, and a new one spread out in its stead." "After a time," He also has written, "all the governments on earth will change. Oppression will envelop the world. And following a universal convulsion, the sun of justice will rise from the horizon of the unseen realm." "The whole earth," He, moreover, has stated, "is now in a state of pregnancy. The day is approaching when it will have yielded its noblest fruits, when from it will have sprung forth the loftiest trees, the most enchanting blossoms, the most heavenly blessings."

(Quoted in Shoghi Effendi, *Promised Day Is Come*, BRL)

Bahá'u'lláh's specific prophecies regarding the immediate destinies of some of the kings and rulers of that day and age need not be recounted here, since to do so would require a detailed explanation of the historical context. Those events, interesting as they are, have come and gone. What remains are the things to come, which are on the historical horizon. Generally speaking, Bahá'u'lláh clearly indicates that the present-day systems are defective, and have failed to serve their purpose. Therefore, they are in a state of disarray and decay, and will eventually be replaced by alternative and far more viable systems of good governance and effective conflict resolution that will prevent wars and usher in a period of peace and prosperity, ultimately leading to a future golden age of world civilization. Bahá'í principles and their social influence will play a significant role in this ideal outcome.

DISCOURSES

Discourses, broadly defined, are explanations of various topics. The following passage is an example of one of Bahá'u'lláh's many discourses on a wide range of topics:

> Intellect hath various degrees. As a discussion of the pronouncements made by the philosophers in this connection would pass beyond the scope of our discourse, we have refrained from mentioning them. It is nonetheless indisputably clear and evident that the minds of men have never been, nor shall they ever be, of equal capacity. The Perfect Intellect alone can provide true guidance and direction. Thus were these sublime words revealed by the Pen of the Most High, exalted be His glory, in response to this question: "The Tongue of Wisdom proclaimeth: He that hath Me not is bereft of all things. Turn ye away from all that is on earth and seek none else but Me. I am the Sun of Wisdom and the Ocean of Knowledge. I cheer the faint and revive the dead. I am the guiding Light that illumineth the way. I am the royal Falcon on the arm of the Almighty. I unfold the drooping wings of every broken bird and start it on its flight."
>
> Consider how clearly the answer hath been revealed from the heaven of divine knowledge. Blessed are those who ponder it, who reflect upon it, and who apprehend its meaning! By the Intellect mentioned above is meant the universal divine Mind.
>
> (Bahá'u'lláh, *Tabernacle of Unity*, BRL)

In this Tablet, revealed on 1 July 1882, Bahá'u'lláh responds to a rather convoluted and obscure question posed by a Zoroastrian leader, Mánikchí Ṣáḥib (Maneckji Limji Hataria, 1813–1890), a Parsee who came to Persia from India in order to assist and "ameliorate" the poor conditions in which the Zoroastrians of Persia existed at that time. In this passage, Bahá'u'lláh contrasts the "lesser intellect" of "human minds" with the supreme "Intellect" of the "universal divine Mind," by which is meant the Prophet of God for that day and age. This response can be considered an allusion to Bahá'u'lláh himself, poetically described as the "Sun of Wisdom" and the "Ocean of Knowledge" and the "royal Falcon on the arm of the Almighty."

Bahá'u'lláh does not claim to be the supreme intellect in a scientific or intellectual sense, but rather with respect to spiritual wisdom, which it was Bahá'u'lláh's mission and purpose to convey to the world at large. Prophets, after all, are not scientists, nor are they philosophers (in the strict sense) nor are they historians, economists, psychologists, sociologists, etc. The knowledge that Bahá'u'lláh revealed is spiritual in nature, and should be understood and appreciated in that light. Bahá'ís consider Bahá'u'lláh's teachings to be divine guidance, which the world needs at this critical juncture in human history.

PRAYERS AND MEDITATIONS

Bahá'u'lláh revealed many prayers and meditations. The translator, Shoghi Effendi, adopted the English style of the King James Version (KJV) of the Bible, since the KJV style itself renders the translations of Bahá'u'lláh's writings easily identifiable as sacred scriptures. Here is an example of a meditation within a prayer:

> I am well aware, O my Lord, that I have been so carried away by the clear tokens of Thy loving-kindness, and so completely inebriated with the wine of Thine utterance, that whatever I behold I readily discover that it maketh Thee known unto me, and it remindeth me of Thy signs, and of Thy tokens, and of Thy testimonies. By Thy glory! Every time I lift up mine eyes unto Thy heaven, I call to mind Thy highness and Thy loftiness, and Thine incomparable glory and greatness; and every time I turn my gaze to Thine earth, I am made to recognize the evidences of Thy power and the tokens of Thy bounty. And when I behold the sea, I find that it speaketh to me of Thy majesty, and of the potency of Thy might, and of Thy sovereignty and Thy grandeur. And at whatever time I contemplate the mountains, I am led to discover the ensigns of Thy victory and the standards of Thine omnipotence.
>
> I swear by Thy might, O Thou in Whose grasp are the reins of all mankind, and the destinies of the nations! I am so inflamed by my love for Thee, and so inebriated with the wine of Thy oneness, that I can hear from the whisper of the winds the sound of Thy glorification and praise, and can recognize in the murmur of the waters the voice that proclaimeth Thy virtues and Thine attributes, and can apprehend from the rustling of the leaves the mysteries that have been irrevocably ordained by Thee in Thy realm.
>
> (Bahá'u'lláh, *Prayers and Meditations*, BRL)

This meditation is rich in nature imagery. The heavens and the earth, the sea and the mountains, the winds and the waves, and the rustling of leaves are all mentioned. Wherever nature is contemplated, everywhere there are attributes of the God that may be appreciated. The beauty and grandeur of nature serve as a reminder of the beauty and grandeur of the Creator.

WRITINGS AND TALKS OF 'ABDU'L-BAHÁ

'Abdu'l-Bahá (1844–1921) was Bahá'u'lláh's eldest son and designated successor, interpreter, and perfect exemplar of Bahá'u'lláh's teachings. While not considered revelation in the strict sense, 'Abdu'l-Bahá's writings and discourses are seen as divine guidance in their own right. In other words, since Bahá'u'lláh appointed 'Abdu'l-Bahá as the infallible exponent of Bahá'u'lláh's teachings, therefore 'Abdu'l-Bahá's statements and explanations, admonitions, and advice, are highly valued. The following three examples will serve as exemplars of 'Abdu'l-Bahá's teachings and wisdom:

TRUE CIVILIZATION

The following passage is from 'Abdu'l-Bahá's treatise, *The Secret of Divine Civilization*, written, at Bahá'u'lláh's personal request, in 1875. Pursuant to Bahá'u'lláh's subsequent instruction, this treatise became the second Bahá'í book to be officially published, in 1882. It was published in Bombay by a printing house run by relatives of the Báb. The passage below is one of the most celebrated, well-known, and often quoted statements by 'Abdu'l-Bahá, which is both a mandate and a prophecy, envisioning a time when a great assemblage—i.e. an international peace summit—would take place when the leaders of the world, or their designated representatives, would convene to conclude a comprehensive and binding international peace pact, that would signalize universal consensus and resolve all remaining territorial and other disputes, once and for all:

> True civilization will unfurl its banner in the midmost heart of the world whenever a certain number of its distinguished and high-minded sovereigns—the shining exemplars of devotion and determination—shall, for the good and happiness of all mankind, arise, with firm resolve and clear vision, to establish the Cause of Universal Peace. They must make the Cause of Peace the object of general consultation, and seek by every means in their power to establish a Union of the nations of the world. They must conclude a binding treaty and establish a covenant, the provisions of which shall be sound, inviolable and definite. They

must proclaim it to all the world and obtain for it the sanction of all the human race. This supreme and noble undertaking—the real source of the peace and well-being of all the world—should be regarded as sacred by all that dwell on earth. All the forces of humanity must be mobilized to ensure the stability and permanence of this Most Great Covenant. In this all-embracing Pact the limits and frontiers of each and every nation should be clearly fixed, the principles underlying the relations of governments towards one another definitely laid down, and all international agreements and obligations ascertained. In like manner, the size of the armaments of every government should be strictly limited, for if the preparations for war and the military forces of any nation should be allowed to increase, they will arouse the suspicion of others. The fundamental principle underlying this solemn Pact should be so fixed that if any government later violate any one of its provisions, all the governments on earth should arise to reduce it to utter submission, nay the human race as a whole should resolve, with every power at its disposal, to destroy that government. Should this greatest of all remedies be applied to the sick body of the world, it will assuredly recover from its ills and will remain eternally safe and secure.

('Abdu'l-Bahá, *Secret of Divine Civilization*, BRL)

Although *The Secret of Divine Civilization* is regarded as a Bahá'í sacred text, the foregoing passage appears to foretell what essentially will be a secular event. Of course, this occurrence has yet to happen. The significance of this passage is to underscore the religious commitment, on the part of all Bahá'ís, to world peace as a sacred undertaking, in which the full force of whatever influence Bahá'ís can contribute will be brought to bear on hastening the advent of world peace itself.

THE RETURN OF THE PROPHETS

Turning now to a text with a definite religious subject matter, 'Abdu'l-Bahá was asked a series of questions by Western Bahá'í, Laura Clifford Barney, in Acre, Palestine (now northern Israel) which 'Abdu'l-Bahá answered in a series of "table talks." Barney, who was conversant in Persian to a certain extent, carried on this series of question-and-answer sessions from 1904–1906. Given her Western background, many of Ms. Barney's questions were on Christian topics. Eventually, the Persian text of 'Abdu'l-Bahá's answers was edited and then published under the title, in English, as *Some Answered Questions*. The style of discourse is somewhat simplified as 'Abdu'l-Bahá gauged the level of his replies in Persian so that Ms. Barney could understand. The excerpt below is in response to a question regarding what the Bible means by the "return" of prophets, such as the "return" of Christ in the Last Day:

THE RETURN OF THE PROPHETS

Question: Will you explain the subject of Return?

Answer: Bahá'u'lláh has set forth a lengthy and detailed explanation of this matter in the *Kitáb-i-Íqán*. Read it, and the truth of this matter will become clear and manifest. But since you have raised the question, a brief explanation will also be provided here.

We will preface our remarks with the text of the Gospel. It is recorded therein that when John the son of Zacharias appeared and announced unto the people the advent of the Kingdom of God, they asked him, "Who art thou? Art thou the promised Messiah?" He replied, "I am not the Messiah." They then asked him, "Art thou Elias?" He replied, "I am not." [104. Cf. John 1:19–21.] These words clearly establish that John the son of Zacharias was not the promised Elias.

But on the day of the transfiguration on Mount Tabor, Christ explicitly said that John the son of Zacharias was the promised Elias. In Mark 9:11 it is said: "And they asked Him, saying, Why say the scribes that Elias must first come? And He answered and told them, Elias verily cometh first, and restoreth all things; and how it is written of the Son of man, that He must suffer many things, and be set at naught. But I say unto you, That Elias is indeed come, and they have done unto him whatsoever they listed, as it is written of him." And in Matthew 17:13 it is said: "Then the disciples understood that He spake unto them of John the Baptist."

Now, they asked John the Baptist, "Art thou Elias?" and he answered, "I am not", whereas it is said in the Gospel that John was the promised Elias himself, and Christ clearly stated this as well. If John was Elias, why did he say he was not, and if he was not Elias, why did Christ say he was?

The reason is that we consider here not the individuality of the person but the reality of his perfections—that is to say, the very same perfections that Elias possessed were realized in John the Baptist as well. Thus John the Baptist was the promised Elias. What is being considered here is not the essence [that is, the individuality of John] but the attributes. …

This is why Christ said, "Ye will witness all that came to pass in the days of the former Prophets." [Cf. Matt. 23:34–6.] …

In the same way, if we consider the individual, it is a different one, but if we consider the attributes and perfections, the same have returned. Thus when Christ said, "This is Elias", He meant: This person is a manifestation of the grace, the perfections, the qualities, the attributes, and the virtues of Elias. And when John the Baptist said, "I am not Elias", he meant, "I am not the same person as Elias." Christ considered their attributes, perfections, qualities, and virtues, and John referred to his own substance and individuality. …

These considerations have been explained at length in the *Kitáb-i-Íqán*.

('Abdu'l-Bahá, *Some Answered Questions*, BRL)

This discourse offers a prime example of the persuasive religious logic with which 'Abdu'l-Bahá approached religious topics in general, and interpretations of prophecies in particular. In this passage, the idea of prophetic "return" is explained as symbolic in nature, ruling out any notion of reincarnation. "Return" is seen as the reappearance of characteristics and qualities that had come before, such as the reemergence of flowers in springtime. By extending this analogy to the notion of prophetic return, 'Abdu'l-Bahá resolves an apparent contradiction between John the Baptist's denial that he was the return of Elijah, and Christ's affirmation that John was indeed the return of Elijah—and how these two seemingly differing statements could best be reconciled. The result is that John the Baptist is presented as the "return" of the "spirit and power" of Elijah. This explanation displays some of 'Abdu'l-Bahá's intellectual prowess and depth of spiritual insight.

PRAYER FOR KNOWLEDGE

Prayer can be spontaneous, or recited from a previously written text. Bahá'ís have many prayers from which to choose. Bahá'í prayer books are seen and used wherever there are Bahá'í gatherings. Many Bahá'ís commit certain prayers to memory. Just as Bahá'u'lláh revealed many prayers, so did 'Abdu'l-Bahá. The following is one example, which is a prayer for knowledge:

> O God, O Thou Who hast cast Thy splendor over the luminous realities of men, shedding upon them the resplendent lights of knowledge and guidance, and hast chosen them out of all created things for this supernal grace, and hast caused them to encompass all things, to understand their inmost essence, and to disclose their mysteries, bringing them forth out of darkness into the visible world! "He verily showeth His special mercy to whomsoever He will." [Qur'án 3:67.]
>
> O Lord, help Thou Thy loved ones to acquire knowledge and the sciences and arts, and to unravel the secrets that are treasured up in the inmost reality of all created beings. Make them to hear the hidden truths that are written and embedded in the heart of all that is. Make them to be ensigns of guidance amongst all creatures, and piercing rays of the mind shedding forth their light in this, the "first life." [Qur'án 56:62.] Make them to be leaders unto Thee, guides unto Thy path, runners urging men on to Thy Kingdom.
>
> Thou verily art the Powerful, the Protector, the Potent, the Defender, the Mighty, the Most Generous.
>
> ('Abdu'l-Bahá, *A Selection of Prayers*, BRL)

Readers will note that this prayer, in passing, cites two brief verses from the Quran, for emphasis and effect. This is clear evidence of the Islamic background of the Bahá'í Faith. As members of an independent world religion, Bahá'ís do not consider themselves to be Muslims. While they respect the Quran, the Quran itself is not considered a Bahá'í holy text, especially since Bahá'í scriptures constitute the Bahá'í sacred canon, as it were. Notwithstanding, Quranic themes, along with explicit citations from time to time, are met with throughout the Bahá'í writings.

WRITINGS OF SHOGHI EFFENDI

As previously explained, Shoghi Effendi (1897–1957) was the great grandson of Bahá'u'lláh, and was 'Abdu'l-Bahá's designated successor. Shoghi Effendi was a student at the University of Oxford when news reached him, in 1921, of the passing of 'Abdu'l-Bahá, and, soon after, of the latter's Will and Testament, naming Shoghi Effendi as the "Guardian" of the Bahá'í Faith. This initially came as quite a surprise and indeed a shock, which took Shoghi Effendi some time to fully absorb and accept. Once he assumed his position as the Guardian, Shoghi Effendi led the Bahá'í world from 1922–1957. Highlights of his life and ministry are given in Chapter Four. As representative examples of Shoghi Effendi's work, a few exemplary passages are quoted below.

RELIGION AND SOCIAL EVOLUTION

The following passage from Shoghi Effendi illustrates the manner in which he introduced, and explained, the relation of the Bahá'í Faith to Christianity, for the benefit of those Bahá'ís whose background was Christian. There are both commonalities and distinctions. In the passage below, Shoghi Effendi points to the emphasis in Christianity on the salvation of the individual, whereas the Bahá'í objective, first and foremost, is on the transformation of society itself which, actually, will have its own formative impact on the individuals of a given society, as well:

RELIGION AND SOCIAL EVOLUTION

The Revelation associated with the Faith of Jesus Christ focused attention primarily on the redemption of the individual and the molding of his conduct, and stressed, as its central theme, the necessity of inculcating a high standard of morality and discipline into man, as the fundamental unit in human society. ... What other interpretation can be given to these words, addressed specifically by Bahá'u'lláh to the followers of the Gospel, in which the fundamental distinction between the Mission of Jesus Christ, concerning primarily the individual, and His own Message, directed more particularly to mankind as a whole, has been definitely established: "Verily, He [Jesus] said: 'Come ye after Me, and I will make you to become fishers of men.' In this day, however, We say: "Come ye after Me, that We may make you to become the quickeners of Mankind."

'Abdu'l-Bahá Himself elucidates this truth in one of His Tablets: "In cycles gone by, though harmony was established, yet, owing to the absence of means, the unity of all mankind could not have been achieved. ... In this day, however, means of communication have multiplied, and the five continents of the earth have virtually merged into one. ... In like manner all the members of the human family, whether peoples or governments, cities or villages, have become increasingly interdependent. ... Hence the unity of all mankind can in this day be achieved. Verily this is none other but one of the wonders of this wondrous age, this glorious century. ... Eventually it will be seen how bright its candles will burn in the assemblage of man."

"Behold," He further explains, "how its light is now dawning upon the world's darkened horizon. The first candle is unity in the political realm, the early glimmerings of which can now be discerned. The second candle is unity of thought in world undertakings, the consummation of which will erelong be witnessed. The third candle is unity in freedom which will surely come to pass. The fourth candle is unity in religion which is the cornerstone of the foundation itself, and which, by the power of God, will be revealed in all its splendor. The fifth candle is the unity of nations—a unity which, in this century, will be securely established, causing all the peoples of the world to regard themselves as citizens of one common fatherland. The sixth candle is unity of races, making of all that dwell on earth peoples and kindreds of one race. The seventh candle is unity of language, i.e., the choice of a universal tongue in which all peoples will be instructed and converse. Each and every one of these will inevitably come to pass, inasmuch as the power of the Kingdom of God will aid and assist in their realization." ...

This is the stage which the world is now approaching, the stage of world unity, which, as 'Abdu'l-Bahá assures us, will, in this century, be securely established.

(Shoghi Effendi, *Promised Day Is Come*, BRL)

The prophetic passage translated in the second and third paragraphs is taken from 'Abdu'l-Bahá's "Tablet" (i.e. epistle or discourse) of the "Seven Candles of Unity" (not formally titled as such, but widely known by this reference), revealed in 1906 to a Bahá'í believer in Edinburgh, Scotland. In this passage, 'Abdu'l-Bahá foresees and foretells a series of seven kinds of unity that will transpire in the fairly near future, as these are inevitable developments, on the historical horizon, in humanity's course of social evolution, which may be further enhanced and accelerated to the degree to which Baha'i ideals and initiatives may succeed in exerting a positive influence in world affairs.

Shoghi Effendi's skill as the inspired translator of the Bahá'í sacred writings (revealed in Persian and in Arabic, with a few texts in (Azeri) Turkish, in the case of 'Abdu'l-Bahá) is also seen here as a key characteristic of Shoghi Effendi's work. His style of English is that "Oxford English," with a heavy reliance on the work of Edward Gibbon as a paradigm, since it is well known that Shoghi Effendi had a great admiration for Gibbon's classic work, *The Decline and Fall of the Roman Empire*, acclaimed as one of the "great books" of Western literature. The style of Shoghi Effendi's translations of Bahá'í scriptures, as previously stated, is modeled on King James English, which is a conscious choice on Shoghi Effendi's part, as translator, to convey the sacred spirit of Bahá'í scriptures in a manner most familiar to readers in the predominantly Christian West.

The Bahá'í doctrine of progressive revelation is also in evidence here, especially in the brief discussion of the role of Islam in the world's religious history. Religion plays a dynamic role in the social evolution of humankind, which is organized and reorganized in increasingly wider social units, from family, clan, tribe, people, nation, until the time becomes ripe for a world civilization. From the Bahá'í perspective, humanity has reached that point in its social evolution where world unity is the next stage of social development.

THE PRINCIPLE OF ONENESS

World unity, from the Bahá'í perspective, is based on the consciousness of the oneness of humankind, which calls for a wider, universal allegiance to the peoples of all nations as a whole. Although a healthy patriotism for one's country is acknowledged and encouraged, an overarching loyalty to the human race is strongly emphasized in the Bahá'í world.

THE PRINCIPLE OF ONENESS

Let there be no mistake. The principle of the Oneness of Mankind—the pivot round which all the teachings of Bahá'u'lláh revolve—is no mere outburst of ignorant emotionalism or an expression of vague and pious hope. Its appeal is not to be merely identified with a reawakening of the spirit of brotherhood and good-will among men, nor does it aim solely at the fostering of harmonious cöoperation among individual peoples and nations. Its implications are deeper, its claims greater than any which the Prophets of old were allowed to advance. … It constitutes a challenge, at once bold and universal, to outworn shibboleths of national creeds—creeds that have had their day and which must, in the ordinary course of events as shaped and controlled by Providence, give way to a new gospel, fundamentally different from, and infinitely superior to, what the world has already conceived. …

It represents the consummation of human evolution—an evolution that has had its earliest beginnings in the birth of family life, its subsequent development in the achievement of tribal solidarity, leading in turn to the constitution of the city-state, and expanding later into the institution of independent and sovereign nations.

The principle of the Oneness of Mankind, as proclaimed by Bahá'u'lláh, carries with it no more and no less than a solemn assertion that attainment to this final stage in this stupendous evolution is not only necessary but inevitable, that its realization is fast approaching, and that nothing short of a power that is born of God can succeed in establishing it.

(Shoghi Effendi, *World Order*, BRL)

In the passage above, Shoghi Effendi explains that the Bahá'í principle of the organic oneness of humankind constitutes a "new gospel." Such a breakthrough achievement in the course of humanity's collective social evolution is not, and will not, be easy. The role of religion is essential in promoting those moral, ethical, and social values necessary to usher in an emerging world civilization which, over the course of time, will evolve and effloresce into a future golden age.

UNITY IN DIVERSITY

Unity is not uniformity. The Bahá'í conception of unity respects diversity. Hence the watchword, "unity in diversity." In the passage below, Shoghi Effendi develops this theme, and accentuates it by translating a poignant passage from the writings of 'Abdu'l-Bahá, in which humanity is compared to a garden of colorful flowers, rich and resplendent in their splendid array of varying hues, which adds charm and delight to the garden as a whole. By analogy, the human race is such a garden, in which all of its intrinsic diversity is highly valued.

UNITY IN DIVERSITY

Let there be no misgivings as to the animating purpose of the world-wide Law of Bahá'u'lláh. Far from aiming at the subversion of the existing foundations of society, it seeks to broaden its basis, to remold its institutions in a manner consonant with the needs of an ever-changing world. It can conflict with no legitimate allegiances, nor can it undermine essential loyalties. Its purpose is neither to stifle the flame of a sane and intelligent patriotism in men's hearts, nor to abolish the system of national autonomy so essential if the evils of excessive centralization are to be avoided. It does not ignore, nor does it attempt to suppress, the diversity of ethnical origins, of climate, of history, of language and tradition, of thought and habit, that differentiate the peoples and nations of the world. It calls for a wider loyalty, for a larger aspiration than any that has animated the human race. It insists upon the subordination of national impulses and interests to the imperative claims of a unified world. It repudiates excessive centralization on one hand, and disclaims all attempts at uniformity on the other. Its watchword is unity in diversity.

(Shoghi Effendi, *World Order*, BRL)

So important is achieving the threshold of world unity that all contrary doctrines, laws, political systems, and economic regimes must give way to this fast-approaching milestone in the course of the world's social evolution. Attachments to any limited, and therefore limiting, doctrine or system must be overcome in an effort to sweep away all those outdated ideas and institutions that might otherwise obstruct and impede the realization of the organic and integral wholeness of the human race, from the Bahá'í perspective. Old ways will give way to new. This appears to be the primary, thematic emphasis of this well-known statement by Shoghi Effendi.

MESSAGES OF THE UNIVERSAL HOUSE OF JUSTICE

"TO THE PEOPLES OF THE WORLD" (OCTOBER 1985)

As stated previously, the Universal House of Justice is the international Bahá'í council, elected every five years, that governs the affairs of the Bahá'í community worldwide. The purpose and mission of the House of Justice, however, is not limited in scope to the Bahá'í community itself. Just as the purpose and mission of the Bahá'í Faith is to promote human solidarity and corresponding world peace, the Universal House of Justice carries forward this mandate at the international level. With this global mission in mind, it makes perfect sense that, at some point in his development, the Universal House of Justice would communicate a message to the world at large. So, in October 1985, the House of Justice issued an open letter addressed to the "Peoples of the World." This remarkable letter is quoted, in part, below:

THE UNIVERSAL HOUSE OF JUSTICE

October 1985
To the Peoples of the World

The Great Peace towards which people of goodwill throughout the centuries have inclined their hearts, of which seers and poets for countless generations have expressed their vision, and for which from age to age the sacred scriptures of mankind have constantly held the promise, is now at long last within the reach of the nations. For the first time in history it is possible for everyone to view the entire planet, with all its myriad diversified peoples, in one perspective. World peace is not only possible but inevitable. It is the next stage in the evolution of this planet—in the words of one great thinker, "the planetization of mankind."

   Whether peace is to be reached only after unimaginable horrors precipitated by humanity's stubborn clinging to old patterns of behavior, or is to be embraced now by an act of consultative will, is the choice before all who inhabit the earth. ...

   Racism, one of the most baneful and persistent evils, is a major barrier to peace. Its practice perpetrates too outrageous a violation of the dignity of human beings to be countenanced under any pretext. Racism retards the unfoldment of the boundless potentialities of its victims, corrupts its perpetrators, and blights human progress. Recognition of the oneness of mankind, implemented by appropriate legal measures, must be universally upheld if this problem is to be overcome.

The inordinate disparity between rich and poor, a source of acute suffering, keeps the world in a state of instability, virtually on the brink of war. Few societies have dealt effectively with this situation. The solution calls for the combined application of spiritual, moral and practical approaches. A fresh look at the problem is required, entailing consultation with experts from a wide spectrum of disciplines, devoid of economic and ideological polemics, and involving the people directly affected in the decisions that must urgently be made. It is an issue that is bound up not only with the necessity for eliminating extremes of wealth and poverty but also with those spiritual verities the understanding of which can produce a new universal attitude. Fostering such an attitude is itself a major part of the solution.

Unbridled nationalism, as distinguished from a sane and legitimate patriotism, must give way to a wider loyalty, to the love of humanity as a whole. Bahá'u'lláh's statement is: "The earth is but one country, and mankind its citizens." The concept of world citizenship is a direct result of the contraction of the world into a single neighborhood through scientific advances and of the indisputable interdependence of nations. Love of all the world's peoples does not exclude love of one's country. The advantage of the part in a world society is best served by promoting the advantage of the whole. Current international activities in various fields which nurture mutual affection and a sense of solidarity among peoples need greatly to be increased.

Religious strife, throughout history, has been the cause of innumerable wars and conflicts, a major blight to progress, and is increasingly abhorrent to the people of all faiths and no faith. Followers of all religions must be willing to face the basic questions which this strife raises, and to arrive at clear answers. How are the differences between them to be resolved, both in theory and in practice? The challenge facing the religious leaders of mankind is to contemplate, with hearts filled with the spirit of compassion and a desire for truth, the plight of humanity, and to ask themselves whether they cannot, in humility before their Almighty Creator, submerge their theological differences in a great spirit of mutual forbearance that will enable them to work together for the advancement of human understanding and peace.

The emancipation of women, the achievement of full equality between the sexes, is one of the most important, though less acknowledged prerequisites of peace. The denial of such equality perpetrates an injustice against one half of the world's population and promotes in men harmful attitudes and habits that are carried from the family to the workplace, to political life, and ultimately to international relations. There are no grounds, moral, practical, or biological, upon which such denial can be justified. Only as women are welcomed into full partnership in all fields of human endeavor will the moral and psychological climate be created in which international peace can emerge.

The cause of universal education, which has already enlisted in its service an army of dedicated people from every faith and nation, deserves the utmost support that the governments of the world can lend it. For ignorance is indisputably the principal reason for the decline and fall of peoples and the perpetuation of prejudice. No nation can achieve success unless education is accorded all its citizens. Lack of resources limits the ability of many nations to fulfill this necessity, imposing a certain ordering of priorities. The decision-making agencies involved would do well to consider giving first priority to the education of women and girls, since it is through educated mothers that the benefits of knowledge can be most effectively and rapidly diffused throughout society. In keeping with the requirements of the times, consideration should also be given to teaching the concept of world citizenship as part of the standard education of every child.

A fundamental lack of communication between peoples seriously undermines efforts towards world peace. Adopting an international auxiliary language would go far to resolve this problem and necessitates the most urgent attention.

Two points bear emphasizing in all these issues. One is that the abolition of war is not simply a matter of signing treaties and protocols; it is a complex task requiring a new level of commitment to resolving issues not customarily associated with the pursuit of peace. Based on political agreements alone, the idea of collective security is a chimera. The other point is that the primary challenge in dealing with issues of peace is to raise the context to the level of principle, as distinct from pure pragmatism. For, in essence, peace stems from an inner state supported by a spiritual or moral attitude, and it is chiefly in evoking this attitude that the possibility of enduring solutions can be found.

There are spiritual principles, or what some call human values, by which solutions can be found for every social problem. Any well-intentioned group can in a general sense devise practical solutions to its problems, but good intentions and practical knowledge are usually not enough. The essential merit of spiritual principle is that it not only presents a perspective which harmonizes with that which is immanent in human nature, it also induces an attitude, a dynamic, a will, an aspiration, which facilitate the discovery and implementation of practical measures. Leaders of governments and all in authority would be well served in their efforts to solve problems if they would first seek to identify the principles involved and then be guided by them. ...

In the earnestness of our desire to impart to you the fervor of our hope and the depth of our confidence, we cite the emphatic promise of Bahá'u'lláh: "These fruitless strifes, these ruinous wars shall pass away, and the 'Most Great Peace' shall come."

[signed: The Universal House of Justice]

(Universal House of Justice, "Promise of World Peace," BRL)

As seen in this letter, several important spiritual and social principles are addressed, which have not often been connected with the issue of world peace itself. Bringing these principles into relevance is a significant contribution to social discourse on peace, not to mention progressive public policy. For instance, the House of Justice strikes a dynamic relationship between the equality of women and men and the pursuit of world peace. In a male-dominated world, war is a norm. But this does not have to be, nor should it be. The contribution and influence of women, once they achieve their full equality, is to resolve conflict without recourse to war. The Bahá'í writings point out that mothers, if given a voice and a choice, will not permit their sons (and, in some cases, daughters) to be used as cannon fodder in the course of prosecuting an unnecessary war. War forces outcomes, but does not resolve the underlying causes of the conflict that gave rise to the war in the first place.

Wars result if problems are not solved. If the root causes are addressed, then wars can be preempted and averted. The Universal House of Justice raises other issues that may risk international conflicts as well, such as global poverty, racism, etc. Taken as a whole, this open letter to the peoples of the world imparts a vision of world peace in which the root causes of war are squarely identified and dynamically interconnected, and solutions for resolving seemingly intractable conflicts are proposed at the level of principle and practice. In this process, the consciousness of the fundamental solidarity of the human race may be the single greatest bulwark in eradicating war, once and for all, because the awareness that the peoples of the world are interrelated is a powerful way to counteract alienation and the inhumane "othering" used as a pretext to create enmity and justify warfare as a result.

"TO THE WORLD'S RELIGIOUS LEADERS" (APRIL 2002)

In the aftermath of terrorist attacks of September 11, 2001, the world's collective attention was—and still is—focused on the problem of religious radicalism and its destructive impacts. Several months later, in April 2002, the Universal House of Justice sent an open letter addressed to "The World's Religious Leaders." While the letter was collegial and supportive of interfaith dialogue, there was a critical dimension in this open message as well (see Buck 2019). One of the fundamental problems of interfaith relations is that of religious prejudice itself. This letter indicates that significant progress in interreligious dialogue is severely limited unless and until the fundamental unity of religions is acknowledged at the level of spiritual, moral, ethical, and social principles. Recognizing any and all shared values constitutes a bedrock, i.e. solid foundation, on which harmonious and potentially productive interfaith relations may be based; the Universal House of Justice therefore calls upon the world's religious leaders to take stock and to contemplate what their respective religions have in common. The following excerpts highlight this significant letter:

THE UNIVERSAL HOUSE OF JUSTICE

April 2002
To The World's Religious Leaders

Tragically, organized religion, whose very reason for being entails service to the cause of brotherhood and peace, behaves all too frequently as one of the most formidable obstacles in the path; to cite a particular painful fact, it has long lent its credibility to fanaticism. We feel a responsibility, as the governing council of one of the world religions, to urge earnest consideration of the challenge this poses for religious leadership. ...

It is to this historic challenge that we believe leaders of religion must respond if religious leadership is to have meaning in the global society emerging from the transformative experiences of the twentieth century. It is evident that growing numbers of people are coming to realize that the truth underlying all religions is in its essence one. ...

As the name implies, religion has simultaneously been the chief force binding diverse peoples together in ever larger and more complex societies through which the individual capacities thus released can find expression. The great advantage of the present age is the perspective that makes it possible for the entire human race to see this civilizing process as a single phenomenon, the ever-recurring encounters of our world with the world of God.

Inspired by this perspective, the Bahá'í community has been a vigorous promoter of interfaith activities from the time of their inception. ... We owe it to our partners in this common effort, however, to state clearly our conviction that interfaith discourse, if it is to contribute meaningfully to healing the ills that afflict a desperate humanity, must now address honestly and without further evasion the implications of the over-arching truth that called the movement into being: that God is one and that, beyond all diversity of cultural expression and human interpretation, religion is likewise one.

With every day that passes, danger grows that the rising fires of religious prejudice will ignite a worldwide conflagration the consequences of which are unthinkable. Such a danger civil government, unaided, cannot overcome. ... The crisis calls on religious leadership for a break with the past as decisive as those that opened the way for society to address equally corrosive prejudices of race, gender and nation. Whatever justification exists for exercising influence in matters of conscience lies in serving the well-being of humankind. At this greatest turning point in the history of civilization, the demands of such service could not be more clear. "The well-being of mankind, its peace and security, are unattainable," Bahá'u'lláh urges, "unless and until its unity is firmly established."

[signed: The Universal House of Justice]

(Universal House of Justice, *April 2002: To the World's Religious Leaders*, BRL)

Although not explicitly stated as such, this open letter may be analyzed, in part, as a response by the Universal House of Justice to 9/11, which shocked the world and focused international attention on the problem of religious fanaticism and sectarianism, leading to terrorism. This open letter to all religious leaders is as ambitious as it is audacious, for it calls for a universal recognition of the moral and ethical unity that comprise the very foundations of religion itself. No significant progress in interfaith dialogue, consensus, and cooperation can take place without consensus on this general theory of religious relativity, openly advocated by the Universal House of Justice.

6

INSTITUTIONS
THE BAHÁ'Í ADMINISTRATIVE ORDER

HOW BAHÁ'Í ADMINISTRATION WORKS

Councils, not clerics, guide Bahá'í administration. So, how does the
Bahá'í Faith operate as an organization, without clergy? It does so
primarily through a series of elected councils—local, regional (which
exist in some countries), national, and international councils. Each of
these Bahá'í councils generates wisdom and makes decisions based on
full and frank consultation, conducted in a spirit of camaraderie and
reciprocal respect, guided by Bahá'í principles, policies, and practices.

Even before Bahá'í councils ever existed, consultation was the
watchword of all Bahá'í decision-making. And so it remains today.
The Bahá'í art of consultation, as well as its system of elections and
councils, is quite unique in the history of religions, and is the subject
of this chapter.

BAHÁ'Í CONSULTATION

Readers, no doubt, are familiar with the expression, "Two heads are
better than one." In other words, collaboration can be a good thing,
especially for problem-solving. Of course, it all depends on the com-
petence of the individuals themselves, and on the quality of their communication and interaction. This principle can be extended to groups

DOI: 10.4324/9780429023088-6

in general, who engage in productive consultation. A prime example is how Bahá'í administration works.

Consultation is a Bahá'í law, first enjoined by Bahá'u'lláh, who wrote: "Say: no man can attain his true station except through his justice. No power can exist except through unity. No welfare and no well-being can be attained except through consultation" (Bahá'u'lláh, quoted in *Consultation: A Compilation*, BRL). Note here that "consultation" is closely connected to the principles of "justice" and "unity." "The Great Being saith: The heaven of divine wisdom is illumined with the two luminaries of consultation and compassion," Bahá'u'lláh further states, adding: "Take ye counsel together in all matters, inasmuch as consultation is the lamp of guidance which leadeth the way, and is the bestower of understanding" (Bahá'u'lláh, *Tablets*, BRL). "Consultation" is closely associated with "compassion." So, it is clear that Bahá'í consultation is characterized by compassion, justice, and unity. This is governance with heart and soul.

Bahá'í consultation is a principled process of enlightened decision-making. Search after truth and consultation, after all, are interrelated and interdependent. Consultation is a "lamp" that illuminates and empowers the conduct and course of Bahá'í administration. "Consultation bestoweth greater awareness and transmuteth conjecture into certitude," Bahá'u'lláh wrote. "It is a shining light which, in a dark world, leadeth the way and guideth." Consultation, moreover, is an indicator of social maturity: "For everything there is and will continue to be a station of perfection and maturity," Bahá'u'lláh declared. "The maturity of the gift of understanding is made manifest through consultation" (Bahá'u'lláh, *Consultation*, BRL). At heart, Bahá'í consultation is therefore spiritual and mature in nature, as applied to practical matters. Such quality of input optimizes favorable outcomes.

The process of Bahá'í consultation is dynamically unique. *Robert's Rules of Order* is not used for the conduct of Bahá'í meetings in which consultation takes place. Bahá'ís reach their decisions through a majority vote, although consensus remains the ideal for any and all Bahá'í decision-making. Before a vote is taken, the issue to be considered by a Bahá'í council is presented for deliberation, the facts are ascertained with due diligence, spiritual principles are identified, a solution is agreed upon, and the decision is then implemented. After a vote is taken and a decision is reached, all agree to carry out the decision in unison.

That said, any prior decision can be revisited and reconsidered later on, if new facts and circumstances warrant. The Bahá'í system of consultation is therefore open-minded, flexible, principled, solution-oriented, creative when necessary, and generally harmonious in nature. Those individuals who offer ideas are taught not to "own" those ideas since, once given, such ideas are considered by the group as a whole. The Bahá'í system of consultation is spiritual in nature and operates with the benefit of clear principles as well.

Marked by civility and guided by such harmonious principles, the Bahá'í process of consultation is conducted in a spirit of goodwill, without engaging in rancor or disputation, with a goal of building consensus. If consensus cannot be achieved, decisions are reached by majority vote. "Such matters should be determined through consultation," Bahá'u'lláh explained, "and whatever emergeth from the consultation of those chosen, that indeed is the command of God, the Help in Peril, the Self-Subsisting" (Bahá'u'lláh, *Tablets*, BRL).

If informed by principle and applied by way of full and frank consultation, decisions are reached through an enlightened process of offering and considering various ideas, purely on their own merit. Candor, as part of civil discourse, is elevated to an art form, whereby honest appraisals are offered in a spirit of respect, with criticism directed at no one and with no great attachment to one's idea.

Consultation takes place not only in Bahá'í councils, but in other Bahá'í contexts as well. For instance, during consultation at Nineteen Day Feasts, Bahá'ís may pass on their recommendations to their "Local Spiritual Assembly" (LSA) for its consideration. The LSA may respond by way of reporting a decision on that recommendation at the next Bahá'í Feast. In this way, the Bahá'í Feast operates somewhat analogously to a "town hall" meeting at which local concerns are voiced and deliberated on. Consultation, moreover, is encouraged for all individuals and institutions throughout society.

The Bahá'í principle and practice of consultation concentrates power in whatever group is responsible for decision-making. Autocratic, dictatorial determinations, therefore, are utterly impossible to imagine in a Bahá'í context. Nor are any polarizing and paralyzing partisan politics involved at all. In fact, Bahá'ís are forbidden to participate in partisan politics, which are inherently divisive and often result in legislative gridlock.

Since the Bahá'í Faith is all about unity, consultation itself must be conducted with cordiality and concord, and be conducive to, and productive of unity. So, both process and outcomes are actuated and guided by Bahá'í principles of unity, as applied to consultation. Bahá'í principles of consultation apply equally to all Bahá'í councils, whether local, regional, national, or international. The only real difference is their jurisdiction and scope. The nature and function of Bahá'í councils will be briefly discussed after the next section, which explains the process of Bahá'í elections, which is distinctive and a form of nonpartisan democracy.

BAHÁ'Í ELECTIONS

The Bahá'í electoral process is as unique as it is democratic. There are no parallels among religious or political institutions. Bahá'í elections are distinctive for their total absence of nominations and campaigning. There is no slate of candidates. No electioneering is allowed, nor fund-raising. No political parties, no primaries, no promises, no platforms, no public spectacles, no media circuses, no contentious contests, no public debates, no open criticisms, no backbiting, no defamatory statements, no insults, no rancor, no *ad hominem* attacks, no controversies, no scandals, no vote-getting, no influence peddling, no lobbying, no corruption. By contrast, Bahá'í elections are conducted in a rarefied and prayerful atmosphere. Although carried out for an important administrative purpose, Bahá'í elections are essentially spiritual in nature. Here is how they work:

Bahá'í councils are elected by plurality vote (rather than majority vote) through secret ballots, with no nominations or campaigning allowed, as previously mentioned. The international Bahá'í council is known as the Universal House of Justice, whose majestic edifice is situated on the sacred slopes of Mount Carmel at the Bahá'í World Centre in Haifa, Israel. National Bahá'í councils are called "National Spiritual Assemblies." Similarly, regional and local Bahá'í councils are known as "Regional Bahá'í Councils" and a "Local Spiritual Assemblies," respectively.

During a Bahá'í election, typically some instructive Bahá'í guidance regarding Bahá'í elections is read aloud to those assembled, after which prayers are said, and then the elections take place in thoughtful silence, in the soulful spirit those prayers ideally create. Tellers are appointed to tally the votes. Those nine individuals who receive the highest number of votes are elected to a given council. If there is a tie in the number of votes between any two individuals—and if one of those individuals belongs to a recognized racial or ethnic minority— the minority member is favored. That is how a tie in a Bahá'í election is often resolved, without recourse to a run-off vote.

In 2005, Arash Abizadeh (Professor, Department of Political Science, Associate Member, Department of Philosophy, McGill University, and former Rhodes Scholar), published a significant article on this topic: "Democratic Elections without Campaigns? Normative Foundations of National Bahá'í Elections," offering an illuminating analysis (Abizadeh 2005).

THE UNIVERSAL HOUSE OF JUSTICE

The Universal House of Justice is the world's first truly global elected body. Elected once in every five years by members of Bahá'í National Spiritual Assemblies from around the world, the Universal House of Justice is the supreme Bahá'í institution in terms of its authority and mandate. House members are therefore elected to five-year terms. In April 1963, the Universal House of Justice was elected, for the first time, by all 56 National Spiritual Assemblies established world-wide at that time. (Today, there are more than 180 National Spiritual Assemblies.) The 2018 election marked the 55th anniversary of the first election of the Universal House of Justice.

Exercising plenary authority, the House oversees the affairs of the Bahá'í world. None of its nine members, whether current or former, have any individual authority or claim to a higher station or to any special dignity apart from being members of the Universal House of Justice itself. The members accept their service on this supreme Bahá'í institution in a spirit of humility and commitment. The Universal House of Justice strives to translate Bahá'u'lláh's vision of world peace into reality.

Decisions by the Universal House of Justice that are general in nature are typically communicated through the dissemination and publication of official, open letters, often directed to specific Bahá'í institutions, as well as to Bahá'ís worldwide. Collections of these letters are published, from time to time, in a series of volumes for ready reference. These decisions constitute a rich body of cumulative wisdom to which Bahá'ís worldwide look for guidance in their activities, administrative affairs, and in their collective efforts to systematically achieve practical goals set forth in collective Baha'i plans of action.

Typically such plans are of five-year duration, as promulgated by the Universal House of Justice.

The Universal House of Justice is the exception to the general rule—that men and women participate in all Bahá'í affairs—in that only men are eligible to serve. The specific reason for this exception is not known. Bahá'ís accept this requirement, clearly established by Bahá'u'lláh, as a matter of faith. In no way does the male-only membership of the Universal House of Justice compromise, or in any way diminish, the full commitment of Bahá'ís worldwide to the fundamental principle of the equality of women and men. Women are also excluded from military combat roles, as 'Abdu'l-Bahá explains:

> In this Revelation of Bahá'u'lláh, the women go neck and neck with the men. In no movement will they be left behind. Their rights with men are equal in degree. They will enter all the administrative branches of politics. They will attain in all such a degree as will be considered the very highest station of the world of humanity and will take part in all affairs. ... No soul can retard or prevent it. But there are certain matters, the participation in which is not worthy of women. For example, at the time when the community is taking up vigorous defensive measures against the attack of foes, the women are exempt from military engagements. ... As regards the constitution of the House of Justice, Bahá'u'lláh addresses the men. He says: "O ye men of the House of Justice!" ... His Holiness Bahá'u'lláh has greatly strengthened the cause of women, and the rights and privileges of women is one of the greatest principles of 'Abdu'l-Bahá. Rest ye assured!
>
> ('Abdu'l-Bahá, *Paris Talks*, BRL)

The wisdom of excluding women from serving on the Universal House of Justice will become clear in the future. Rather than a contradiction, this policy constitutes the proverbial "exception that proves the rule"—in that this exception, under these parameters, proves that the Bahá'í principle of the equality of women and men works in all other circumstances (with the other exception being military combat).

Chapter Five included excerpts from "The Promise of World Peace" (October 1985)—the first official public statement issued by the Universal House of Justice since its inception in 1963—and the "Letter to the World's Religious Leaders" (Universal House of Justice, April 2002, BRL). Chapter Four presents part of the mission statement set forth in "The Constitution of the Universal House of Justice," adopted and signed on 26 November 1972. In the exercise of its governance, members of the House vote according to the dictates of their conscience.

THE NATIONAL SPIRITUAL ASSEMBLY

Each National Spiritual Assembly (NSA) is elected by a convention of delegates every year in April. For instance, the National Spiritual Assembly of the Bahá'ís of the United States is the nine-member elected governing body of the US Bahá'í community. At the time of this writing, the US-NSA was most recently elected during the 111th Annual Bahá'í National Convention (25–28 April 2019), at the Bahá'í House of Worship in Wilmette, Illinois. Each NSA oversees the affairs of the region or country under its Bahá'í jurisdiction. NSA members therefore are elected to one-year terms. Today, there are many NSAs across the world.

THE REGIONAL BAHÁ'Í COUNCIL

Regional Bahá'í Councils (RBCs) exist in several countries around the world today. For instance, RBCs were first established in the United States in 1997, by permission of the Universal House of Justice. In 2002, Canada became one of the earliest countries to see the emergence of Bahá'í Regional Councils. There are RBCs in Australia as well, and elsewhere (although the present writer is not aware of a comprehensive list of RBCs that is publicly available). The creation of Regional Bahá'í Councils occurs only in countries where conditions make this step necessary and advantageous. Typically, these Regional Bahá'í Councils are elected Bahá'í institutions, serving under the direction of their respective National Spiritual Assembly. RBC members are elected to one-year terms. Regional Bahá'í Councils serve to encourage and promote the success of current Bahá'í plans and advise and assist in the successful initiation and multiplication of local Bahá'í "core activities" in Bahá'í "clusters" (geographic areas) within their designated regions.

THE LOCAL SPIRITUAL ASSEMBLY

Each Local Spiritual Assembly deliberates and decides on the affairs of the local Bahá'í community within its given jurisdiction. LSA members are elected to one-year terms. As an elected body, the LSA is responsible for the spiritual welfare of the local Bahá'í community itself and, beyond that, of the spiritual health of the citizens of the local community at large. The Bahá'í Faith, after all, exists to make the world a better place, as part of its mission and mandate. In this respect, little or no distinction is made between Bahá'ís and non-Bahá'ís. The overarching Bahá'í mission is to unify the world through the progressive and powerful social and moral principles that Bahá'ís do their best to promote.

THE INSTITUTION OF THE COUNSELORS

The "Bahá'í Administrative Order" features both elected and appointed institutions. In Bahá'í parlance, "the Rulers and the Learned" euphemistically refers to these elected councils ("the Rulers") and appointed branches (i.e. "the Learned"), respectively. This expression comes from Bahá'u'lláh's will and testament, the "Book of the Covenant" (*Kitáb-i-'Ahd*) which states, in a pertinent part: "Blessed are the rulers and the learned among the people of Bahá" (Bahá'u'lláh, *Tablets* BRL, and *Kitáb-i-Aqdas*, BRL), which 'Abdu'l-Bahá has interpreted as follows:

> In this holy cycle the "learned" are, on the one hand, the Hands of the Cause of God, and, on the other, the teachers and diffusers of His teachings who do not rank as Hands, but who have attained an eminent position in the teaching work. As to the "rulers" they refer to the members of the Local, National and International Houses of Justice. The duties of each of these souls will be determined in the future.
>
> ('Abdu'l-Bahá, quoted in Bahá'u'lláh, *Kitáb-i-Aqdas*, BRL)

Here, the "Hands of the Cause of God" refer to those select handful of distinguished individuals—three contingents of whom were successively appointed by Bahá'u'lláh, 'Abdu'l-Bahá, and Shoghi Effendi—who were charged with the twin duties of propagating the Bahá'í Faith and protecting it (from schism). Furthering their work, the Bahá'í administrative system developed the institution of the Counselors.

In June 1968, the Universal House of Justice first established the institution of the Counselors. Every five years, the Universal House of Justice appoints a total of 81 Counselors, who serve on five Continental

Boards: Africa, the Americas, Asia, Australasia, and Europe. These Counselors, in turn, operate through five Continental Boards of Counselors, whose work is guided by the "International Teaching Centre," based at the Bahá'í World Centre. The International Teaching Centre's nine members are appointed by the Universal House of Justice for a five-year term, soon after the "International Bahá'í Convention," with the 12th International Bahá'í Convention having taken place on 2 May 2018. The Boards then appoint "Auxiliary Boards for Protection and Propagation" members (who may appoint their own assistants), who serve in designated geographical areas within their respective continental regions

The Counselors promote the spiritual, intellectual, and social life of the Bahá'í community worldwide. These individuals serve in a purely advisory capacity. In other words, the Counselors have no legislative, executive, or judicial authority. From the grassroots to the international level, the institution, as a whole, plays a vital role in advancing the interests of the Bahá'í Faith. The Counselors exert a positive influence on the life of the Bahá'í community by offering advice to Spiritual Assemblies, promoting learning within the Bahá'í community, inspiring individual initiative, and enhancing the capacity of the Bahá'í community to develop and carry out systematic plans of action, and to learn from experience in their community-building efforts. Together with the members of the Auxiliary Boards and their assistants, the Counselors endeavor to promote the growth and vibrancy of the Bahá'í community worldwide. The mission and mandate of the Counselors, and those who work under their direction, is to promote the development of Bahá'í spiritual, intellectual, and social life, and to contribute to the betterment of wider societies at large. (Bahá'u'lláh, *Kitáb-i-Aqdas*, BRL)

SUMMARY

- Councils, not clerics, guide Bahá'í administration.
- Consultation is a Bahá'í law, first enjoined by Bahá'u'lláh.
- Bahá'u'lláh wrote, "Say: no man can attain his true station except through his justice."
- Bahá'u'lláh also stated, "No power can exist except through unity."

- Bahá'u'lláh further declared, "No welfare and no well-being can be attained except through consultation."
- Search after truth and consultation, after all, are interrelated and interdependent.
- Consultation is a "lamp" that illuminates and empowers the conduct and course of Bahá'í administration.
- Bahá'í councils are elected by plurality vote (rather than majority vote) through secret ballots.
- Elected Bahá'í councils include local, regional (which exist in some countries), national, and international councils.
- The international Bahá'í council is known as the Universal House of Justice.
- The Universal House of Justice is the world's first truly global elected body.

BUILDING COMMUNITY
WHAT BAHÁ'ÍS DO

Readers will recall that Chapter Two introduced the disease/cure model for understanding religious worldviews. The "human predicament," from a Bahá'í perspective, is seen as profound disunity, from family relations to international relations. "Disunity is the crux of the problems which so severely afflict the planet. It permeates attitudes in all departments of life," the Universal House of Justice points out, adding,

> It is at the heart of all major conflicts between nations and peoples. More serious still, disunity is common in the relations between religions and within religions, vitiating the very spiritual and moral influence which it is their primary purpose to exert
> (Universal House of Justice, November 1992, BRL).

The Bahá'í solutions to these overarching global problems, therefore, are profound principles of unity, from family relations to international relations—put into action. This chapter, "Building Community: What Bahá'ís Do," demonstrates how some of these Bahá'í principles of unity are being effectively and creatively implemented, as Bahá'ís endeavor to create social models that work and are worthy of emulation and replication.

DOI: 10.4324/9780429023088-7

The Bahá'í social universe is rapidly expanding. The Bahá'í community is open-armed and ever-widening in its social outreach. Bahá'í locales are welcoming and embracing, dedicated to enhancing individual and social transformation. "Service"—to neighborhoods, communities of interest, and other social spaces, whether personal or professional—is the watchword of homespun, group Bahá'í endeavors and individual initiatives. Bahá'í social orbits are increasingly inclusive within their interpersonal constellations. In other words, Bahá'ís are encouraged to interact with their friends, neighbors, and colleagues in a spirit of unity, worship, education, and service.

Thousands of Bahá'í communities worldwide have been engaging in local service projects as part of an overarching process of "community building," where "community" is broadly defined. Community building means enhancing both the spiritual and material nature of the local community through a grassroots approach. Educational classes and service opportunities are offered to children and youth, as well as to adults. According to Bahá'í scholar Moojan Momen, "This is new. In the entire scope of human history, no organization or faith has ever implemented anything like it—a simultaneous worldwide social development program designed to carry forward an ever-advancing global civilization" (Momen 2018). A Bahá'í's sense of community is one of solidarity, given the emphasis on unity and of the oneness of humankind that is central to the Bahá'í teachings and worldview. This sense of solidarity extends to friends of the Faith and to other contacts as well. Far from insular, Bahá'í communities are social spaces without borders—communities of friends, making new friends.

Local Bahá'í communities host regular events and special events that enrich and enhance the vibrancy of spiritual and social life. This chapter highlights "essential activities" and "core activities" that animate, educate, and elevate the Bahá'í experience throughout the world. The term, "essential activities," is used in a letter, dated 27 December 2005, from the Universal House of Justice to the Conference of the Continental Boards of Counselors. This is not a hard-and-fast distinction and is adopted here primarily for organizational reasons. Bahá'í community life consists of such essential activities as Nineteen Day Feasts and Bahá'í Holy Days, while Bahá'í core activities consist of devotionals, study circles, children's classes, and youth classes. Taken together, these constitute "local Bahá'í activities."

ESSENTIAL ACTIVITIES

BASIS: THE BAHÁ'Í CALENDAR

The rhythm of Bahá'í worship and spiritual life is based on a special and rather unique Bahá'í Calendar. Just about every world religion has its own sacred calendar. The Bahá'í Faith is no exception. Originally created by the Báb, then adapted by Bahá'u'lláh, the Bahá'í Calendar consists of 19 months of 19 days, with several "Intercalary Days" rounding out the solar year (see Keil 2008). The Bahá'í New Year (Naw-Rúz, Persian for "New Day") begins on the vernal equinox (which is astronomically determined and falls on 19, 20, or 21 March on the Gregorian calendar). Although not strictly astronomical (since 19-day months are neither solar nor lunar), the Bahá'í Calendar is heavenly in the spiritual sense. In every way, it reminds one of God, and of all that is angelic, noble, and virtuous.

The Bahá'í Calendar is distinctive in several respects. The Bahá'í Calendar charts not only chronological time but marks the progress of the soul as well. Each weekday, each day of the month, each month, each year, and each cycle of 19 years is given a special name—a "Name of God," meaning an attribute of God that can also be manifested as a human virtue. For example, the Gregorian calendar date of Sunday, 21 March 2010, may be expressed as follows in the Bahá'í Calendar: The weekday of "Beauty" (*Jamál*, i.e. Sunday), the (first) day "Splendor" (*Bahá*) in the (first) month of "Splendor" (*Bahá*) in the year (15th) of "Affection" (*Vidád*), in the cycle (19 years) of "Unity" (*Váhid*) of the first Grand Cycle (361 years) of "All Things" (Arabic, *Kullu Shay'*; Persian, *Kull-i-Shay'*). The original terms, although foreign, are familiar in English.

The Bahá'í Calendar transforms time into opportune moments for reflection on matters of spirit, which are both timely and timeless alike. Originally called the "Wondrous (*Badí'*) Calendar" when it was first created by the Báb (and later adopted and adapted by Bahá'u'lláh), the Bahá'í Calendar invests time with spiritual significance by naming weekdays, days of the month, months, years, and cycles of years after godly perfections. These Names of God represent far more than simple designations of units of time. They connect to the timeless, yet timely, progress of the soul in its spiritual growth and advancement throughout life. This is because these godly qualities—which represent spiritual energies—can be translated into an array of goodly virtues. This Bahá'í almanac, therefore, inspires spiritual progress by associating time with reminders of God and all that enhances human nobility, i.e. of saintly qualities. By and through the progressive spiritualization of all persons—and, indeed, of all things—the Báb wished to transform all of social and physical reality into "mirrors"—reflecting the perfections represented by these divine names, as expressed in action and function. The present writer has devoted a series of short articles on each of these names in the Bahá'í Calendar (see Buck, *Transforming Time: Turning Godly Perfections into Goodly Actions*).

In this wondrous calendric system, each and every unit of time gives pause for spiritual thought and reflection. This is part of the Báb's comprehensive system of precepts and practices, all calculated to keep the believer in a constant, God-conscious frame of mind. Each of these dynamic names of God highlights a distinctive quality of sterling character and human nobility—which not only may be invoked in prayer and meditation but may be evoked in thought and action. In doing so, the mirror of the human heart, or soul, may reflect a ray of the spiritual sun. With this background in mind, highlights of Bahá'í essential activities may be presented as follows.

NINETEEN DAY FEASTS

As in other faiths, Bahá'ís worship individually and collectively. At the heart of Bahá'í community life is the Nineteen Day Feast, when the local Bahá'í community meets for worship, consultation, and fellowship. As the name suggests, the Bahá'í Feast is held once every nineteen days—that is, in each and every Bahá'í month, usually at the beginning of each Bahá'í month. Typically, a Bahá'í Feast is conducted in three parts: (1) devotions; (2) consultation; and (3) fellowship. In other words, the Feast begins with the reading (and often chanting) of Bahá'í sacred scriptures (especially prayers), followed by consultation on community affairs, ending with food and fellowship (social), although this order of events may be varied. Although the Feast offers physical repast—in the form of refreshments served during the social portion—the primary emphasis is on spiritual nourishment through prayers and readings invoked and recited during devotions. This is the real food for the soul!

One of the most beloved of Bahá'u'lláh's prayers is this short passage, which is the opening prayer in the standard US Bahá'í prayerbook:

> Blessed is the spot, and the house, and the place, and the city, and the heart, and the mountain, and the refuge, and the cave, and the valley, and the land, and the sea, and the island, and the meadow where mention of God hath been made, and His praise glorified.
>
> (Bahá'u'lláh, *A Selection of Prayers*, BRL)

Although Bahá'í prayers seek blessings from God, the very act of praying itself is a blessing. So, the place where the Feast is held is transformed into a sacred space. "Round about whatever dwelling the friends of God may enter, and from which their cry shall rise as they praise and glorify the Lord," Bahá'u'lláh elsewhere writes, "shall circle the souls of true believers and all the favoured angels" (Bahá'u'lláh, *Bahá'í Meetings*, BRL). Ideally, the devotional portion of the Feast—when a spirit of reverence is created—has an uplifting spiritualizing effect. That is the purpose and goal of engaging in Bahá'í worship, which creates and sustains a rarefied spiritual atmosphere—thereby enhancing the consultative phase as well, which comes next.

Consultation—the "business" portion of a Bahá'í Feast—is typically led by a designated member of the Local Spiritual Assembly (LSA) and functions somewhat like a "town hall meeting," but is all the while conducted with civility and respect. International and national Bahá'í news may be shared with the Bahá'í friends who are present at that gathering. The local Bahá'í treasurer gives a report on the Bahá'í Fund (local, national, and international), to which Bahá'ís only may contribute. The affairs, goals, and plans of the local Bahá'í community are discussed, with individual suggestions and group recommendations noted, for consideration by the LSA, later on. Ideally, the LSA's decisions on prior Feast recommendations are reported back to the community at the next Feast, both as a courtesy and as evidence of the importance the LSA places on the concerns and ideas of the local Bahá'í community. Therefore, the consultative portion of Feast is far from "business as usual," since the purpose of the Bahá'í community, generally speaking, is to promote spiritual and social health and vibrancy of the community itself—including, ideally, the wider community in that locale.

Last but not least, a Bahá'í Feast typically ends with the social portion. The host serves the refreshments. In the food and fellowship that follow, a spirit of camaraderie and solidarity emerges. Bahá'í identity, both individual and collective, is thereby strengthened and reinforced. The local Bahá'í community is quickened and consolidated. Bahá'í social life is nourished and reinvigorated. As a result, the local Bahá'í community is refreshed, energized, and more united. If so, then a major purpose of the Feast is fulfilled.

HOLY DAYS

Another essential activity of Bahá'í community life is the observance and celebration of Bahá'í Holy Days (including several Bahá'í Festivals). There are nine Bahá'í Holy Days during which work is suspended and children are exempted from attending school. In historical order, they are as follows:

1. Birth of Bahá'u'lláh (12 November 1817; "Festival of the Twin Holy Birthdays").
2. Birth of the Báb (20 October 1819; "Festival of the Twin Holy Birthdays").
3. Naw-Rúz (21 March 1844; "Festival of Naw-Rúz").
4. Declaration of the Báb (23 May 1844; "Festival of the Declaration of the Báb").
5. Martyrdom of the Báb (9 July 1850).
6. Declaration of the Bahá'u'lláh, First Day of Riḍván (21 April 1863; "Festival of Riḍván").
7. Ninth Day of Riḍván (29 April 1863; "Festival of Riḍván").
8. Twelfth Day of Riḍván (2 May 1863; "Festival of Riḍván").
9. Ascension of Bahá'u'lláh (29 May 1892).

What follows are brief descriptions of each of the Bahá'í Holy Days, as faithfully observed by Bahá'ís around the world. For historical details of events that each of the following Bahá'í Holy Days commemorate, see Chapter Four: "History, Bahá'u'lláh and His Covenant" and Buck and Melton, *Religious Celebrations*, 2011.

Festival of the Twin Holy Birthdays: Historically, the birth of the Báb (20 October 1819) and the birth of Bahá'u'lláh (12 November 1817) took place two years apart on two consecutive days—1 and

2 Muharram, respectively—according to the Islamic lunar calendar. These Holy Days are celebrated by Bahá'ís worldwide on the first and second days of the eighth lunar month after Naw-Rúz, and may fall as early as 20–21 October and as late as 11–12 November. In 2017, Bahá'ís around the world celebrated the Bicentenary of the Birth of Bahá'u'lláh, and, in 2019, honored the Bicentenary of the Birth of the Báb.

Festival of the Birth of the Báb: For the occasion of the Birth of the Báb, Bahá'u'lláh revealed a joyful Tablet that begins as follows:

> In the name of the One born on this day, Him Whom God hath made to be the Herald of His Name, the Almighty, the All-Loving!
>
> This is a Tablet We have addressed unto that night wherein the heavens and the earth were illumined by a Light that cast its radiance over the entire creation.
>
> Blessed art thou, O night! For through thee was born the Day of God, a Day which We have ordained to be the lamp of salvation unto the denizens of the cities of names, the chalice of victory unto the champions of the arenas of eternity, and the dawning-place of joy and exultation unto all creation.
>
> (Bahá'u'lláh, *Days of Remembrance*, BRL)

Note that Bahá'u'lláh honors the Birth of the Báb by calling that sacred occasion the "lamp of salvation unto the denizens of the cities of names." There are a number of other such celebratory eulogies of the Báb by Bahá'u'lláh as well.

Festival of the Birth of the Bahá'u'lláh: For Bahá'ís, there is something cosmic about Bahá'u'lláh's earthly birth, insofar as it coincides with, if not inaugurates, a new birth of global self-consciousness and intrinsic unity, to be expressed extrinsically. At dawn, on 12 November 1817, Bahá'u'lláh (first known by his given name, Ḥusayn-'Alí Núrí) was born in Tehran, the capital of Persia (now Iran), in the district known as the Darvázih Shimrán, which was at the edge of the city. His father, Mírzá Buzurg, was a Persian nobleman, most notably the Vazír of Núr (a province in Persia). Khadíjih Khánum, Bahá'u'lláh's mother, was, Mírzá Buzurg's second wife. As a child, the young Ḥusayn-'Alí never cried, it was said, nor showed restlessness. His father's ancestral home was in the village of Tákur, in the province of Núr, where the young boy would spend his idyllic summers. Bahá'u'lláh recounts one memorable event that resulted in a spiritual awakening in the form of a profound realization, which took place on the last of seven days of festivities of the marriage of one of his older brothers:

> When I was still a child and had not yet attained the age of maturity, ... it was announced that the play "Sháh Sultán Salím" would be presented. ... After this the king held audience with his court, during which intelligence was received that a rebellion had broken out on a certain frontier. ... A few moments later cannons were heard booming from behind the tent, and it was announced that a battle had been engaged. This Youth regarded the scene with great amazement. When the royal audience was ended, the curtain was drawn, and, after some twenty minutes, a man emerged from behind the tent carrying a box under his arm. "What is this box," I asked him, "and what was the nature of this display?" "All this lavish display and these elaborate devices," he replied, "the king, the princes, and the ministers, their pomp and glory, their might and power, everything you saw, are now contained within this box." ... Ever since that day, all the trappings of the world have seemed in the eyes of this Youth akin to that same spectacle.
>
> (Bahá'u'lláh, *Summons*, BRL)

As a young nobleman, Bahá'u'lláh was known as the "Father of the Poor" for his beneficence and munificence in Tákur and its vicinity. Bahá'u'lláh also showed great sagacity and mastery of argument. He later became a prominent figure in the Bábí religion.

Festival of Naw-Rúz (20 or 21 March): This is a day of joy for Bahá'ís, family, and friends, and is celebrated by Bahá'ís worldwide. The Bahá'í New Year, happily, coincides with nature's new year, i.e. the vernal (spring) equinox in the northern hemisphere, in which spiritual renewal and natural renewal are celebrated on the same occasion. Called "Naw-Rúz" (literally, in Persian, "New Day"), this holy day is held either on 20 or 21 March, depending on the astronomical timing of the first day of spring. It is a festive, yet dignified occasion, especially considering the fact that, during the preceding nineteen days, Bahá'ís have been observing the Bahá'í Fast by abstaining from food, water, and beverages from sunrise to sunset, as this excerpt from a Bahá'í prayer illustrates: "Praised be Thou, O my God, that Thou hast ordained Naw-Rúz as a festival unto those who have observed the Fast for love of Thee and abstained from all that is abhorrent unto Thee," Bahá'u'lláh writes, adding: "Grant, O my Lord, that the fire of Thy love and the heat produced by the Fast enjoined by Thee may inflame them in Thy Cause, and make them to be occupied with Thy praise and with remembrance of Thee" (Bahá'u'lláh, *Days of Remembrance*, BRL). While there is not a Bahá'í tradition of New Year's resolutions as there is in the Gregorian new year each January 1st, the Bahá'í New Year is nevertheless a time for reflection and resolve to make the next year even better.

Festival of the Declaration of the Báb (23 or 24 May): The Bahá'í Faith is one religion, with two messengers. Not only was the Báb the herald of Bahá'u'lláh, but was also in an independent prophet and spiritual lawgiver, who created the original version of what is now the Bahá'í Calendar, and contributed a number of what became Bahá'í laws, ethics, doctrines, and social principles. Thus, Shoghi Effendi designated the Báb as the "the martyr Prophet and co-founder of their Faith" (Shoghi Effendi, *Unfolding Destiny*, BRL; see also Buck, "The Báb's Living Legacy").

The Declaration of the Báb—celebrated by Bahá'ís the world over—is one of the "two Most Great Festivals" which, in the words of Bahá'u'lláh, is

> that day on which We [Bahá'u'lláh] raised up the One [the Báb] Who announced unto mankind the glad tidings of this Name [Bahá'u'lláh], through which the dead have been resurrected and all who are in the heavens and on earth have been gathered together.
>
> (Bahá'u'lláh, *Kitáb-i-Aqdas*, BRL) ([brackets added])

This Holy Day commemorates the evening of 22 May 1844 (two hours and 11 minutes after sunset), when the Báb—in Shiraz, Persia (now Iran)—announced his mission to prepare the world for the imminent advent of "Him Whom God shall make manifest"—who came to be regarded as Bahá'u'lláh. Bahá'í history—and therefore the Bahá'í Calendar—was inaugurated on this historic occasion.

Martyrdom of the Báb (9 or 10 July): Solemnly observed by Bahá'ís globally, this occasion commemorates the death of the Báb—the herald of Bahá'u'lláh—which took place on 9 July 1850, in Tabriz, Persia (now Iran) when the Báb was publicly executed, at the age of 31, by a firing squad of 750 soldiers, under some rather extraordinary facts and circumstances, the most notable of which is that the Báb emerged unscathed from the first attempt at executing him. According to Nader Saiedi, Taslimi Foundation Professor of Bahá'í Studies, Department of Near Eastern Languages and Cultures at UCLA:

> The Báb consistently rejected miracles as the proof of the truth of the Prophet of God. But the Báb goes further than this. He forbids His followers to attribute any miracle to Him. And therefore, the final event in the life of the Báb is not defined as a miraculous event. Yet there is really no plausible explanation for that. And, therefore, it remains a mysterious event in the sacred history of the world.
>
> (Dr. Nader Saiedi, February 2017, Los Angeles; quoted. in Price, 2018)

Festival of Riḍván (1st Day—20 or 21 April; 9th Day—28 or 29 April; 12th Day—1 or 2 May): The two most important Bahá'í Holy Days are what Bahá'u'lláh calls the two "Most Great Festivals"— commemorating the Declaration of the Báb in Shiraz in 1844 and the Declaration of Bahá'u'lláh in Baghdad in 1863. The latter is known as the "Festival of Riḍván" and is acclaimed by Bahá'u'lláh as the "King of Festivals" (Bahá'u'lláh, *Kitáb-i-Aqdas*, BRL). To state the obvious, this means that the Festival of Riḍván is the most important of all Bahá'í holy days. As the name "Festival" indicates, this is another joyous occasion celebrated by Bahá'ís worldwide—one which lasts for 12 days, in fact.

Like most holy days of other world religions, this period of time commemorates an important historical occasion, endowed with great religious significance. The Bahá'í Festival of Riḍván ("Paradise") celebrates the declaration of Bahá'u'lláh on 22 April 1863 in Baghdad—"in the garden of Najíb Páshá, which hath been designated as the Garden of Riḍván" (Bahá'u'lláh, *Days of Remembrance*, BRL)—proclaiming that he was the "Promised One"—or "Him Whom God shall make manifest"—foretold by the Báb. Although "public" to a limited degree, Bahá'u'lláh's disclosure (to a handful of Bábís, i.e. followers of the Báb) was somewhat private in nature, at the time. News of Bahá'u'lláh's momentous announcement, as would be expected, rapidly spread throughout the Bábí community. Four years later, beginning in 1867, Bahá'u'lláh publicly proclaimed his mission to the world's political and religious leaders—in a series of open epistles (letters) that would be published later on—as the "Promised One" foretold in the sacred scriptures of all world religions.

"The Divine Springtime is come, O Most Exalted Pen, for the Festival of the All-Merciful is fast approaching," Bahá'u'lláh proclaims, in the opening of a prayer revealed for this occasion, continuing: "Bestir thyself, and magnify, before the entire creation, the name of God, and celebrate His praise, in such wise that all created things may be regenerated and made new" (Bahá'u'lláh, *Days of Remembrance*, BRL). In this passage, Bahá'u'lláh addresses his "Most Exalted Pen"—a poetic device that adds poetic and rhetorical luster to this remarkable prayer. Regarding the First Day of Riḍván, Bahá'u'lláh elsewhere recounts:

> On the first day that the Ancient Beauty [Bahá'u'lláh] ascended His Most Great Throne in the garden named Riḍván, the Tongue of Glory gave utterance to three blessed words. First, that in this Revelation the law of the sword hath been annulled. Second, that ere the expiration of one thousand years whosoever advanceth a prophetic claim is false. By "year" a full year is intended, and no exegesis or interpretation is permitted in this matter. And third, that at that very hour God, exalted be His Glory, shed the full splendour of all His names upon all creation.
>
> (Bahá'u'lláh, *Days of Remembrance*, BRL)

In other words, on the afternoon of 22 April 1863, Bahá'u'lláh did the following (1) abolished the Islamic law of holy war (*jihād*); (2) declared himself to "Him Whom God shall make manifest," and that God would not send another messenger until at least full 1,000 years later; and (3) announced that God had, at that sacred moment, blessed all of creation—and, in another Tablet, purified all of creation—thereby abolishing the Shí'í Islamic law of ritual impurity (Arabic: *najis*). In a later Tablet revealed for the Festival of Riḍván, Bahá'u'lláh expanded his initial Baghdad declaration—as "Him Whom God shall make manifest" foretold by the Báb—to an even greater, more universal announcement as the "Promised One" of all religions. For instance, in this Riḍván Tablet, Bahá'u'lláh proclaimed his fulfillment of the prophecies of Jesus, as follows:

This is the Day whereon the Spirit [Jesus Christ] proclaimed from the midmost heart of heaven: "O concourse of creation! He Who is the sovereign Ruler of all hath been made manifest. That which pertaineth to the Kingdom of My Lord hath been fulfilled. He Who is the Beloved of My heart and the Helper of My Cause is now come. Follow Him, and be not of those that have turned aside." ... "It is for His sake that I adorned the cross with My body and then arose from the dead to perfect His remembrance amongst men." ... "O people of the Gospel! Take heed lest ye direct your prayers towards Me after having turned away from Mine all-glorious Father, Who changed, through His love, Abraham's fire into light. He who awaiteth another when once He hath appeared is indeed in grievous error." ... "Thus commandeth you the Spirit, Who offered up His life that the world might be quickened and that the Desire of every heart might appear."

(Bahá'u'lláh, *Days of Remembrance*, BRL)

Since there is not a specific Bahá'í Holy Day that commemorates Bahá'u'lláh's later proclamations (c. 1867–1873) to the world's political and religious leaders (i.e. in 1867, when Bahá'u'lláh was exiled to Edirne, Turkey, and then, in 1868 to Acre, Palestine/Israel), celebrating the Festival of Riḍván, as indicated by the passage above, memorializes not only Bahá'u'lláh's original 1863 declaration in Baghdad, but also, by extension, his subsequent proclamations in Edirne and Acre, wherein the intended audience ("kings and ecclesiastics") is greatly expanded, and the announcement profoundly augmented—in what the present writer has previously called a "multiple-messiahship." As a matter of faith, this proclamation by Bahá'u'lláh was a momentous announcement—indeed a stupendous truth-claim of world-historical proportions. In other words, in 1863, Bahá'u'lláh declared himself to be "Him Whom God shall make manifest," as foretold by the Báb, while, later on, during 1867–1873, Bahá'u'lláh identifies himself as several messiahs at one and the same time:

[1] To Israel He was neither more nor less than the incarnation of the "Everlasting Father," the "Lord of Hosts" come down "with ten thousands of saints"; [2] to Christendom Christ returned "in the glory of the Father," [3] to Shí'ah Islám the return of the Imám Ḥusayn; [4] to Sunní Islám the descent of the "Spirit of God" (Jesus Christ); [5] to the Zoroastrians the promised Sháh-Bahrám; [6] to the Hindus the reincarnation of Krishna; [7] to the Buddhists the fifth Buddha.

(Shoghi Effendi, *God Passes By*, BRL)

Bahá'u'lláh, in various passages, proclaims himself to be the first five messiahs, listed above, whereas the sixth and seventh messiahs were identified with Bahá'u'lláh during the ministry of 'Abdu'l-Bahá. Even more messianic associations were added as the Bahá'í Faith continued to expand, in the course of its missionary outreach, to the followers of other religions, who were not a part of Bahá'u'lláh's social world during his lifetime, which is why they were not directly addressed by Bahá'u'lláh at that time. (See Buck 2004 and *Figuring Out Prophecy*.)

As to its timing, the Festival of Riḍván begins at sunset on the 32nd day of the Bahá'í year (20 April in the Gregorian calendar, although the dates will vary slightly from year to year) and ends at sunset 12 days later (1 or 2 May). It is the most important of the annual Bahá'í festivals. Three of these twelve Festival days—the first (20 or 21 April), ninth (28 or 29 April), and twelfth (1 or 2 May)—are set aside as distinct Bahá'í Holy Days in their own right. On these sacred occasions, as mentioned, Bahá'ís take their days off work in order to participate in these religious observances. Bahá'í children stay home from school, as they typically do on other Bahá'í Holy Days as well. During this twelve-day festival, Bahá'í elections are held at local, national, and international levels, thereby adding a whole new dimension to these occasions, during which these important elections take place.

Ascension of Bahá'u'lláh (28 or 29 May): On this solemn, sacred occasion, Bahá'ís the world over observe the anniversary of the passing of Bahá'u'lláh, on 29 May 1892 (at 3:00 a.m.), just outside of Akko (also known as Akka or Acre), in what was then Ottoman Palestine, now northern Israel. Local Bahá'í communities worldwide therefore gather at that time (3:00 a.m.) to commemorate their founder with Bahá'í prayers and scriptures, usually culminating in the chanting in Arabic, or recitation in translation, of what is known as the "Tablet of Visitation," a special prayer reserved for honoring and eulogizing Bahá'u'lláh (as well as the Báb).

Festival of the Day of the Covenant (25 or 26 Nov.): This Bahá'í Festival, also observed by Bahá'ís globally, commemorates Bahá'u'lláh's appointment of His eldest son, 'Abdu'l-Bahá, as the Center of His Covenant. For a full discussion of this historic and religiously unique designation of successorship, please see "The 1893 Russian Publication of Bahá'u'lláh's Last Will and Testament: An Academic Attestation of 'Abdu'l-Baha's Successorship" (Buck and Ioannesyan 2017).

Ascension of 'Abdu'l-Bahá (27 or 28 Nov.): On this solemn occasion, Bahá'ís around the world observe the anniversary of the death of 'Abdu'l-Bahá—Bahá'u'lláh's eldest son and designated successor—on 28 November 1921, in Haifa, Ottoman Palestine (now northern Israel). As mentioned in Chapter 4 above, Cambridge Orientalist, Edward Granville Browne—in "Sir 'Abdu'l-Bahá Abbás: Died 28th November, 1921," an obituary published in 1922 in the Journal of the Royal Asiatic Society—claimed that 'Abdu'l-Bahá "has probably exercised a greater influence not only in the Orient but in the Occident than any Asiatic thinker and teacher of recent times" (Browne 1922).

Ayyám-i-Há or Intercalary Days (varies between 25 Feb. and 1 March): Ayyám-i-Há, or "Days of Ha"—celebrated by Bahá'ís worldwide during the four days (five in a leap year) before the last month of the Bahá'í Calendar—are days of good cheer, gift-giving, hospitality, and charity, prior to the Bahá'í Nineteen Day Fast. A Bahá'í festival that serves calendrical and community purposes, the Bahá'í Intercalary Days offer a season of joy and giving that precedes the Nineteen Day Bahá'í Fast, in which Bahá'ís abstain from food and drink, from sunrise to sunset, as a spiritual exercise. This time of festivity ("good cheer") is not only to have a good time, but to do some good at the same time, by giving to the less fortunate. A season of jubilance and benevolence, Ayyám-i-Há, reaching out to those in need enriches the quality of this time and renders it all the more worthwhile. For Bahá'ís, personal salvation is bound up with social salvation, in that personal transformation is dynamically related to social transformation. The Bahá'í Intercalary Days are therefore all about good cheer and doing good, when celebrations and service go together. The more good service, the more there is to rejoice.

THE FOUR CORE ACTIVITIES

Bahá'ís worldwide are engaged in a process of "community building" which has been described as "Love in Action" on the US Bahá'í website. (See Bahá'ís of the United States, 2019.) The four core activities of Bahá'í community life are: (1) devotional gatherings; (2) study circles; (3) children's classes; and (4) junior youth groups.

Since 1996, Bahá'ís have embarked on a grand developmental initiative being orchestrated on a world scale. At the heart of this program is the key concept that the diffusion of knowledge—spiritual, social, and intellectual—is central to bettering society. This educational effort is carried out in three stages to meet the developmental needs of differing ages—of children, of young adolescents, youth, and adults. At the heart of this process is the social commitment to providing a tangible service to others. As such, this Bahá'í program seeks to inspire a desire to engage in a wide array of community service efforts for the common good—and to increase the capacity to do so. In addition to social action, Bahá'ís also engage in the public discourses of society in a variety of venues and social spaces, both local and virtual (i.e. online). In this way, the spiritual, moral, and social principles of the Bahá'í Faith are gradually translated into practical models of a new social reality.

DEVOTIONAL GATHERINGS

Bahá'í-inspired devotionals are informal prayer-gatherings. They are interpersonal, inclusive, and interfaith in nature. Bahá'ís host these gatherings, usually in their homes and neighborhoods. In these informal and welcoming settings, Bahá'ís invite their family, friends, and fellow Bahá'ís to join them in worship. United in spirit, participants engage in earnest prayers, and often in meaningful, soulful conversations as well. Yet there are no rituals, no clergy, no formalities. A spirit of shared worship prevails. The consciousness of all present is elevated and enriched. For the most part, most of the prayers and readings are read from the Bahá'í sacred texts. Quite often, guests will choose some of their favorite passages as well, including from other faith traditions.

Prayer creates a space for inspiration as well as spiritual rejuvenation, not to mention the spirit of fellowship that devotional gatherings promote socially. Friendship deepens. Solidarity is strengthened. A sense of community is reinforced. In this sense, prayer is a valuable, if not indispensable, "inner resource" on which each person can draw and derive motivational strength, guided by clarity of purpose and vision. Action completes prayer. The fundamental Bahá'í principle is that work, performed in the spirit of service, is seen as an act of worship of God, in and of itself. Thus, prayer and service go together, hand in hand. In Bahá'í community life, worship and service are dynamically integrated. For greater outreach to the wider community, Bahá'ís are encouraged to "multiply" the number of devotional gatherings in any given locale.

STUDY CIRCLES

All over the world, Bahá'ís engage in "study circles" as one of their "core activities." Educators—especially teachers engaged in adult education initiatives in rural settings—are generally quite familiar with study circles. A study circle is a small, diverse group of participants, who meet regularly and focus on topics and matters of common interest and purpose.

In the Bahá'í context, the Ruhi Institute has developed a special curriculum—a sequence of courses generally referred to as the "Ruhi books." Thus, the term, "institute process," is more or less synonymous with study circles. At the time of this writing, the Ruhi books are 11 in number, with more to follow. As the Ruhi Institute explains: "The books are intended to be used as the main sequence of courses in a systematic effort to enhance capacity for service" (Ruhi Institute *Overview*).

The first Ruhi book is called *Reflections on the Life of the Spirit*. This resource is basically a collection of selected Bahá'í readings, interspersed with some explanatory commentary, and followed by a series of study questions to reinforce the learning process. Each study circle develops a special skill. When participants go through the entire sequence of Ruhi books, they develop a set of special skills in the process. These skills are put to good use, and contribute to the process of community building, which local Bahá'í communities across the world are engaged in doing. The main sequence of courses is as follows: Book 1: *Reflections on the Life of the Spirit*; Book 2: *Arising to Serve*; Book 3: *Teaching Children's Classes, Grade 1*; *Teaching Children's Classes, Grade 2: A Branch Course of Book 3* (pre-publication edition); *Teaching Children's Classes, Grade 3: A Branch Course of Book 3* (pre-publication edition); Book 4: *The Twin Manifestations*; Book 5: *Releasing the Powers of Junior Youth;* Book 6: *Teaching the Cause*; Book 7: *Walking Together on a Path of Service*; Book 8: *The Covenant of Bahá'u'lláh* (pre-publication edition); Book 9: *Gaining an Historical Perspective* (material in development); Book 10: *Building Vibrant Communities* (pre-publication edition); Book 11: *Material Means* (material in development) (Ruhi Institute "Overview").

Typically, a tutor or facilitator leads and guides these small group readings and discussions based on the readings. The tutor does not lecture. Rather, the tutor fosters the group learning dynamic. The institute process is geared towards skill development in the context of equipping individuals to engage in community service. The Ruhi Institute's sequence of courses is the outcome of pilot projects, initiated under special pedagogical considerations and philosophy of education, which includes a spiritual and moral dimension, complementing the traditional and standardized academic curricula. As just one example of the rich offerings of this sequence of courses, in Ruhi Book 3, participants "learn to teach simple children's classes consisting of memorization of prayers and quotations, songs, stories, games and coloring." As a practical measure, the book offers "15 Lessons for Children." "Lesson 9," for instance, includes this song:

> Prefer Your Brother
>
> I am thirsty, I am thirsty
> But my brother, he comes first
> So I offer him the water
> That will quench his thirst
> > Chorus
> > It is a blessing to prefer your brother
> > This is a way to show you care
> > It is a blessing to prefer your sister
> > You are richer, the more you share
> I am hungry, I am hungry
> And my sister, she is too
> So I give her some of my food
> That's what's best to do
> > Chorus
>
> *(Ruhi Institute "Brother")*

The Bahá'í-inspired institute process is a grand social experiment that is being developed, expanded, and refined globally. In this sense, the Bahá'í community, as a whole, is even more of a "social experiment" than it was previous to the sea-change in Bahá'í community life that began in 1996. This also represents part of a greater effort, on the part of the Bahá'í administration, to adopt and carry out a "systematic" series of learning activities aimed at increasing individual and group capacity for community service, in the path of individual and social transformation, whereby personal development and growth is enhanced by study and service.

CHILDREN'S CLASSES

Children are the future of the world. They are our most precious resource. They are a great responsibility. "Children are the most precious treasure a community can possess, for in them are the promise and guarantee of the future," the Universal House of Justice writes, further stating: "They bear the seeds of the character of future society which is largely shaped by what the adults constituting the community do or fail to do with respect to children. They are a trust no community can neglect with impunity" (Universal House of Justice, *Turning Point*, BRL). For children to be raised to become productive citizens and future leaders in the next generation, they must be properly raised and educated. On this important issue, Bahá'u'lláh teaches that "the greatest means" for "the advancement of the world of being and the uplift of souls" is the "education of the child" (Bahá'u'lláh, *Bahá'í Education*, 1976).

The education of children consists not only in the usual academic skills of reading, writing, and arithmetic, but of moral and spiritual education as well. The most fundamental form of moral and spiritual education is the teaching of virtues. Virtues education is typically not taught in public schools. Therefore, when Bahá'ís offer virtues education to children in their respective neighborhoods, this is a significant contribution to the moral and spiritual development of children in their early years and instills and awakens within them their spiritual identity.

Around the world, Bahá'ís host children's classes in their local neighborhoods. The children's classes are for spiritual education. They primarily consist in teaching virtues, i.e. noble qualities of a sterling character. This is part of the moral education of children and contributes to the uplift of the children who participate in these children's classes, and has a leavening effect on their families and, more widely, the local community itself.

JUNIOR YOUTH GROUPS

The "Junior Youth Spiritual Empowerment Program" is focused on "junior" youth, aged 12 to 15. This is an important, indeed critical, time of life in the formation of an individual's character and may set the stage for an individual's course of life to follow. This stage is a great opportunity to foster character development in youth, who are beginning to ask questions and think about their respective roles and place in society.

In these small groups, pre-teen and teenage youth discuss ideas and issues of common interest and concern and, in the process, form a strong moral identity. Younger youth look up to older youth. In this program, the older youth—who serve as mentors to the junior youth—are each referred to as an "Animator." An Animator assists participating junior youth to develop their own capacities, and to instill in each youth a sense of spiritual identity, moral clarity, and a commitment to contribute to the betterment of society. This program encourages youth to question the world around them, and to independently and responsibly make decisions in their own best interest, and in the best interests of the community at large, in order to make the world a better place.

The current titles in this sequence of courses are: (1) "Breezes of Confirmation"; (2) "Glimmerings of Hope"; (3) "Thinking About Numbers"; (4) "Walking the Straight Path"; (5) "Learning About Excellence"; (6) "Observation and Insight"; (7) "The Human Temple"; and (8) "Drawing on the Power of the Word." These titles have a general orientation. Although they are inspired by the Bahá'í teachings, there is little, if any, explicit Bahá'í content in this series. This curriculum for the "spiritual empowerment" of junior youth is universal in its scope and reach. This material therefore can be, and actually has been, adopted and adapted by a number of educational institutions around the world. At this critical age, such ethical and moral training can make a real difference in the lives of youth everywhere.

SUMMARY

- "Disunity is the crux of the problems which so severely afflict the planet. It permeates attitudes in all departments of life," according to the Universal House of Justice.
- Bahá'ís endeavor to create social models that work and are worthy of emulation and replication.
- "Service"—to neighborhoods, communities of interest, and other social spaces, whether personal or professional—is the watchword of homespun, group Bahá'í endeavors, and individual initiatives.
- "Community building" means enhancing both the spiritual and material nature of the local community through a grassroots approach.
- The four "core activities" of Bahá'í community life are (1) devotional gatherings; (2) study circles; (3) children's classes; and (4) junior youth groups.

8

SOCIAL ACTION
SOCIAL AND ECONOMIC DEVELOPMENT

Bahá'ís are committed to social and economic development, locally and globally. "That one indeed is a man who, today, dedicateth himself to the service of the entire human race," Bahá'u'lláh declares in the "Tablet of Maqṣúd," adding: "The Great Being saith: Blessed and happy is he that ariseth to promote the best interests of the peoples and kindreds of the earth" (Bahá'u'lláh, Tablets, BRL). At both grassroots and international levels, Bahá'ís sponsor and carry out various community service projects, as part of an overall "culture of growth," in which service to others plays a central role. Some of these Bahá'í-inspired projects include individual initiatives, while others are formal, Bahá'í-sponsored projects at the institutional level. Together, these contribute to the betterment of society. For the most part, these are small-scale projects on a large scale (i.e. collectively, worldwide in distribution). Many of these projects are creative and innovative. This direct approach, however, steers clear of politics. Bahá'ís avoid partisan politics, seen as divisive in nature, and therefore contrary to the primary Bahá'í purpose, which is to promote unity and justice throughout the world, i.e. for "the body politic." If there is genuine government interest and cooperation—as in the case of the Republic of Kiribati (see below)—then all the better, so long as such involvement is for the common good. Bahá'í social and economic development projects are prime examples—and prospective models—of faith-based initiatives, *par excellence*.

DOI: 10.4324/9780429023088-8

As a world religion, the Bahá'í Faith is a global community—not only geographically, but institutionally and developmentally. Bahá'í community life is a rich tapestry of devotion to God and inspired desire to serve the community. This dedication lends spiritual impetus in launching and sustaining a systematic, replicable matrix of "core activities," in addition to "essential activities." As discussed in Chapter Seven, essential activities include Bahá'í Nineteen-Day Feasts (monthly meetings where members worship, consult, and socialize) and Bahá'í Holy Days—among other activities, including administrative pursuits. The core activities (introduced in the preceding chapter)—animate Bahá'í life through and through. The core activities include children's classes, junior youth spiritual empowerment groups, devotional meetings, and study circles. These core activities often inspire community service projects—and some of these, in turn, can be further evolved into social and economic development projects, although these can be launched independently as well.

Study circles train and encourage participants to serve their Bahá'í and greater communities through various activities enhanced by the development of interpersonal social skills, such as "home visits" for strengthening bonds of friendship and for "nurturing" new believers in the fundamental tenets and practices of Bahá'í life. These core activities go far in "consolidating" Bahá'í communities internally and expanding their outreach externally. These core activities are complemented by special events and occasions such as conferences, Bahá'í summer and winter schools, and other edifying events. The congregational (or "church") model—so traditional within popular religious experience—is dismissed in favor of neighborhood gatherings, without clergy. This model is a truly alternative one that is being carried out by Bahá'í clusters the world over. The results are dramatic in some communities, while nascent and emerging in others. It is all part of a new social outreach, as experimental as it is well intentioned and promising. In all these core activities, the Bahá'í emphasis is on building community bonds and contributing service, not conversion.

These core activities—children's classes, junior youths groups, study circles, and devotional meetings—are both systematic and creative in nature. This constellation of activities is also evaluated every three months by each local Bahá'í "cluster" (a group of regionally adjacent Bahá'í communities) in what are called "reflection meetings," as part of an overarching "culture of learning." At a reflection meeting, grassroots Bahá'ís discuss their successful and not-so-successful efforts (as the case may be), with the goal of trying to learn from their individual and collective experiences. After full and frank consultation, community members then propose new approaches that might prove to be more effective. This is an ongoing feedback and improvement process, in which each Bahá'í community learns from its prior experiences. This same consultation, evaluation, and planning process can easily be extended to service projects of a more formal, ambitious, and sustained nature.

As one might expect, Bahá'í dedication to community service sometimes takes the form of social and economic development projects, resources permitting. Involvement in the life of society, after all, is a natural outgrowth of Bahá'í ideals of community outreach and social uplift. Local Bahá'í community service projects are strongly encouraged as part of a wider commitment to social and economic development. As a framework for social action at the neighborhood level—through a process of action, reflection, consultation, and shared decision-making—Bahá'ís engage in grassroots social action initiatives in order to better their local communities through such service projects as literacy programs, environmental clean-up efforts, health and hygiene education, and agricultural development, to cite just a few examples.

The main point here is that the current Bahá'í emphasis on service has fostered an orientation and outlook that optimize opportunities and initiatives to render service, wherever and whenever feasible. Bahá'ís everywhere invite individuals as well as "communities of interest" to participate in any and all of the core activities and to collaborate in service projects for the wider community for the greater good. Thus, the boundaries of each Bahá'í community are open, permeable, and vitalizing. Bahá'ís regard non-Bahá'í participants as neighbors, friends, colleagues, associates, collaborators, coworkers, kindred spirits, and fellow world citizens. Such positive and productive social orientations may be characterized as pragmatic cosmopolitanism—quintessentially egalitarian in nature and scope. Going far beyond mere tolerance and tacit equality, Bahá'ís cultivate mutually enhancing friendships and reciprocity. In short, the Bahá'í friends befriend their wider communities, in which some community-building activities evolve into social action projects.

By orientation and inclination, Bahá'í communities are thus outwardly directed. So inspired, they collectively desire and aspire to transform and edify society. This is accomplished through promoting, practicing, and pragmatically applying Bahá'í spiritual and practical teachings that readily translate into civic virtues and values, such as unity, justice, dignity, and a host of other noble virtues—all of which have ennobling effects on positive character development, social progress, and the advancement of civilization.

FOUNDATIONS FOR SOCIAL SERVICE AND PROGRESS

On 9 November 2018, the Universal House of Justice announced that "the [former] Office of Social and Economic Development now effloresces into a new world-embracing institution established at the World Centre, the Bahá'í International Development Organization." This new Bahá'í institution replaces the former Office of Social and Economic Development. Beyond establishing the Bahá'í International Development Organization itself, a "Bahá'í Development Fund" will also be inaugurated. The Bahá'í Development Fund is a financial resource on which the Bahá'í International Development Organization will draw, and to which Bahá'í individuals and institutions may contribute. At the time of this writing, little further information is available, beyond the announcement itself. This agency will likely monitor and, to certain extent, oversee and/or advise Bahá'í-inspired educational, economic, and social development projects around the world, a few examples of which are offered below, being the subject and focus of this chapter.

SOCIAL AND ECONOMIC DEVELOPMENT PROJECTS

Bahá'ís worldwide have established various social and economic development projects, as stated earlier. Bahá'í-inspired service projects are for the betterment of local communities and thereby the world, cumulatively and collectively considered. In this sense, Bahá'ís are generally and genuinely motivated to selflessly do their part to improve the conditions of society as best they can. This chapter therefore partly addresses the question that naturally arises in the minds of observers: "What do Bahá'ís to do to make this world a better place?" To illustrate, some selected, ongoing Bahá'í-inspired social and economic development projects are highlighted in this chapter, as follows.

EDUCATION

Education enlightens society. Indeed, education is an engine of individual and social progress. Education enhances the future by enriching the younger generation. Enlightened education of children and youth—in addition to optimal adult education and higher education—is of pivotal importance. Consider the opposite situation, i.e. the relative lack of education throughout many developing countries today. Ignorance benights society. The choice is stark: Either educate or suffer the social consequences. Since education is a foundation and bedrock for individual and social progress, it comes as no surprise to find that the Bahá'í teachings are clear on this point: Education is of paramount importance.

Prioritizing education as a social goal is one thing. Implementing and effectively promoting education is what must come next. Strategies need to be developed in accordance with the facts and circumstances of a given social situation. This is where Bahá'í-inspired educational projects assume great importance, even if they are only experimental. Five examples of such Bahá'í-inspired educational projects include: (1) Olinga Foundation for Human Development (Ghana); (2) Parent University (Savannah, Georgia, USA); (3) Núr University (Bolivia); (4) Mongolian Development Center (MDC) (Mongolia); and (5) Bahá'í Academy (India). Ten Bahá'í-inspired academic schools include (1) Ocean of Light International School (Tonga); (2) Brilliant Star School (Tabuariki, Solomon Islands); (3) Townshend International School (Czech Republic); (4) Nancy Campbell Academy (Canada); (5) School of the Nations (Brasilia, Brazil); (6) Bambino Private Schools (Lilongwe, Malawi); (7) Lycée Enoch Olinga (Niamey, Niger); (8) Mazin Academy (Jogi Moor, Pakistan); (9) School of the Nations (Macau); and (10) Ruhi Arbab School (Colombia). These Bahá'í-inspired initiatives are bound to evolve and multiply over time.

A prime example of such educational projects is Bolivia's Núr University (Spanish name: Universidad Nur), founded in 1982 in Santa Cruz de la Sierra (Bolivia's largest city). Núr University is "the first [private university] to be established by a presidential decree" and, in 1986, "set up the first graduate school of any kind in Bolivia" (BIC, Núr University). With well over 3,000 students today, Núr University offers undergraduate, graduate, and professional degree programs in such academic and professional disciplines areas as law, public health management, teaching, social and economic development, administration, marketing, auditing, and consulting and coaching. The university integrates academic knowledge with both practical experience and basic moral principles, and emphasizes community service, social justice, and a respect for human diversity. For instance, in hundreds of rural communities across Bolivia, teachers and government administrators have participated in a specialized program that Núr University has developed for training in moral leadership. In so doing, the university has also collaborated with educational institutions and nongovernmental organizations in other countries on research and development projects to promote literacy, public health, the advancement of women, moral leadership, public administration and governance, and sustainable development (BIC, *For the Betterment of the World*). On Núr University's Transformative Leadership Program—"used in approximately sixty projects or workshops in forty countries in North and South America, Europe, Africa, and Asia"—see Hernandez 2018.

HEALTH

The importance of health to the well-being of individuals and society is obvious. Promoting health education, such as good hygiene, is a key to promoting health itself. While governments are expected to provide basic health services, often that is not enough. Faith-based organizations, such as the Bahá'í Faith itself, can—and should—contribute to health awareness and best practices for fostering health at the grassroots level (BIC, *For the Betterment of the World*).

Two Bahá'í-inspired health projects include (1) Health for Humanity, United States (see Health for Humanity) and (2) the Fondation Graine d'Espoir ("Seed of Hope Foundation"), Democratic Republic of the Congo. Founded on 19 January 1992, "Health for Humanity" was formed by around 20 physicians. Inspired by the vision of ophthalmologist and co-founder, Dr. Mary Khadem, the "Program Focus" is as follows:

- Health for Humanity focuses its work on meeting [the] unmet, urgent need of providing training for health professionals in the developing world through partnerships with health care institutions.
- Modern cataract surgery in Albania and Mongolia.
- Eradication of river blindness in Cameroon.
- Voluntary testing and counseling centers for HIV/AIDS in China.
- Vocational training for single adolescent mothers in Cameroon.
- Conflict resolution skills for immigrant children in California and New Mexico.
- Reading readiness for economically disadvantaged preschool children in Illinois.
- Gap Community Project mentoring program in Bronzeville, Chicago. (See Health for Humanity.)

Such focused and strategic medical training can make a world of difference in advancing interventional medical services in developing countries. "Health for Humanity's foundation is inspired by the vision of the organic oneness of mankind presented in the Bahá'í Faith," the Health for Humanity website explains, adding: "Although Health for Humanity's values and origins are found within the Bahá'í teachings, … this organization's work is service undertaken for the love of humanity and we openly encourage participation from a diverse cross-section of interested people and colleagues." (See Health for Humanity.) As a faith-based, Bahá'í-inspired initiative, Health for Humanity is a model social development project.

AGRICULTURE

A productive and prosperous system of agriculture is foundational to society. Social development in this area is a priority. Given the challenges that societies worldwide face today—such as climate change and dominant market economies that make it difficult for traditional family farms to remain viable—agricultural development can make a qualitative and strategic difference in the rural population, especially in less developed countries (BIC, *For the Betterment of the World*).

One Bahá'í-inspired agricultural project is the Kimanya-ngeyo Foundation for Science and Education (Uganda). One of the Kimanya-ngeyo Foundation's primary projects is the "Preparation for Social Action" (PSA) program in Uganda. The PSA program sponsors individual and collective agricultural projects. PSA promotes organic farming as a standard (rather than using chemical fertilizers), teaches how to test soil qualities and how to experiment with polycropping systems, such as organic milpa (i.e. maize, beans, and squash). Originated by the Colombian Foundation for the Advancement and Teaching of the Sciences (FUNDAEC), PSA is a non-formal (non-degree) education program for youth and adults that encourages and guides engagement in community life, by seeing and supporting PSA participants as "promoters of community well-being." See the outside program assessment, "The Preparation for Social Action Program (PSA) Kimanya Ngeyo Evaluation Report" (Jinja, Uganda, March 2018) (Murphy-Graham and Taylor 2018).

The Kimanya-ngeyo Foundation's PSA project is a prime example of Bahá'í-inspired agricultural projects. This is just one of a number of PSA projects worldwide. Based in Cali, Columbia, FUNDAEC (acronym in Spanish for "Foundation for the Application and Teaching of the Sciences") has developed the PSA model, which is an alternative, secondary tutorial school system that enhances the capacity of young people to further their own progress and development. Since 2006, the PSA program has been established in 17 countries in Africa, Asia, Latin America, and the Pacific, with over 10,000 participants so far. Besides Uganda, PSA-participating countries include Colombia, Ecuador, Panama, Bolivia, Costa Rica, Zambia, Cameroon, Democratic Republic of the Congo, Kenya, Central African Republic, Papua New Guinea, Vanuatu, Philippines, Cambodia, Malaysia, and India, with steps taken to initiate PSA projects in a further 15 countries, in response to their requests.

ECONOMIC LIFE OF COMMUNITIES

Prosperity depends on the economic health of a given population and society. Promoting prosperity is the overarching goal of most, if not all, economic development projects. Creative and resourceful thinking, planning, and implementing are crucial (BIC, *For the Betterment of the World*). Three Bahá'í-inspired economic development projects include: (1) Supporting Community Leaders (SCL), a program of FUNDAEC (Colombia); (2) Education, Curriculum, and Training Associates (ECTA) (Nepal); and (3) Asociación Bayán (Honduras). For instance, in Nepal, ECTA developed a community banking program that trains groups of 10 to 30 participants in skills of sound financial management and encourages them to establish or expand their own businesses. Individuals learn to save small sums of money and then make modest loans available to community bank members at a reasonable rate of interest. Managed entirely by the members themselves, these small-scale community banks are profitable. Interest earned is apportioned according to the savings that each participant holds. In a novel form of profit-sharing, a portion of the profits is put into a social and economic development fund for the community at large (BIC, *For the Betterment of the World* 2018).

ARTS AND MEDIA

Art has the potential to inspire admirers to aspire to truth and beauty in their own lives. Therefore, art that contributes to social uplift should not be seen as marginal, or as a frivolous past-time and pursuit. Art has the potential and capacity to awaken and enlighten society on a large scale, if effectively executed and promoted. Art has its own place of importance in the Bahá'í outlook (BIC, *For the Betterment of the World* 2018).

Four Bahá'í-inspired arts and media projects include (1) Radio Bahá'í (Soloy, Panama); (2) Children's Theater Company (New York, USA); (3) Illumine Media Project (Toronto, Canada); and (4) People's Theater (Germany). Media can play a significant role in contributing to the material and spiritual progress of society. Bahá'í radio stations have been established in Latin America and Asia. In the 1980s, Radio Bahá'í in Soloy, Panama, was founded "to give voice to and serve as an educational and cultural channel for indigenous peoples." Broadcasting in both Spanish and Ngäbere (the language of the local population), Radio Bahá'í Panama has at least 7,000 listeners, including children, youth, and women. Producing programs in the form of interviews, announcements, and original songs and skits, Radio Bahá'í airs content focused on spiritual themes, including virtues education for moral character development, and content that stresses the importance of contributing service to one's local community (BIC, *For the Betterment of the World*).

ADVANCEMENT OF WOMEN

The advancement of women is of paramount importance. Since women constitute half of society, at the very least they should not be worse off than men. If society is to aspire to new heights, its wings (using the metaphor of a bird) must be equally developed in order to take flight and soar aloft. Achieving equality of women in all fields of endeavor benefits society as a whole. Men should also see this as a priority, even if only out of enlightened self-interest. Promoting the advancement of women is good social policy, redounds to the advantage of all, and is necessary and essential to all social progress (BIC, *For the Betterment of the World*).

Two Bahá'í-inspired advancement of women projects include (1) The Barli Development Institute for Rural Women (India) and (2) the Tahirih Justice Center (United States). Based in Indore, the Barli project, has been "empowering Women since 1985." The Barli projects include: (a) a "Personality Development" program; (b) a "Health and Hygiene" initiative (including educational programs for teaching pre-natal and post-natal care); (c) a "Caring for the Environment" program and (d) a "Solar Cooking and Vegetable Drying" educational program as well.

The Tahirih Justice Center "stands alone as the only national, multi-city organization providing a broad range of direct legal and social services, policy advocacy, and training and education to protect immigrant women and girls fleeing violence." Since its inception in 1997, the Tahirih Justice Center—a national non-profit, non-partisan, tax-exempt 501(c) charitable organization—has assisted over 25,000 women escaping violence, most of whom have sought and have been granted asylum as refugees on grounds of gender-based violence. (See Tahirih Justice Center 2019; and Cooper *et al.* 2013, "Reducing Gender-Based Violence.")

STRENGTHENING COMMUNITY SCHOOLS
THROUGH TEACHER TRAINING

At all institutional levels, the quality of education depends on effective schools, and effective schools depend upon well-trained and highly motivated teachers. Teacher training enhances teaching effectiveness and strengthens educational programs. Therefore, the education of teachers is at the core of developing effective instruction, especially at the pre- and primary school levels (BIC, *For the Betterment of the World* 2018).

A prime example of a Bahá'í-inspired educational development project is the Rays of Light Foundation (Milne Bay Province, Papua New Guinea), established with the guidance and financial support of the Office of Social and Economic Development, Bahá'í World Centre, and affiliated with Columbia's FUNDAEC. Instituted in 2008 as a private non-profit organization, the Rays of Light Foundation works to provide social and economic development to Papua New Guinea and the Solomon Islands primarily by working with children and youth, in practical furtherance of the Bahá'í principle of offering universal education for all. To assist in this process, a PSA program (see the section on "Agriculture" above) has been developed, along with an "Elementary Teacher Training" (ETT) program as well. (See Rays of Light Foundation 2019.)

THE MORAL AND SPIRITUAL EMPOWERMENT OF JUNIOR YOUTH

The future of any given society depends greatly on preparing youth to assume their future roles as the leaders of society. To educate is to empower. Instilling in youth a clear sense of purpose and moral values—of how to set long-term goals and make wise decisions—can be a great service to society as a whole. In their local neighborhoods, Bahá'ís around the world have offered, and continue to offer, junior youth "spiritual empowerment" programs. This process, in turn, releases the potential of youth, and orients them to contribute to society by way of service. In these spiritual empowerment programs, youth study together specially developed materials that facilitate group discussions and inspire and equip youth to pursue a path of service, thereby making their lives more worthwhile, productive, enriching, and rewarding (BIC, *For the Betterment of the World*).

The Ootan Marawa Educational Institute—in the Republic of Kiribati (33 far-flung coral islands and atolls coral islands in the heart of the Pacific Ocean, halfway between Hawaii and Australia)—has attracted the admiration and respect of the indigenous community there. The efforts of Bahá'ís on the island of South Tarawa are also featured in *A Widening Embrace*, a 77-minute film commissioned by the Universal House of Justice and released in May 2018, which shows how the Bahá'í community cooperates with government and schools to orchestrate a Bahá'í-inspired educational program in schools. The

Bahá'í Faith is the fourth-largest religious community in Kiribati, after the Roman Catholic, Protestant, and Mormon faith-communities.

On 28 April 2019, at the closing session of the Bahá'í community's national convention—held in a traditional island meeting house—Kiribati's President, Taneti Maamau, officially greeted the attendees on behalf of the government. This Bahá'í national convention was held to elect the National Spiritual Assembly (NSA) of the Bahá'ís of the Republic of Kiribati and to consult on issues of importance to Kiribati. (Bahá'ís worldwide hold similar national conventions in their home countries, to elect their respective NSAs and to consult on significant issues of the day as well.) Previously, in October 2017, President Maamau had also attended Kiribati's celebration of the "Bicentenary of the Birth of Bahá'u'lláh" and sent a special message of congratulations to the Universal House of Justice. "I commend your contributions shared through Bahá'u'lláh's teachings of unity and peace to our youth and community," President Maamau wrote, adding: "I have confidence that this will go a long way towards strengthening harmonized living, respectful practices, love, and peace in our society" (BIC, Kiribati: Stories of Celebration). President Maamau's reference to "your contributions shared through Bahá'u'lláh's teachings of unity and peace to our youth" no doubt refers to the the Ootan Marawa Educational Institute's Bahá'í-inspired school programs.

OVERVIEW OF BAHÁ'Í DEVELOPMENT ACTIVITIES

This chapter has highlighted some of the more well-known projects. Others exist as well. For instance, the Banani International School (Lusaka, Zambia) is a non-profit residential school for girls from Grades 5 to 12, "open to girls of all religious, cultural and ethnic backgrounds." (See Banani International School 2019.) This is yet another instance of a Bahá'í-inspired "social action" initiative. Many others may be cited. Many more will likely follow. As an "Overview of Bahá'í Development Activities," the Bahá'í International Community states,

> Bahá'í efforts in the field of development comprise a spectrum of activities. Generally speaking, they are initiated by individuals and small groups of friends in a locality, or by the Faith's administrative institutions—local or national governing councils. The vast majority are simple grassroots endeavors of limited duration. Conservative

estimates indicate that there are close to 40,000 such activities under-taken over the course of a year. ... Some efforts evolve into projects of a more sustained nature, with a commensurate degree of adminis-trative structure. Examples may include schools, radio stations, and community gardens. Over 1,400 sustained projects of this scale are currently being carried out addressing any one of several areas of com-munity life such as education, health, agriculture, or media. In more than 130 instances, projects have developed further—typically over the course of many years coordinating a growing number of lines of action—and taken the form of nonprofit, nongovernmental organiza-tions. Generally referred to as "Bahá'í-inspired organizations," these entities operate at a higher level of sophistication and often manage several programs and projects.

(BIC, *For the Betterment of the World*)

These statistics give a fair impression of the nature and relative number of these Bahá'í-inspired social and economic development projects. Given that the Bahá'í population worldwide is estimated at around seven million adherents, the sum total of these initiatives is respect-able, if not impressive, and, ideally, if not foreseeably, will continue to multiply and magnify in number and in scope.

This chapter selectively highlights several Bahá'í-inspired social and economic development projects. This is a mere sampling of a few out of many such activities and projects. For an overview—with added breadth and depth—readers are encouraged to consult the spe-cial report "For the Betterment of the World: The Worldwide Bahá'í Community's Approach to Social and Economic Development" (BIC, *For the Betterment of the World*) and view the documentary film *A Widening Embrace* (Universal House of Justice, *Widening Embrace*, BRL), that survey and portray Bahá'í core activities and Bahá'í-inspired social and economic development projects, where the latter is often an outgrowth of the former.

SUMMARY

- Bahá'ís are committed to spiritual, social, and economic develop-ment, locally and globally.
- Bahá'ís avoid partisan politics, seen as divisive in nature.
- The primary Bahá'í purpose is to promote unity and justice throughout the world—i.e. "the body politic."

- Bahá'í social and economic development projects are prime examples—and prospective models—of faith-based initiatives, *par excellence*.
- On 9 November 2018, the Universal House of Justice announced the establishment of the "Bahá'í International Development Organization," which replaces the former Office of Social and Economic Development at the Bahá'í World Centre in Haifa, Israel.
- Bahá'ís worldwide have established various social and economic development projects.
- Conservative estimates indicate that there are close to 40,000 Bahá'í-inspired social and economic development projects—such as schools, radio stations, and community gardens—which mostly are simple, grassroots endeavors of limited time span.
- Over 1,400 sustained projects are currently being carried out in such areas of community life such as education, health, agriculture, or media.
- More than 130 projects have developed further, typically taking the form of non-profit, non-governmental organizations.

PUBLIC DISCOURSE
THE BAHÁ'Í INTERNATIONAL COMMUNITY AND THE INDIVIDUAL

The world is in crisis. Social unrest, civil wars, religious sectarianism, structured economic injustice, racism, political corruption, moral decay, and a host of other global problems are signs and symptoms of a world in travail. Nothing short of a worldwide, concerted effort to bring about its transformation can ever hope to resolve this global crisis. The Bahá'í Faith is doing what it can to promote positive social change. Closely allied with Bahá'í-inspired social and economic development projects is public discourse on important issues of this day and age. Engaging in the public discourses of society is another way to exert a positive, leavening and progressive social influence. One goal, or outcome, of public discourse is to promote further social action and transformation for the common good.

The Bahá'í Faith exists for the betterment of the world. The will of God for this day and age, Bahá'ís believe, is for humanity to realize the reality of its own inherent unity—i.e., to become fully alive to the oneness of humankind—and then, energized and empowered by this fundamental principle, to actively take measures to dispel any and all prejudices that stand in the way of human solidarity, peace, and prosperity. For this to happen, individual and social transformation is needed. This spiritual and societal quest is necessary not only for the well-being of society, but for the continued survival of our planet as well.

DOI: 10.4324/9780429023088-9

The Bahá'í Faith offers a vision, hope, and assurance of world peace and prosperity, leading ultimately to a golden age of civilization. It is not a matter of if and why, but of how and when. Bahá'í social principles serve as guideposts in steering the course of world affairs in the right direction. Bahá'ís do not have any magic formulas, mystic powers, or silver bullets wherewith to accomplish these objectives. Rather, Bahá'ís realize that all must work together, in concert, to achieve the betterment of society in an orchestrated way. For this, some profound spiritual insights that the Bahá'í Faith offers can make a world of difference in how best to bring about social transformation, global peace, and prosperity.

"Participation in the discourses of society" (Universal House of Justice, Riḍván 2010: To the Bahá'ís of the World, BRL) is now a ubiquitous and vibrant watchword in the Bahá'í community worldwide. Discourse is dialogue—a reciprocal exchange of views. As such, Bahá'í engagement in public discourses addresses how relevant Bahá'í principles may be applied to the needs and problems of society today. It is also a way to learn from the ideas and experiences of others in an interactive process of dialogue and consultation, at international, national, local, and individual levels, and in professional societies, workplaces, and in informal social settings as well. This chapter highlights how Bahá'ís, at all levels, are engaging in the public discourses of society, with meaningful dialogues and proposals for practical applications in the process of social transformation—a process that is as dynamically evolving as it is challenging.

BAHÁ'Í PUBLIC DISCOURSE AT THE INTERNATIONAL LEVEL: COLLABORATION WITH THE UNITED NATIONS

At the institutional, international level of world affairs, the Bahá'í International Community (BIC) officially represents the Bahá'í Faith. The BIC is the focal and vocal voice of the worldwide Bahá'í community and operates under the auspices of the Universal House of Justice. Established as a non-governmental organization (NGO) in 1948, the BIC has consultative status with a number of United Nations (UN) agencies, including the United Nations Economic and Social Council (ECOSOC), the United Nations Children's Fund (UNICEF), the United

Nations Environmental Program (UNEP), and the United Nations Department of Public Information (DPI). The Bahá'í International Community also engages and collaborates with other UN specialized agencies, as well as with UN member states, intergovernmental and non-governmental organizations, and with academia.

From time to time, the Bahá'í International Community issues formal statements of an advisory nature. These authorized communications not only are official in nature—insofar as they represent Bahá'í positions on a wide range of topics of contemporary interest and importance—but may serve as useful models of public discourse for use by Bahá'ís in all social spaces, especially when they engage in the discourses of society at professional and personal levels. The BIC's formal position papers fall within certain focus areas, as set forth below.

FOCUS AREAS

Public discourse addresses the needs of society, and proposes possible solutions. Public discourse typically focuses on specific topics of social importance. The Bahá'í International Community has prioritized six major "Focus Areas" of social concern, each of which has global significance. These are (1) Realizing the equality of women and men; (2) Human rights and the well-being of humankind; (3) Development and community building; (4) Youth as protagonists of constructive change; (5) Religion in the life of society; and (6) Situation of Bahá'ís in Iran. (BIC, *Persecution*). Each of these focus areas will be discussed below.

Realizing the Equality of Women and Men

Women obviously are half of the world's population. Therefore, the issue of women's equality affects humanity as a whole. Inequality of the sexes deprives humanity of the tremendous potential of women to contribute to the well-being of society as a whole. Unless and until such equality is actively promoted and implemented, the world will be at a social disadvantage in a globally fundamental way. Women should be given equal educational, vocational, economic, scientific, political, and other social opportunities. Not to do so is to deprive the world of a great social resource—one that is greatly needed today. Various sectors of society are affected by this very issue, in fact. From the well-being of the family to the development of the intellectual life of society as a whole, the equality of women and men is central to the future development of humanity and to the further advancement of social progress.

The equality of women and men is a fundamental Bahá'í principle of universal social importance. Without claiming superiority on this basis, it would be fair to say that, in the history of religions, the Bahá'í Faith may well be the first world religion to fully advocate and advance the equality of women and men, from the very beginning of the religion itself. Of course, this issue is a fairly "modern" question, which is why it makes perfect sense that the Bahá'í Faith, appearing as it did in the 19th century—in the full glare of modern history—would address this timely and pressing issue of gender equality and give it such prominence today.

What the BIC actively promotes is a reflection of spiritual and social priorities of the global Bahá'í community at large, writ large. In fact, what the BIC has to offer to the international community at the UN derives, in large part, from the insights gained from Bahá'í initiatives and efforts at the grassroots level which, in some ways, are social experiments that endeavor to bring about those social transformations that are necessary in order to realize not only the goal, but the reality, of the equality of women and men.

The UN Commission on the Status of Women focuses on women's rights and empowerment. As such, the Commission is the single largest international forum dedicated to promoting women's equality, attracting the participation of representatives of numerous UN member states and other international actors. For instance, in 2017, the Commission held a forum on the theme of "Women's Economic Empowerment in the Changing World of Work." At this prestigious forum, Ms. Saphira Rameshfar represented the BIC and spoke on its behalf. For this event—the Commission on the Status of Women's Sixty-first Session (13–24 March 2017)—the BIC contributed a formal statement, "Toward Prosperity: The Role of Women and Men in Building a Flourishing World Civilization" (BIC, *Toward Prosperity*). This is a much-needed reminder of the importance of gender equality. In this statement, the BIC's clarion call serves to awaken and sustain social conscience at the international level. Calling for the need to acknowledge and act on the principle of the equality of women and men serves to keep this issue alive and at the forefront of all UN endeavors. This wings of a bird metaphor is a familiar Bahá'í teaching that was often used by 'Abdu'l-Bahá. Note that this statement from "Toward Prosperity" advocates the advancement of women in all areas of human life and endeavor for "the greater good" and as a necessary precondition for ushering in a "flourishing world civilization."

A flourishing world civilization will draw on the participation of all people, whose skills and talents should be harmonized with the needs of the greater good. This will increasingly become possible as all children are given access to a quality education that helps them develop their intellectual and moral capabilities. Moreover, as women are the first educators of rising generations, their educational opportunity should be given emphasis in all communities. The caring, conciliatory qualities that women can bring to the workforce, indeed, to every sphere of life, have long been undervalued, and humanity has subsequently suffered. Can we foresee the fruits that will grow when true partnerships between men and women emerge in all dimensions of life? Humanity can be likened to a bird with two wings, the male and the female, that has struggled to take flight because the female wing has been suppressed for so long. Who can fully envision the great heights to which humanity will soar when both wings are coordinated and strong?

Safeguarding Human Rights and the Well-being of Humankind

In 1948, the UN's Universal Declaration of Human Rights was a milestone of social progress and established a framework for the protection of human rights under international law. But the Declaration itself required implementation and further action in order for the human rights enshrined in this historic document to be fully respected and realized. The litmus test of human rights is the rights of minorities in any given society. After all, the human rights most often violated are those of minorities, not of majorities.

Ensuring human rights requires ongoing vigilance and activism, so that "human rights machinery" (BIC, Bahá'í International Community and International Organizations)—i.e., efforts to strengthen the mechanisms for full implementation of the human rights promulgated by the Universal Declaration of Human Rights—may be safeguarded and strengthened. Toward this end, the BIC participates actively in meetings of the Human Rights Council, its Special Procedures, and the Universal Periodic Review. BIC representatives, moreover, engage regularly with the UN, the Office of the High Commissioner for Human Rights, and with the Committee on Economic Social and Cultural Rights, among others.

One human rights issue that makes news headlines today is that of migration and immigration. On 12 July 2018, the BIC addressed this issue by presenting a paper entitled, "Migration: A Chance to Reflect on Global Well-Being," to the Sixth Intergovernmental Negotiations on the Global Compact for Migration, in Geneva (BIC, *For the Betterment of the World*). The BIC points out that nations often get in the way of resolving the international migration crisis, which requires—indeed, demands—a global solution. The number of refugees claiming asylum and other migrants is growing exponentially, as civil wars and economic crises throughout the world continue to exacerbate an already intractable problem. Invoking the principle, as revoiced and emphasized by Shoghi Effendi—that "the advantage of the part is best to be reached by the advantage of the whole"—implies that state interests may ultimately best be served by international interests. In any case, no nation is an island. From a Bahá'í perspective, international consultations, resolutions, and implementations—in concerted and coordinated efforts to resolve the international migration crisis—can best succeed only when state interests are subordinated to global interests.

Furthering Development and Community Building

"Development and community building" is the third pillar of the BIC's six "focus areas of public discourse. The BIC connects the issue of "development" with the idea of "community building." The latter is an important concept in local Bahá'í efforts across the world today. The BIC has been active in the UN Commission on Social Development and the Commission on Sustainable Development. On 29 January 2019, the BIC released "Billions Arising: Releasing the Universal Capacity for Transformative Social Change," a statement from the Bahá'í International Community to the 57th session of the Commission for Social Development, an excerpt of which is provided below.

The building of capacity in local communities, on the one hand, and the government's discharge of its rightful duties, on the other, can sometimes be placed in opposition to one another. But this duality ultimately proves false, for some of the most notable instances of rapid progress have sprung from the convergence of enlightened policy and empowered populations. Communities flourish as they develop the capacities—intellectual, social, technical, and moral—to make informed decisions about how their agency will be exercised in ways that both contribute to and are enhanced by state services. For its part, the government's objective of broad-based social advancement is best served when local populations have the capability and volition to resolve problems on their own. In this light, social and economic policies become vital means for the state to enhance the partnership between itself and the communities it supports and serves.

(BIC, *Billions Arising*)

The title, "Billions Arising," implies that social development is primarily a grassroots endeavor, in which people at the local level are the principal actors and agents of social change, at least potentially, in translating enlightened social principles and policies into concrete and practical outcomes. The role of governments is to adopt and implement "policy tools" in order to foster and further social development "on the ground." (BIC, *Billions Arising*). Here, the BIC urges government agencies to help "unlock the transformative power of local communities and individuals" rather than "simply providing and funding." This is exactly what the Bahá'í community is fostering at the grassroots level through its systematic, yet innovative "community building" efforts. It is hoped that these efforts, taken as a whole—or at least the most successful parts of these projects—may serve as social models and exemplars that may attract the interest of government policymakers, to encourage a dynamic partnership between local initiatives and state support.

Empowering Youth as Protagonists of Constructive Change

Empowering youth is a worldwide Bahá'í endeavor. Youth, by nature, tend to be idealistic. Youth are a largely untapped, relatively undeveloped, and often poorly guided segment of society. Yet potentializing the power of youth to contribute to the transformation of society is a worthy, if not necessary, undertaking. On 30–31 January 2018, the 2018

(7th Annual) ECOSOC Youth Forum was held in New York. Attended by over 700 participants, the Forum is the largest single, annual gathering of youth and youth representatives at the United Nations. The BIC contributed to this 2018 event by presenting a special statement, "Rising Generations: Weaving a New Tapestry of Community Life," along with four videos (BIC, *Rising Generations*):

> A practical way to engage various members of the community to help set goals and execute plans is to create spaces for consultation. Whether concerned with analysing a specific situation, trying to gain a fuller understanding of a given issue, exploring a possible course of action, or arriving at a decision, consultation may be seen as a collective search for truth. The participants in a consultative process are not interested in exercising power over one another or convincing one another of the validity of their perspectives. Rather, they participate with an understanding that different people see reality from different points of view, and as these views are examined and understood, new insights emerge and clarity is gained. Some consultative spaces might bring together groups of parents who would like to share concerns about and aspirations for their children. Other spaces might bring together groups of friends providing similar types of service to the community – teachers of classes for children and youth, friends tending to gardens and farms together, entrepreneurs identifying unique resources their community can contribute to enrich the society around them. Periodic spaces where these different groups can all come together and reflect on the current state of the community as a whole while planning for the months ahead would also contribute to the flourishing of a healthy, interconnected and united community.
>
> (BIC, *Rising Generations*)

Advancing Religion in the Life of Society

A fifth pillar of the BIC's six focus areas of public discourse is the issue of religion in the life of society. Religion has a key role to play today in advancing the common good. This is done, in large part, through increasing public awareness that human life is fundamentally spiritual as well as material in nature. The spiritual dimension carries with it some key universal principles, human values, and important ideas and ideals.

On the issue of religion in society, on 6 September 2015, Chong Ming Hwee (a BIC representative) presented a perspective paper, "Re-examining the role of religion in world peace," to the 1st Annual Malang International Peace Conference. This paper was first published in the *Jakarta Post* on 18 September 2015, in which Mr. Hwee concludes, "It is timely, if not overdue, for us to critically re-examine the role of religion in the cultivation of lasting world peace" (BIC, *Re-examining*).

Mitigating the Situation of Bahá'ís in Iran

The year 2019 marked the 40th anniversary of the 1979 Iranian Revolution, which resulted, in part, in systematic persecution against Bahá'ís in Iran. In Iran, the following violations, among others, of Bahá'í human rights under international law and civil rights under Iranian law—persecution that has been perpetrated and perpetuated by the Islamic Republic of Iran ever since the 1979 Islamic Revolution—have been well documented, to wit: barring Bahá'í administrative and group religious activities; incitement to hatred (by anti-Bahá'í propaganda); harassment; arbitrary arrests and detentions; indictments under false and/or pretextual charges; denial of due process, including lawful criminal procedure; denial of legal representation; imprisonment; failure to investigate and prosecute attacks and assaults; expulsion from civil service; expulsion from universities, if admitted, and often denial of admission in other cases if the applicant is known to be a Bahá'í; mass closure of private businesses; denial of pensions; denial of rightful inheritances; monitoring of bank accounts, movements, and activities; denial of access to publishing or copying facilities for Bahá'í literature; confiscation and/or destruction of Bahá'í properties, including cemeteries and Bahá'í holy places; denial of Bahá'í prisoners of access to and treatment by medical specialists; severe limitations of various civil rights and liberties; intimidation of Muslims who associate with Bahá'ís; harsh interrogation, including beatings and psychological torture; physical torture; execution; and mutilation.

Although, historically, Bahá'ís have been persecuted in Iran throughout Bahá'í history, widespread persecution of Bahá'ís under the current regime has significantly intensified and become more systematic. (See Vahman 2019; Iran Press Watch 2019; Bahá'í International Community, *Archives*; Buck 2008; Ghanea 2003.) The BIC's statement, "UN Human Rights Council—39th Session, September. Item 4: Human rights situations that require the Council's attention," presented in Geneva on 18 September 2018, stresses the enormity and gravity of the plight of the Bahá'ís of Iran (BIC, *Persecution*). This appeal calls upon the UN Human Rights Council to refocus international attention on the plight of the Bahá'ís in Iran today. This, of course, is one of many situations in which human rights are still being violated around the world. That said, the BIC's advocacy on behalf of the beleaguered Bahá'í community of Iran is timely. Continuing focus on this long-standing problem is necessary in order to keep this issue alive at the international level. International attention and pressure have been shown to have a mitigating influence in the past.

The foregoing makes it clear why the Bahá'í International Community has prioritized this sixth major issue of social concern, which is an ongoing problem that demands a solution, and which requires vigilant and unrelenting perseverance in drawing international attention to the plight of religious minorities in Iran (as everywhere), until international pressure succeeds in mitigating or resolving this problem altogether. Conscience dictates that the Bahá'ís of Iran not be forgotten. In so doing, the Bahá'í International Community and other Bahá'í agencies also include the plight of other religious minorities as well. Even though persecution of Bahá'ís appears to be the most egregious and systematic of Iran's violations of the human rights of its religious minorities—especially those that are "unrecognized," i.e., excluded from the Constitution of the Islamic Republic of Iran, by design—the religious minority rights of all of these oppressed communities must be addressed and redressed as well. Article 13 of the Constitution of the Islamic Republic of Iran explicitly states:

> Zoroastrian, Jewish, and Christian Iranians are the only recognized religious minorities, who, within the limits of the law, are free to perform their religious rites and ceremonies, and to act according to their own canon in matters of personal affairs and religious education
>
> (Constitute, *Iran*).

This excludes Iranian Bahá'ís from civil recognition and constitutional rights afforded to Zoroastrians, Jews, and Christians.

BAHÁ'Í PUBLIC DISCOURSE AT THE NATIONAL LEVEL: FIVE "LINES OF ACTION"

In 2013, the Universal House of Justice established the Office of Public Discourse, which works with national and international bodies, providing guidance and expertise. For instance, in 2019, the following "lines of action" were identified by the Office of Public Discourse at the Bahá'í World Centre to increase capacities for engaging in effective American race relations discourses—as well as other public discourse issues of contemporary interest—at the national level:

- Reading the reality of society and its discourses on race.
- Entering established social spaces, such as conferences and workshops.
- Developing sincere friendships with people active in social justice work.
- Convening spaces for a variety of people and agencies and creating content to stimulate sharing of thoughts.
- Learning how to engage small, knowledgeable groups of Bahá'ís. (Bahá'ís of the United States, 2019.)

In 2018, the National Spiritual Assembly (NSA) of the Bahá'ís of the United States appointed two race discourse officers, who operate within the Bahá'í Office of Public Affairs (OPA) in Washington, DC. This is part of an ongoing and evolving process in preparation for a national conference on race unity, envisioned by the NSA in 2017. This forthcoming conference will provide a platform "where people active on the national level can share learning and connections" as to improving race relations in America, in a process "parallel with the general Bahá'í community's efforts to address racism through community building, social action and participation in discourse." Consistent with the "lines of action" identified above, Anthony N. Vance, Director of Public Affairs, National Spiritual Assembly of the Bahá'ís of the United States (Washington, D.C.), responded to the present writer's queries as to the efforts (i.e., lines of action) of the Office of Public Affairs, pursuant to the advice and recommendations by the Office of Public Discourse, as follows:

We have been relayed a request from you regarding lines of action that we are pursuing in public discourse at the national level. Specifically, you are interested in knowing what those lines of action, identified for our office by the Office of Public Discourse at the Bahá'í World Centre, currently are. They are as follows:

- Reading society
- Entering social spaces
- Building relationships
- Working with collaborators from within the Bahá'í community
- Developing content. (Vance, 2019)

Mr. Vance then comments as to the dynamic interrelationships among these five lines of action, noting that, "to varying degrees," these lines of action are "dependent on each other and intersect." Mr. Vance notes "a mutual process of learning," which is a hallmark and benchmark of Bahá'í interaction with like-minded organizations and leaders of thought (Vance 2019).

BAHÁ'Í PUBLIC DISCOURSE AT THE INDIVIDUAL LEVEL: THREE EXAMPLES

INSTITUTE FOR STUDIES IN GLOBAL PROSPERITY (ISGP)

The Institute for Studies in Global Prosperity was founded in 1999, and works in cooperation with the Bahá'í International Community. The Institute, moreover, is engaged in training young adults by conducting a series of seminars for undergraduate students, graduate students, and young professionals. The Institute also participates in discourses focused on social transformation in four areas: (1) Science, Religion and Development (with programs taking place in ten countries around the world); (2) Governance; (3) Equality of Women and Men; and (4) Overcoming Oppression (Institute for Studies in Global Prosperity, 2019).

ASSOCIATION FOR BAHÁ'Í STUDIES (ABS)

Founded in 1975 in Canada, the Association for Bahá'í Studies was established to promote advanced studies of the Bahá'í Faith and to explore its application to the needs of the world. Having expanded to serve North America, the Association engages participants from across Canada and the United States by holding annual conferences and by publishing a peer-reviewed journal, *The Journal of Bahá'í Studies*, along with other publications. At its 43rd Annual Conference, held 8–11 August 2019 in Ottawa, Canada, the theme for the 2019 Association for Bahá'í Studies Conference was "Beyond Critique: Laying the Groundwork for Social Transformation." Papers were presented on a wide array of disciplines addressing a range of social issues such as economics, healthcare, education, law, and the media.

BAHAITEACHINGS.ORG

One platform on which individuals may engage in contributing to the discourses of society is BahaiTeachings.org, which is the most popular Bahá'í website in the world today. Although it has no official status, it appears that BahaiTeachings.org has earned the respect of Bahá'í institutions.

BahaiTeachings.org endeavors to address its audience with love, warmth, respect, openness, consideration and kindness—avoiding any preachy tone of overweening religiosity or triumphalism. Instead, authors who contribute articles try to employ a humble posture of sharing thoughts. Striving to offer the highest quality articles possible, this website publishes essays that will have a long life and a wide reach on the internet, teaching the Faith for potentially many years to come. BahaiTeachings.org's vision of quality is guided by these words of the Universal House of Justice, i.e. to "aim to raise consciousness without awakening the insistent self, to disseminate insight without cultivating a sense of celebrity, to address issues profoundly but not court controversy, to remain clear in expression but not descend to crassness prevalent in common discourse" (from a letter dated 4 April 2018 written on behalf of the Universal House of Justice to a National Spiritual Assembly).

BAHÁ'Í PUBLIC DISCOURSE AT ALL LEVELS OF SOCIETY: ADVICE BY THE BAHÁ'Í INTERNATIONAL COMMUNITY

The Bahá'í International Community explains how the process of Bahá'í participation in the public discourses ideally should work. Bahá'ís are encouraged to do so with an open mind, to be ready to learn from others, as well as to contribute their own experiences and insights, and do so for altruistic reasons rather than for public relations credit (BIC, What *Bahá'ís Do. Involvement in the Life of Society. Participation in the Discourses of Society*). Bahá'ís are encouraged to engage in the public discourses of society in order to learn to be more effective as catalysts and agents of social change. Transformation of society cannot occur without enlightened discourse and consequent social action. Those change agents, i.e., the social actors themselves, must be drawn from all walks of life and from all persuasions.

The Bahá'í Faith offers some powerful social principles to help affect social transformation. These principles require practical application. The Bahá'ís cannot accomplish this on their own. Like anybody else, Bahá'ís can benefit from learning from others in further exploring these topics in conversation within social spaces that are conducive to such consultation. Reciprocally, others can derive insights and inspiration from Bahá'í community-building efforts all over the world, especially as they gain experience, and as such activities multiply and magnify, with some emerging as models of exemplars of effective and profound social transformation. This arena of Bahá'í endeavor is still developing, evolving, and unfolding.

Public discourse strives to keep certain key social issues in the forefront of civil discourse, where the voices of civil society are brought to bear on discussions at local, national, and international levels. What the BIC does at the international level, and in its work with the UN, can, and should, be replicated at the national and local levels, with thoughtful and creative approaches that optimize the chances of success in furthering social action and progress on any given issue of social importance.

SUMMARY

- "Participation in the discourses of society" is now a ubiquitous watchword in the Bahá'í community worldwide.
- This approach focuses on addressing how relevant Bahá'í principles may be applied to the needs and problems of society today.
- It is also a way to learn from the ideas and experiences of others in an interactive process of dialogue and consultation, at international, national, local, and individual levels, and in professional societies, workplaces, and in informal social settings as well.
- At the institutional, international level of world affairs, the "Bahá'í International Community" (BIC) represents the Bahá'í Faith.

- Established as a non-governmental organization in 1948, the BIC is the voice of the worldwide Bahá'í community and operates under the auspices of the Universal House of Justice.
- From time to time, the Bahá'í International Community promulgates formal statements of an advisory nature.
- The Bahá'í International Community has prioritized six major issues of social concern, each of which has global significance, to wit: (1) Realizing the equality of women and men; (2) Human rights and the well-being of humankind; (3) Development and community building; (4) Youth as protagonists of constructive change; (5) Religion in the life of society; and (6) Situation of Bahá'ís in Iran.

VISION
FOUNDATIONS FOR A FUTURE GOLDEN AGE

A VISION OF THE FUTURE

Bahá'ís have a clear vision of the future. As previously said, Bahá'ís are building the future in the present. Bahá'ís adopt short-term goals to achieve long-term objectives. This is accomplished by a series of well-thought-out and goal-driven plans issued, usually once every five years, by the Universal House of Justice. These global plans provide a framework for concerted, systematic actions by Bahá'ís worldwide in furtherance of community development and sustained growth. They see a dynamic connection between present-day efforts and future outcomes. In other words, Bahá'ís are pursuing short-term objectives for long-term individual and social transformation.

On 11 March 1936, Shoghi Effendi wrote an impressive and remarkably detailed vision statement of the future golden age, toward which the human race ideally is heading. Originally written as a letter addressed to Western Bahá'ís ("To the beloved of God and the handmaids of the Merciful throughout the West"), this vision statement—which takes the form of a definite and definitive prophecy—was later published as "The Unfoldment of World Civilization," reprinted as the final section in the anthology of selected letters by Shoghi Effendi to America, *The World Order of Bahá'u'lláh.* The central part of this extraordinary vision of the future "world commonwealth" is as follows:

DOI: 10.4324/9780429023088-10

> The unity of the human race, as envisaged by Bahá'u'lláh, implies the establishment of a world commonwealth in which all nations, races, creeds, and classes are closely and permanently united, and in which the autonomy of its state members and the personal freedom and initiative of the individuals that compose them are definitely and completely safeguarded. This commonwealth must, as far as we can visualize it, consist of a world legislature, whose members will, as the trustees of the whole of mankind, ultimately control the entire resources of all the component nations, and will enact such laws as shall be required to regulate the life, satisfy the needs and adjust the relationships of all races and peoples.
>
> (Shoghi Effendi, *World Order*, BRL)

This utopian vision appears to be entirely secular in form but is actually religious in its origin. Shoghi Effendi connects this vision to Bahá'u'lláh's teachings. For the most part, Shoghi Effendi makes explicit what Bahá'u'lláh made implicit, although there is considerable overlap. As the designated "Guardian" of the Bahá'í Faith, and in his capacity as an inspired interpreter and translator of the sacred writings of the three "Central Figures" of the Bahá'í Faith, i.e. the Báb, Bahá'u'lláh, and 'Abdu'l-Bahá—and "tasked with applying the principles, promulgating the laws, protecting the institutions, and adapting the Bahá'í Faith to the requirements of an ever-advancing society" as well (Universal House of Justice, *October 1963*, BRL)—Shoghi Effendi effectively was mapping onto the future world some of the direct and foreseeable social implications of Bahá'u'lláh's and 'Abdu'l-Bahá's principles, precepts, and prophecies.

The very idea of a world commonwealth presupposes some kind of world unity, and such world unity is predicated on the consciousness of the oneness of humanity, which the Bahá'í Faith is endeavoring to promote. This vision continues:

> A world executive, backed by an international Force, will carry out the decisions arrived at, and apply the laws enacted by, this world legislature, and will safeguard the organic unity of the whole commonwealth. A world tribunal will adjudicate and deliver its compulsory and final verdict in all and any disputes that may arise between the various elements constituting this universal system. A mechanism of world inter-communication will be devised, embracing the whole planet, freed from national hindrances and restrictions, and functioning with

marvellous swiftness and perfect regularity. A world metropolis will act as the nerve center of a world civilization, the focus towards which the unifying forces of life will converge and from which its energizing influences will radiate. A world language will either be invented or chosen from among the existing languages and will be taught in the schools of all the federated nations as an auxiliary to their mother tongue. A world script, a world literature, a uniform and universal system of currency, of weights and measures, will simplify and facilitate intercourse and understanding among the nations and races of mankind. In such a world society, science and religion, the two most potent forces in human life, will be reconciled, will coöperate, and will harmoniously develop. The press will, under such a system, while giving full scope to the expression of the diversified views and convictions of mankind, cease to be mischievously manipulated by vested interests, whether private or public, and will be liberated from the influence of contending governments and peoples. The economic resources of the world will be organized, its sources of raw materials will be tapped and fully utilized, its markets will be coördinated and developed, and the distribution of its products will be equitably regulated.

(Shoghi Effendi, *World Order*, BRL)

This vision of the future world commonwealth includes: a "world legislature"; a "world executive"; a "world tribunal"; a "world intercommunication" system; a "world metropolis"; a "world civilization"; a "world language"; a "world script"; a "world literature"; a "universal system of currency, of weights and measures"; a free press; and a world economic system. The benefits that this world system will confer are as follows:

National rivalries, hatreds, and intrigues will cease, and racial animosity and prejudice will be replaced by racial amity, understanding and coöperation. The causes of religious strife will be permanently removed, economic barriers and restrictions will be completely abolished, and the inordinate distinction between classes will be obliterated. Destitution on the one hand, and gross accumulation of ownership on the other, will disappear. The enormous energy dissipated and wasted on war, whether economic or political, will be consecrated to such ends as will extend the range of human inventions and technical development, to the increase of the productivity of mankind, to the extermination of disease, to the extension of scientific research, to the raising of the standard of physical health, to the sharpening and refinement of the human brain, to the exploitation of the unused and unsuspected resources of the planet, to the prolongation of human life, and to the furtherance of any other agency that can stimulate the intellectual, the moral, and spiritual life of the entire human race.

(Shoghi Effendi, *World Order*, BRL)

The foregoing statement speaks for itself. It is a preview of what world peace will look like, and of the infrastructures and institutions required to maintain and sustain world order. Shoghi Effendi concludes this vision of the future world commonwealth so:

A world federal system, ruling the whole earth and exercising unchallengeable authority over its unimaginably vast resources, blending and embodying the ideals of both the East and the West, liberated from the curse of war and its miseries, and bent on the exploitation of all the available sources of energy on the surface of the planet, a system in which Force is made the servant of Justice, whose life is sustained by its universal recognition of one God and by its allegiance to one common Revelation—such is the goal towards which humanity, impelled by the unifying forces of life, is moving.

(Shoghi Effendi, *World Order*, BRL)

This is the ideal society of the future that Bahá'ís are now establishing the basic groundwork for, in a global process called "community building." (See Chapter Seven, "Building Community: What Bahá'ís Do.") This vision is grand, but not grandiose. It is a serious, earnest, and carefully conceived vision of a future global society. The primary "data, as it were, on which Shoghi Effendi relied were the Bahá'í scriptures themselves, which provide a rich resource for social, as well as individual development. For those who are drawn to this vision, the Bahá'í Faith offers a global community of kindred spirits who are inspired, one and all, by this compelling and promising vision of the future of our planet.

EMERGENCE FROM OBSCURITY

So, how can this grand and glorious vision be achieved? The answer is step-by-progressive-step, as the Bahá'í community grows in size and influence.

Many people have not heard of the Bahá'í Faith. Yet it is emerging from its former obscurity. "One telling indicator of progress was the numerous places where it became clear that the Faith had emerged from obscurity at the national level," the Universal House of Justice wrote in a 2018 message to the Bahá'ís of the world, adding: "There were government leaders and leaders of thought who stated publicly—and sometimes emphasized privately—that the world stands in need of Bahá'u'lláh's vision and that the Bahá'ís' endeavours are admired and should be expanded" (Universal House of Justice, April 2018, BRL). Such public recognition of the Bahá'í Faith typically goes unreported by the press and other media. As one would expect, such recognition, from time to time, is noted in Bahá'í media.

To illustrate the House's point, on Sunday, 27 October 2019, the President of Israel, Reuven Rivlin, visited Haifa to honor the 200th anniversary of the birth of the Báb. "The values of tolerance and respect are well integrated into the two cities where the Bahá'í World Centre is based—Akka and Haifa," President Rivlin remarked during his visit to Haifa, further remarking: "The State of Israel is proud and delighted to host Bahá'í believers and the World Centre for the Bahá'í Faith, which promotes values of peace and unity among different religions" (BIC, *News*). President Rivlin's tribute to Bahá'í contributions to peace is especially significant in the Middle East, where peace among religions is sorely needed. *The Jerusalem Post* briefly reported this visit: "At the beginning of the week, President Reuven Rivlin was in Haifa to pay his respects to the Bahá'í community, which is marking the 200th anniversary of the Birth of the Báb, prophet-herald of the Bahá'í faith" (*Jerusalem Post*, 2019).

As another instance, on 12 February 2018, the President of Ireland, Michael D. Higgins, welcomed a delegation of some 50 Bahá'ís, including children, youth, and adults, at a formal reception at his official residence, where Brendan McNamara, on behalf of the National Assembly of the Bahá'ís of Ireland, presented President Higgins with a hand-bound collection of selected Bahá'ís writings the "Irish language" (also known as "Gaeilge" (pronounced Gwal-gah), not "Gaelic") coinciding with the country's effort to promote the indigenous Irish language. The President said that he and his wife, Sabina, know many members of the Bahá'í Faith, and that he had first met Bahá'ís in 1967 at Indiana University in Bloomington (where he was a graduate student in sociology at that time) where a number of Bahá'ís were part of the School of Music, with whom he had regular contacts

(Higgins 2018; see also BIC 2018b). In appreciation, President Higgins commended the Bahá'ís of Ireland, saying: "I know you will continue to inspire and motivate young people, and ensure the Bahá'í Faith will go from strength to strength, continuing to bring people together here and around the world" (BIC, *News*).

At that time, President Higgins had known Bahá'ís for over 50 years. So, he knew much about which he was speaking. A video of President Higgins (in Irish and in English) is available online (Higgins 2018).

This chapter highlights some of the ways in which the Bahá'í Faith contributes to world peace, especially at the grassroots level, but also at national and international levels as well. Bahá'í peace-building efforts have a long history, in which 1985 was a milestone year, as will be discussed in the next section.

THE PROMISE OF WORLD PEACE—THEN AND NOW

In Chapter Five, "The Promise of World Peace"—the October 1985 message by the Universal House of Justice addressed "To the Peoples of the World"—was quoted, at length. In its global message, the House stated: "World peace is not only possible but inevitable. It is the next stage in the evolution of this planet—in the words of one great thinker, 'the planetization of mankind'" (Universal House of Justice, October 1985, BRL). Here, the House was quoting Pierre Teilhard de Chardin's celebrated essay, "A Great Event Foreshadowed: The Planetization of Mankind" (25 December 1945). Although the House stated that world peace is "inevitable," it really is a matter of time, and circumstance. The conditions must first be right and the time ripe.

At that time, the House offered Bahá'í community as a model of a global society in which unity, and therefore peace, is possible for the world at large. Pointing to the Bahá'í community as an exemplar of a peaceful society was probably intended to give some assurance to the peoples of the world that it is possible to create a unified and peaceful society. It is that assurance on which the promise of world peace is largely based. Of course, both Bahá'u'lláh and 'Abdu'l-Bahá, as well as Shoghi Effendi, had previously foretold the advent of world peace and of a future golden age of world civilization. The Bahá'í social model has since been refined.

In a letter dated 18 January 2019 (written on the occasion of the centenary of the Paris Peace Conference and the Treaty of Versailles), the Universal House of Justice referred back to its 1985 message and then updated its perspective on world peace. In this 2019 letter, the House states that the road to peace may well be "tortuous." The House further points out that the world is "gripped by a crisis of identity, as various peoples and groups struggle to define themselves," but that what is needed is a "vision of shared identity and common purpose." "The establishment of peace is a duty to which the entire human race is called," the Universal House of Justice is quick to point out, and hastens to add:

> The responsibility that Bahá'ís bear to aid that process will evolve over time, but they have never been mere spectators—they lend their share of assistance to the operation of those forces leading humanity towards unity. They are summoned to be as leaven to the world.
>
> (Universal House of Justice, January 2019, BRL)

Elaborating on how Bahá'ís today are building communities that are bastions and beacons of peace, the House describes the nature of contemporary Bahá'í communities as follows:

> "The Promise of World Peace", the message we addressed to the peoples of the world in 1985, set out the Bahá'í perspective on the condition of the world and the prerequisites of universal peace. It also offered the global Bahá'í community as a model for study that could reinforce hope in the possibility of uniting the human race. In the years since, the followers of Bahá'u'lláh have been patiently refining that model and working with others around them to build up and broaden a system of social organization based on His teachings. They are learning how to nurture communities that embody those prerequisites of peace we identified in 1985.
>
> (Universal House of Justice, 18 January 2019: *To the Bahá'ís of the World*, BRL)

The Bahá'í community has been evolving since that time. Yet the prerequisites for peace, set forth by the Universal House of Justice, have not changed. Among others, there are eight major prerequisites to peace that the House highlighted in 1985, to wit:

1. *Recognizing the Oneness of Humanity*: "Acceptance of the oneness of mankind is the first fundamental prerequisite for reorganization and administration of the world as one country, the home of humankind."

2. *Eradicating Racism*: "Racism, one of the most baneful and persistent evils, is a major barrier to peace."

3. *Overcoming Religious Strife*: "Religious strife, throughout history, has been the cause of innumerable wars and conflicts, a major blight to progress, and is increasingly abhorrent to the people of all faiths and no faith."

4. *Reducing Poverty*: "The inordinate disparity between rich and poor, a source of acute suffering, keeps the world in a state of instability, virtually on the brink of war."

5. *Widening Patriotic Loyalty*: "Unbridled nationalism, as distinguished from a sane and legitimate patriotism, must give way to a wider loyalty, to the love of humanity as a whole."

6. *Achieving Gender Equality*: "The emancipation of women, the achievement of full equality between the sexes, is one of the most important, though less acknowledged prerequisites of peace."

7. *Providing Universal Education*: "The cause of universal education, which has already enlisted in its service an army of dedicated people from every faith and nation, deserves the utmost support that the governments of the world can lend it."

8. *Adopting an International Language*: "A fundamental lack of communication between peoples seriously undermines efforts towards world peace. Adopting an international auxiliary language would go far to resolving this problem and necessitates the most urgent attention." (Universal House of Justice, October 1985, BRL) (Italics side headings added)

Since then, the methods and means of the application of these eight peace prerequisites have become more focused and systematic in nature, starting with children. The sea change, or paradigm-shift, in Bahá'í culture took place in 1996. Ever since then, nurturing the moral education of children (by teaching virtues in neighborhood children's classes), developing the character of youth (through Junior Youth Spiritual Empowerment Programs," deepening spiritual dedication (through regular devotionals), and building capacity for service to others (through close-knit study circles), has been the new order of the day within Bahá'í community life worldwide.

Some correspondences may be drawn to the eight prerequisites of peace set forth in the House's 1985 open letter to the peoples of the world. For instance, the phrase, "children can be raised untainted by any form of racial, national, or religious prejudice" corresponds to peace prerequisites 2, 5, and 3. "They champion the full equality of women with men" correlates to prerequisite 6, "programs of education" to prerequisite 7, and so on. Taken together, these community-building activities are creating a foundation for peace and justice. The House notes that the "Local Spiritual Assembly" is called upon to "govern in servitude, to resolve conflicts, and to build unity," where the "the foundational recognition that all of humanity are the children of one Creator" relates back to peace prerequisite number 1. The House commends "the community's increased ability to make meaningful contributions to various important discourses prevalent in society" and to generally advance the "discourses of society," especially "discourses directly related to peace" (Universal House of Justice, January 2019, BRL).

To recapitulate, the House points to several distinctive features that characterize Bahá'í community life, such as raising children happily and free of all prejudice, championing full gender equality, offering programs of transformative education, pursuing various forms of social action to address the ills of society, hosting inspirational devotional meetings for people of all faiths (or none), consciously building and evolving their local communities on spiritual and service-based foundations, conducting peaceful elections of local Bahá'í councils, all of which are done with the recognition that all of humankind "are the children of one Creator."

This depiction of Bahá'í community life is not far-fetched, but is true to life. Note that Bahá'í community life today is peaceful and harmonious. As such, this is a "model" of domestic peace that is replicated internationally. It does not demonstrate peace in the political sense, however. Such is a matter of statecraft, as was the Treaty of Versailles, the centenary of which occasioned this letter from the House. This exemplary Bahá'í model, when further evolved, may well attract the attention of various world leaders. If impressed, such a result could have an indirect impact on the path to world peace, since leaders can see for themselves and appreciate what a peaceful community can look like, and what the community-building process was that led to such remarkable and exemplary results. For instance, on 31 July 2017, Singapore's Prime Minister, Lee Hsien Loong, addressed an open message to the Bahá'í community of his country, recognizing Bahá'í contributions to "enhancing mutual respect in a multi-faith society and strengthening Singapore's social harmony" (Bahá'í World News Service 2017(b)).

Another instance of a world leader recognizing Bahá'í contributions to world peace took place on 30 August 2017, when the Prime Minister of India, Narendra Modi—on the occasion of the 200th anniversary of the birth of Bahá'u'lláh—addressed an official message to the Bahá'í community of India, stating that the "Bahá'í faith has found wholehearted acceptance in India," wherein Bahá'í "institutions and missions are much revered in our nation," and along with the "Lotus Temple," positively "epitomise this spirit of fellowship and universal brotherhood" (Bahá'í World News Service 2017(a)).

Films documenting Bahá'í community-building efforts have been produced, such as *A Widening Embrace* (2018) and others. Commissioned by the Universal House of Justice, this 77-minute film highlights Bahá'í efforts to bring about social transformation in 24 Bahá'í communities around the world, representing different cultural realities and contexts. By visiting various rural and urban settings, neighborhoods and villages, this film captures Bahá'í community-building experiences and insights by focusing on: (1) the grassroots process itself; (2) the role of youth in service to their communities; and (3) Bahá'í-inspired social and economic development projects (Universal House of Justice, *A Widening Embrace*).

BUILDING THE FUTURE IN THE PRESENT: CHANGING SOCIAL REALITY

The future has its roots in the present. In their community-building efforts, Bahá'ís are laying some solid foundations for creating a peaceful world. This takes a lot of work, time, and energy, and requires dedication and perseverance. The Bahá'ís cannot create a peaceful world on their own. The Bahá'í Faith offers a blueprint for achieving world peace. Pertinent and timely directions are given. Yet the Bahá'í teachings, no matter how practical and necessary, cannot change the world on their own. Social changes that are needed to bring about peace and prosperity will not happen miraculously. A universal effort is called

for. Such an undertaking will benefit from a clear vision and coordi-
nation, for which the Bahá'í teachings offer valuable insights. For the
practical application of Bahá'í teachings, Bahá'ís are now collaborat-
ing with their neighbors, with friends and family, and with their colleagues, in shaping and consolidating and uplifting their respective
communities, for all to see.

In his 2005 paper, Bahá'í scholar Moojan Momen describes, theo-
retically and phenomenologically, how the Bahá'í world is effectively
changing social reality—a reality that itself is socially created. How
does social change occur? What are its dynamics? Dr. Momen begins
by noting how sociologists Peter Berger and Thomas Luckmann in
their 1966 sociological classic, *The Social Construction of Reality*,
demonstrated how people create their own cultures, which later generations take for granted as social reality (Momen 2005). Although
Momen does not mention this, Berger, in his next book, *The Sacred
Canopy: Elements of a Sociological Theory of Religion* (1967) called
this process of social construction, "world-building," as stated in the
very first sentence of his book: "Every human society is an enterprise
of world-building." In the very next sentence, Berger connects this
process with religion: "Our main purpose here is to make some general statements about the relationship between human religion and
human world-building" (Berger 1967, 3).

As applied to the Bahá'í religion, Momen states his objective so:

> I wish to look at one aspect of this concept of the social construction of
> reality and the idea of a change in this reality that has not been studied
> much: the question of how a group can set out deliberately to change
> reality.
>
> (Momen 2005, 16)

In other words, Dr. Momen demonstrates how Bahá'ís are shaping
their own social reality and, in so doing, trying to effect social transformation in their surrounding social orders as well.

In this way, Bahá'ís are "building up a non-hierarchical administrative system where individuals do not have either power or authority," along with engaging in "consultative decision-making processes"
that "encourage those who often feel most oppressed and alienated
in modern society to express themselves and participate in social
action"; and, moreover, by establishing "institutions that aim to serve

rather than to exert power and authority"; and by promoting "a new global consciousness of human unity," whereby "a new social reality is slowly but steadily emerging within the Bahá'í community"—one that "the Universal House of Justice has already spoken of presenting ... as a model for how the global unity advocated by Bahá'u'lláh over one hundred years ago can be achieved" (Momen 2005, 31–32).

Bahá'ís firmly believe that Bahá'u'lláh has come to unify the world. The Bahá'í vision of the future, therefore, is that of a golden age—a world commonwealth—in which that vision of unity will come to fruition and, in the fulness of time, be fully realized. The process of creating that future is long and arduous. Nothing short of such clarity of vision and commitment to unifying principles can achieve it. This is the primary contribution of the Bahá'í Faith to the world today. The Bahá'í teachings aim to raise, to a superlative degree, the consciousness of the oneness of humanity, and to develop those organic processes and institutions that will ensure harmony and justice for all. It is a grand vision and a promising undertaking. The Bahá'ís, of course, will not—and cannot—achieve this alone. But, by promoting this vision—and by systematically applying the powerful socio-moral principles underpinning it—the Bahá'ís are contributing, in their own special way, to the betterment of our world. Bahá'ís have a clear sense of the social and spiritual "evolution" of our planet, and are working to accelerate the process of unity and peace. Time will tell to what extent this ideal vision of world unity can be translated into reality. But, in this grand process of individual and social transformation, the global effort is well worth the noble endeavor.

SUMMARY

- On 11 March 1936, Shoghi Effendi wrote an impressive and remarkably detailed vision statement of the future golden age, toward which the human race ideally is heading.
- This is the ideal society of the future that Bahá'ís are now establishing the basic groundwork for, in a global process called "community building." (See Chapter Seven, "Building Community: What Bahá'ís Do.)
- The Bahá'í Faith is emerging from its former obscurity.
- The Universal House of Justice wrote in a 2018 message to the Bahá'ís of the world, pointing out their endeavors are attracting

significant recognition and respect on the part of some leaders across the world: "There were government leaders and leaders of thought who stated publicly—and sometimes emphasized privately—that the world stands in need of Bahá'u'lláh's vision and that the Bahá'ís' endeavours are admired and should be expanded" (Universal House of Justice).

- In its 1985 message, the House stated, "World peace is not only possible but inevitable. It is the next stage in the evolution of this planet—in the words of one great thinker, 'the planetization of mankind'" (Universal House of Justice 1985).

- At that time, the House offered Bahá'í community as a model of a global society in which unity, and therefore peace, is possible for the world at large.

- Eight prerequisites of peace are:
    1. Recognizing the oneness of humanity.
    2. Eradicating racism.
    3. Overcoming religious strife.
    4. Reducing poverty.
    5. Widening patriotic loyalty.
    6. Achieving gender equality.
    7. Providing universal education.
    8. Adopting an international language.

- In the Universal House of Justice's letter dated 18 January 2019 (written on the occasion of the centenary of the Paris Peace Conference and the Treaty of Versailles), some correspondences may be drawn to the eight prerequisites of peace drived from the House's 1985 open letter to the peoples of the world.

- For instance, the phrase, "children can be raised untainted by any form of racial, national, or religious prejudice" corresponds to peace prerequisites 2, 5, and 3.

- "They champion the full equality of women with men" correlates to prerequisite 6, "programs of education" to prerequisite 7, "devotional meetings followers of all faiths and none" to prerequisite 3, and so on.

- Taken together, these community-building activities are creating a "foundation" for "peace and justice."

- By promoting this vision—and by systematically applying the powerful socio-moral principles underpinning it—the Bahá'ís are contributing, in their own special way, to the betterment of our world.

REFERENCES

'Abdu'l-Bahá. *Extract from a Tablet of 'Abdu'l-Bahá* (a.k.a. "Tablet to Amír Khán"). Additional Tablets, Extracts and Talks. Bahá'í Reference Library ("BRL"). https://www.bahai.org/library/authoritative-texts/abdul-baha/additional-tablets-extracts-talks/169212878/1#341827961.

'Abdu'l-Bahá. *Paris Talks*. Bahá'í Reference Library ("BRL"). https://www.bahai.org/library/authoritative-texts/abdul-baha/paris-talks/.

'Abdu'l-Bahá. *Promulgation of Universal Peace*. ("*Promulgation*.") Bahá'í Reference Library. https://www.bahai.org/library/authoritative-texts/abdul-baha/promulgation-universal-peace/.

'Abdu'l-Bahá. *Secret of Divine Civilization, The*. Bahá'í Reference Library. https://www.bahai.org/library/authoritative-texts/abdul-baha/secret-divine-civilization/.

'Abdu'l-Bahá. *Selections from the Writings of 'Abdu'l-Bahá*. ("*Selections*.") Bahá'í Reference Library. https://www.bahai.org/library/authoritative-texts/abdul-baha/selections-writings-abdul-baha/.

'Abdu'l-Bahá. *Some Answered Questions*. Bahá'í Reference Library. https://www.bahai.org/library/authoritative-texts/abdul-baha/some-answered-questions/.

'Abdu'l-Bahá. *Tablets to the Hague*. Bahá'í Reference Library. https://www.bahai.org/library/authoritative-texts/abdul-baha/tablets-hague-abdul-baha/.

Abizadeh, Arash. "Democratic Elections without Campaigns? Normative Foundations of National Bahá'í Elections." *World Order* 37, no. 1 (2005): 7–49.

Abizadeh, Arash. "How Bahá'í Voters Should Vote." *Journal of Bahá'í Studies* 18, no. 1–4 (2008): 77–94.

Asociación Bayán/The Bayán Association (La Ceiba, Honduras). http://www.bayanhn.org/home.

Báb, The. *Selections from the Writings of the Báb.* ("*Selections.*") Bahá'í Reference Library ("BRL"). https://www.bahai.org/library/authoritative-texts/the-bab/selections-writings-bab/.

Badiee, Julie and the Editors. "Mashriqu'l- Adhkár (Arabic: 'Dawning Place of the Praise of God')." Bahá'í Encyclopedia Project. http://www.bahai-encyclopedia-project.org/attachments/Mashriqul-Adhkar.pdf

Bahá'í Academy (Shivajinagar, Panchgani, Maharashtra, India). http://www.bahaiacademy.org/bahaiacademy/.

Bahá'í Community of Toronto. A space to study, reflect and consult. https://www.bahaitoronto.org/reflection-meeting/.

Bahá'í International Community ("BIC"). *Archives of Bahá'í Persecution in Iran.* https://iranbahaipersecution.bic.org/.

Bahá'í International Community ("BIC"). "Bahá'í Administrative Order, The." https://www.bahai.org/beliefs/essential-relationships/administrative-order/

Bahá'í International Community ("BIC"). "The Bahá'í Faith: The Website of the Worldwide Bahá'í Community." 2020.

Bahá'í International Community ("BIC"). *Bahá'í International Community and International Organizations.* 28 February 1995. https://www.bic.org/statements/bah%C3%A1%C3%AD-international-community-and-international-organizations.

Bahá'í International Community ("BIC"). *Bahá'í World News Service.* https://news.bahai.org/.

Bahá'í International Community ("BIC"). *Billions Arising: Releasing the Universal Capacity for Transformative Social Change,* January 29, 2019. https://www.bic.org/statements/billions-arising-releasing-universal-capacity-transformative-social-change.

Bahá'í International Community ("BIC"). Community Building and Fostering Mutual Support. https://www.bahai.org/action/youth/community-building-fostering-mutual-support.

Bahá'í International Community ("BIC"). *Focus Areas.* https://www.bic.org/focus-areas.

Bahá'í International Community ("BIC"). *For the Betterment of the World: The Worldwide Bahá'í Community's Approach to Social and Economic Development.* 3rd ed. New York: Bahá'í International Community, Released online on April 27, 2018. https://www.bahai.org/documents/osed/betterment-world.pdf.

Bahá'í International Community ("BIC"). *Human Rights Situations That Require the Council's Attention.* https://www.bic.org/statements/un-human-rights-council-39th-session-september.

Bahá'í International Community ("BIC"). Kiribati: Stories of Celebration. https://stories.bicentenary.bahai.org/kiribati/.

Bahá'í International Community ("BIC"). *Migration: A Chance to Reflect on Global Well-Being*, July 12, 2018. https://www.bic.org/news/migration-chance-reflect-global-well-being.

Bahá'í International Community ("BIC"). *Nur University: Training a New Generation of Leaders. One Country: Newsletter of the Bahá'í International Community*, Vol. 13, Issue 4, January–March 2002. https://www.onecount ry.org/story/nur-university-training-new-generation-leaders.

Bahá'í International Community ("BIC"). *Re-Examining the Role of Religion in World Peace*, September 24, 2015. https://www.bic.org/perspectives/re -examining-role-religion-world-peace.

Bahá'í International Community ("BIC"). *Rising Generations: Weaving a New Tapestry of Community Life*, January 25, 2018. https://www.bic.org/ statements/rising-generations-weaving-new-tapestry-community-life.

Bahá'í International Community ("BIC"). *Toward Prosperity: The Role of Women and Men in Building a Flourishing World Civilization*, March 3, 2017. https://www.bic.org/publications/toward-prosperity-role-women-and -men-building-flourishing-world-civilization.

Bahá'í International Community ("BIC"). The Training Institute. https:// www.bahai.org/action/response-call-bahaullah/training-institute

Bahá'í International Community ("BIC"). Transforming Collective Deliberation: Valuing Unity and Justice. https://www.bic.org/statements/transforming-collective-deliberation-valuing-unity-and-justice

Bahá'í International Community ("BIC"). *What Bahá'ís Do. Involvement in the Life of Society. Participation in the Discourses of Society*. https://www.bah ai.org/action/involvement-life-society/participating-discourses-society.

BahaiTeachings.org. "The views expressed in our content reflect individual perspectives and do not represent the official views of the Baha'i Faith." bahaiteachings.org.

Bahá'í World News Service. *Construction advances on historic first national Baha'i House of Worship*. November 24, 2019. https://news.bahai.org/ story/1374/.

Bahá'í World News Service. *Design of national temple unveiled at Naw-Ruz amidst great joy*. March 21, 2018. https://news.bahai.org/story/1246/.

Bahá'í World News Service. *Design of Vanuatu Temple unveiled*. June 18, 2017. https://news.bahai.org/story/1175/.

Bahá'í World News Service. *Design unveiled for first Baha'i Temple in the DRC*. July 2, 2020. https://news.bahai.org/story/1438/.

Bahá'í World News Service. *Houses of Worship*. https://news.bahai.org/me dia-information/houses-worship/.

Bahá'í World News Service. *Local Temple design unveiled in Kenya*. April 15, 2018. https://news.bahai.org/story/1251/.

Bahá'í World News Service. *UN to Iran: End Human Rights Violations Against Bahá'ís*. https://news.bahai.org/story/1372/.

Bahá'í World News Service. "New Film Gives Voice to Communities Around the World." May 2, 2018a. https://news.bahai.org/story/1260/. The film may be viewed online here: https://www.bahai.org/widening-embrace/.

Bahá'í World News Service. "Irish President Urges Bahá'ís to Press On." February 18, 2018b. https://news.bahai.org/story/1239/.

Bahá'í World News Service. "India's Prime Minister and New President Pay Tribute to Bahá'u'lláh." September 4, 2017a. https://news.bahai.org/story/1193/.

Bahá'í World News Service. "Singapore's Prime Minister Honors Bicentenary Anniversary." August 15, 2017b. https://news.bahai.org/story/1186/.

Bahá'í World News Service. "President of Israel visits World Centre to Honor Bicentenary amid Wave of Commemorations in Haifa and Across the Globe." October 28, 2019. https://news.bahai.org/story/1367/.

Bahá'u'lláh. *Bahá'í Meetings*. Bahá'í Reference Library. https://www.bahai.org/library/authoritative-texts/compilations/bahai-meetings/bahai-meetings.pdf?e4125f73.

Bahá'u'lláh. *Call of the Divine Beloved, The*. Bahá'í Reference Library. https://www.bahai.org/library/authoritative-texts/bahaullah/call-divine-beloved/.

Bahá'u'lláh. *Consultation: A Compilation*. Bahá'í Reference Library. https://www.bahai.org/library/authoritative-texts/compilations/consultation/.

Bahá'u'lláh. *Days of Remembrance*. Bahá'í Reference Library. https://www.bahai.org/library/authoritative-texts/bahaullah/days-remembrance/.

Bahá'u'lláh. *Epistle to the Son of the Wolf*. Bahá'í Reference Library. https://www.bahai.org/library/authoritative-texts/bahaullah/epistle-son-wolf/.

Bahá'u'lláh. *Gleanings from the Writings of Bahá'u'lláh*. Bahá'í Reference Library. https://www.bahai.org/library/authoritative-texts/bahaullah/gleanings-writings-bahaullah/.

Bahá'u'lláh. *Hidden Words, The*. Bahá'í Reference Library. https://www.bahai.org/library/authoritative-texts/bahaullah/hidden-words/.

Bahá'u'lláh. *Ishráqát wa chand Lawḥ-i dígar*. Bombay: Náṣirí Press, 1893.

Bahá'u'lláh. *Kitáb-i-Aqdas*. Bahá'í Reference Library. https://www.bahai.org/library/authoritative-texts/bahaullah/kitab-i-aqdas/.

Bahá'u'lláh. *Kitáb-i-Íqán*. Bahá'í Reference Library. https://www.bahai.org/library/authoritative-texts/bahaullah/kitab-i-iqan/.

Bahá'u'lláh. *Prayers and Meditations by Bahá'u'lláh*. Bahá'í Reference Library. https://www.bahai.org/library/authoritative-texts/bahaullah/prayers-meditations/.

Bahá'u'lláh. *Summons of the Lord of Hosts, The.* Bahá'í Reference Library. https://www.bahai.org/library/authoritative-texts/bahaullah/summons-lord-hosts/.

Bahá'u'lláh. *Tablets of Bahá'u'lláh.* Bahá'í Reference Library. https://www.bahai.org/library/authoritative-texts/bahaullah/tablets-bahaullah/.

Bahá'u'lláh. *Tabernacle of Unity.* Bahá'í Reference Library. https://www.bahai.org/library/authoritative-texts/bahaullah/tabernacle-unity/.

Bahá'u'lláh, The Báb, and 'Abdu'l-Bahá. *A Selection of Prayers Revealed by Bahá'u'lláh, the Báb, and 'Abdu'l-Bahá.* Bahá'í Reference Library. https://www.bahai.org/library/authoritative-texts/prayers/bahai-prayers/.

Bahá'u'lláh, 'Abdu'l-Bahá, and Shoghi Effendi. *A Compilation on Bahá'í Education.* Bahá'í Reference Library. https://reference.bahai.org/en/t/c/BE/.

Balyuzi, Hasan M. *'Abdu'l-Bahá: The Centre of the Covenant of Bahá'u'lláh.* 2nd ed. Oxford: George Ronald, 1987.

Balyuzi, Hasan M. *Bahá'u'lláh: The King of Glory.* Oxford: George Ronald, 1991.

Balyuzi, Hasan M. *The Báb: The Herald of the Day of Days.* Oxford: George Ronald, 1973.

Bambino Private Schools (Lilongwe, Malawi). http://www.bambinoschools.com/.

Banani International School, 2019. https://bananischool.org/.

Barli Development Institute for Rural Women (Indore, India). https://www.barli.org/.

Berger, Peter. *The Sacred Canopy: Elements of a Sociological Theory of Religion.* New York: Doubleday, 1967.

Brilliant Star School (Tabuariki, Solomon Islands). http://www.friendsofbrilliantstar.org/History-of-Brilliant-Star-School.php.

Braun, Eunice. *From Vision to Victory: Thirty Years of the Universal House of Justice.* Oxford: George Ronald, 1993.

Browne, Edward Granville. "Introduction." In *'Abdu'l-Bahá, A Traveller's Narrative Written to Illustrate the Episode of the Báb (Maqálah-'i shakhṣí-i sayyáḥ kih dar qaẕíyah-'i Báb nivishtah ast).* Edited in the original Persian, and translated into English, with an Introduction and Explanatory notes, edited by Edward G. Browne. Volume 2: English Translation and notes. Cambridge: Cambridge University Press, 1891/2012; paperback edition, 2012.

Browne, Edward Granville. "Sir 'Abdu'l-Bahá Abbás: Died 28th November, 1921." *Journal of the Royal Asiatic Society of Great Britain and Ireland,* n.s., 1 (January 1922): 145–146.

Buck, Christopher. "'Abdu'l-Bahá's 1912 Howard University Speech: A Civil War Myth for Interracial Emancipation." In *'Abdu'l-Baha's Journey West:*

The Course of Human Solidarity, edited by Negar Mottahedeh, 111–144. New York: Palgrave Macmillan, 2013.

Buck, Christopher. "Bahá'í Contributions to Interfaith Relations." *Journal of Ecumenical Studies*, 54, no. 2 (Spring 2019): 260–277.

Buck, Christopher. "Bahá'í Myths and Visions of America (Chapter 12)." In *God & Apple Pie: Religious Myths and Visions of America*, 296–343. Kingston, NY: Educator's International Press, 2015a.

Buck, Christopher. "Deganawida, the Peacemaker." In *American Writers: A Collection of Literary Biographies*, Supplement XXVI, 81–100, edited by Jay Parini. Farmington Hills, MI: Scribner's Reference/The Gale Group, 2016.

Buck, Christopher. "Fifty Bahá'í Principles of Unity: A Paradigm of Social Salvation." *Bahá'í Studies Review* 18 (2015b): 3–44 (cover date, 2012; publication date, 2015). https://www.academia.edu/35016378/_Fifty_Baha_i_Principles_of_Unity_A_Paradigm_of_Social_Salvation_2017_update_.

Buck, Christopher et al. *Figuring Out Prophecy* (65 articles, as of 16 Aug. 2020). https://bahaiteachings.org/series/figuring-out-prophecy/.

Buck, Christopher. "Religious Minority Rights." In *The Islamic World*, edited by Andrew Rippin, 638–655. London/New York: Routledge, 2008. [Final chapter.]

Buck, Christopher. "Science and Religion Are Complementary." In *World Religions: Belief, Culture, and Controversy.* edited by David Tipton, Joseph Laycock, Dale McGowan, and J. Gordon Melton (Academic Edition). Santa Barbara, CA: ABC-CLIO, 2013b.

Buck, Christopher. et al. *The Báb's Living Legacy* (8 articles). https://bahaiteachings.org/series/the-babs-living-legacy/.

Buck, Christopher. "The Eschatology of Globalization: Bahá'u'lláh's Multiple-Messiahship Revisited." In *Studies in Modern Religions, Religious Movements and the Bábí-Bahá'í Faiths*, edited by Moshe Sharon, 143–178. Leiden: Brill Academic Publishers, 2004.

Buck, Christopher. et al. *The Universal Emancipation Proclamation* (57 articles, as of 4 Sept. 2020). https://bahaiteachings.org/series/the-universal-emancipation-proclamation/.

Buck, Christopher. *Transforming Time: Turning Godly Perfections into Goodly Actions* (40 articles). https://bahaiteachings.org/series/transforming-time-turning-godly-perfections-into-goodly-actions/.

Buck, Christopher and Youli A. Ioannesyan. "Bahá'u'lláh's *Bishárát* (Glad-Tidings): A Proclamation to Scholars and Statesmen." *Bahá'í Studies Review*, 16 (2010): 3–28.

Buck, Christopher and Youli A. Ioannesyan. "Scholar Meets Prophet: Edward Granville Browne and Bahá'u'lláh (Acre, 1890)." *Bahá'í Studies Review* 20 (2018): 21–38. (cover date, 2014; publication date, 2018).

Buck, Christopher and Youli A. Ioannesyan. "The 1893 Russian Publication of Bahá'u'lláh's Last Will and Testament: An Academic Attestation of 'Abdu'l-Baha's Successorship." *Bahá'í Studies Review* 19 (2017): 3–44 (cover date, 2013; publication date, 2017).

Buck, Christopher and Kevin Locke, et al. *Indigenous Messengers of God* (70 articles, as of 23 Sept. 2020). https://bahaiteachings.org/series/indigenous-messengers-of-god/.

Buck, Christopher and J. Gordon Melton. "Bahá'í Calendar and Rhythms of Worship." In *Religious Celebrations: An Encyclopedia of Holidays, Festivals, Solemn Observances, and Spiritual Commemorations*, edited by J. Gordon Melton, Vol. I, 79–86. Santa Barbara, CA: ABC-CLIO, 2011. See also idem, "'Abdu'l-Bahá, Ascension of"; "Ayyám-i-Há (Bahá'í Intercalary Days)"; "Báb, Festival of the Birth of the"; "Báb, Festival of the Declaration of the"; "Báb, Martyrdom of the"; "Bahá'í Fast"; "Bahá'u'lláh, Ascension of"; "Bahá'u'lláh, Festival of the Birth of"; "Covenant, Day of the"; "Naw-Rúz, Festival of"; "Nineteen-Day Feast (Bahá'í)"; "Race Unity Day"; "Ridván, Festival of"; "World Religion Day."

Children's Theater Company (New York, USA). http://www.childrenstheatercompany.org/.

Closson, Rosemary R. and Sylvia Kaye. "Understanding the Bahá'í Ruhi Institute: A Global Faith-Based Adult Education Process." *Adult Learning*, 18(1/2) (Winter/Spring 2007): 9–11.

Cooper, Laurie Ball, Elizabeth Levy Paluck and Erin K. Fletcher. "Reducing Gender-Based Violence." In *The SAGE Handbook of Gender and Psychology*, edited by Michelle K. Ryan and Nyla R. Branscombe, 359–377. Thousand Oaks, CA: SAGE Publications, 2013.

Dahl, Gregory C. *One World, One People: How Globalization is Shaping our Future*. Wilmette, IL: Bahá'í Publishing, 2008.

Education, Curriculum, and Training Associates (ECTA) (Nepal). https://www.onecountry.org/story/ecta-focuses-grassroots-empowerment-nepal.

Eschraghi, Armin. "'Undermining the Foundations of Orthodoxy': Some notes on the Báb's Shari'ah (Sacred Law)." In *A Most Noble Pattern: Essays in the Study of the Writings of the Báb*, edited by Todd Lawson. Oxford: George Ronald, 2011.

Esslemont, John E. *Bahá'u'lláh and the New Era: An Introduction to the Bahá'í Faith*. Bahá'í Reference Library. https://www.bahai.org/library/other-literature/publications-individual-authors/bahaullah-new-era/1#773046298.

Ewing, Sovaida Ma'ani. *Collective Security within Reach*. Oxford: George Ronald, 2009.

Fondation Graine d'Espoir ("Seed of Hope Foundation"), Democratic Republic of the Congo. https://www.bahai.org/documents/osed/betterment-world.pdf.

Ghanea, Nazila. *Human Rights, the U.N. and the Bahá'ís in Iran*. Oxford: George Ronald, 2003.

Health for Humanity (Wadsworth, IL, USA). http://www.healthforhumanity. us/. See also "Oneness of Mankind: The Bahá'í Faith." http://www.healthfor humanity.us/the-bahai-faith.html. Health for Humanity (Wadsworth, IL, USA). http://www.healthforhumanity.us/. See also "Oneness of Mankind: The Bahá'í Faith." http://www.healthforhumanity.us/the-bahai-faith.html.

Hernandez, Joan Barstow. "Transformative Leadership: Its Evolution and Impact." *Journal of Bahá'í Studies*, 28(3) (Fall 2018): 55–85.

Higgins, Michael D. *Speech by President Higgins to Representatives of the Bahá'ís of Ireland*, 2018. https://www.youtube.com/watch?v=Vf3exE9CMBI.

Illumine Media Project (Toronto, Canada). https://illuminemediaproject.b andcamp.com/.

Iran Press Watch. *Documenting the Persecution of the Bahái Community in Iran*. http://iranpresswatch.org/.

Constitute (Comparative Constitutions Project). *Iran (Islamic Republic of) 1979 (rev. 1989)*. https://www.constituteproject.org/constitution/Iran_1989.

Institut Technique Agricole Tshilaka (Democratic Republic of the Congo). https://www.facebook.com/Institut-Technique-Agricole-De-Larache-G ranja-663528843693723/.

Jerusalem Post, The. *Grapevine*, October 31, 2019. https://www.jpost.com/J-S pot/Releasing-women-from-bondage-606515.

Karlberg, Michael. *Beyond the Culture of Contest: From Adversarialism to Mutualism in an Age of Interdependence*. Oxford: George Ronald, 2004.

Kassindja, Fauziya and Layli Miller Bashir. *Do They Hear You When You Cry*. New York: Dell/Random House, 1999.

Kazemzadeh, Firuz. "'Abdu'l-Bahá Abbás (1844–1921)." *Bahá'í Encyclopedia Project*. http://www.bahai-encyclopedia-project.org/attachments/Abdul-Bahá_Abbas.pdf.

Keil, Gerald. *Time and the Bahá'í Era: A Study of the Badí' Calendar*. Oxford: George Ronald, 2008.

Khadem, Riaz. *Shoghi Effendi in Oxford*. Oxford: George Ronald, 1999.

Kimanya-ngeyo Foundation for Science and Education (Jinja, Uganda). https://www.kimanya.org/.

Lample, Paul. *Revelation & Social Reality: Learning to Translate What is Written into Reality*. West Palm Beach, FL: Palabra Publications, 2009.

Lawson, Todd. *A Most Noble Pattern: Essays in the Study of the Writings of the Báb*, edited by Todd Lawson. Oxford: George Ronald, 2011.

Lawson, Todd. *Being Human: Bahá'í Perspectives on Islam, Modernity, and Peace*. Los Angeles, CA: Kalimát Press, 2019.

Lawson, Todd. *Gnostic Apocalypse and Islam: Qur'an, Exegesis, Messianism, and the Literary Origins of the Bábí Religion*. London and New York: Routledge, 2011.

Locke, Alain. "Impressions of Haifa." https://bahai.works/Bah%C3%A1% E2%80%99%C3%AD_World/Volume_2/Impressions_of_Haifa.

Loehle, Craig. *Blueprint for a New World: Using the Power of the Revelation of Bahá'u'lláh to Revitalize the Individual and Society.* Oxford: George Ronald, 2007.

Lycée Enoch Olinga (Niamey, Niger). http://www.lycee-enoch-olinga.org/.

Mazin Academy (Jogi Moor, Pakistan). https://www.facebook.com/ mazinacademy.

McLean, Jack. *A Celestial Burning: A Selective Study of the Writings of Shoghi Effendi.* New Delhi: Bahá'í Publishing Trust of India, 2012.

Mitchell, Glenford E. "Administration, Bahá'í," Bahá'í Encyclopedia Project. http://www.bahai-encyclopedia-project.org/attachments/Administration_ Bahái.pdf.

Momen, Moojan. *A Short Introduction to The Bahá'í Faith.* Oxford: Oneworld, 1997. http://bahai-library.org/books/introduction/.

Momen, Moojan. *Building a Global Culture of Learning,* 2018. https://bahaite achings.org/building-global-culture-learning/.

Momen, Moojan. "Changing Reality: the Bahá'í Community and the Creation of a New Reality." *História: Questões & Debates,* 43 (2005): 13–32.

Mongolian Development Centre (MDC) (Mongolia). https://www.facebook .com/pg/BASEDUK/photos/?tab=album&album_id=194663147288077.

Mottahedeh, Negar, ed. *'Abdu'l-Bahá's Journey West: The Course of Human Solidarity.* New York: Palgrave Macmillan, 2013.

Murphy-Graham, Erin and Alice Taylor. *The Preparation for Social Action Program (PSA) Kimanya Ngeyo Evaluation Report,* 2018. https://drive.g oogle.com/file/d/1Lsd3YOTjXZ9s8FFwCoB532v2wLZPBHBZ/view.

Nabíl-i-Zarandí (a.k.a. Nabíl-i-A'ẓam). *The Dawn-Breakers: Nabíl's Narrative of the Early Days of the Bahá'í Revelation,* translated by Shoghi Effendi. Wilmette, IL: Bahá'í Publishing Trust, 1932. (With extensive footnotes, drawn from a wide range of scholarly sources.)

Nancy Campbell Academy (Stratford and Aurora, Ontario, Canada). http:// www.nancycampbell.ca/.

Núr University (Santa Cruz and La Paz, Bolivia). https://www.nur.edu/.

Ocean of Light International School (Nuku'alofa, Tongatapu, Tonga). http:// www.oceanoflight.to/.

Olinga Foundation for Human Development (Accra-North, Ghana). http:// www.olingafoundation.org/new/.

Palmer, David A. "From 'Congregations' to 'Small Group Community Building': Localizing the Bahá'í Faith in Hong Kong, Taiwan and Mainland China." *Chinese Sociological Review,* 45(2) (Winter 2013): 78–98.

Parent University (Savannah, Georgia, USA). http://internet.savannah.chath am.k12.ga.us/schools/parentuniv/default.aspx.

People's Theater (Offenbach, Germany). 2008. http://www.peoples-theater.de/.

Phelps, Steven. *A Partial Inventory of the Works of the Central Figures of the Bahá'í Faith, Compiled from Public Domain Sources, With a Subject Classification Scheme for the Bahá'í Writings*. Version: 8 February 2020, 2020. http://blog.loomofreality.org/.

Rabbaní, Rúhíyyih. *The Priceless Pearl*. London: Bahá'í Publishing Trust, 1969.

Radio Bahá'í (Soloy, Panama/República de Panamá). https://en.wiki pedia.org/wiki/Bah%C3%A1%27%C3%AD_Faith_in_Panama# Bah%C3%A1'%C3%AD_Radio.

Rays of Light Foundation (Lae, Morobe Province, Papua New Guinea). http://raysoflight.org/.

Reingold, Edward M. and Nachum Dershowitz. "The Bahá'í Calendar." In *Calendrical Calculations: The Millennium Edition*, 223–231. Cambridge: Cambridge University Press, 2001.

Ruhi Arbab School (Jamundi-Robles, Colombia). https://bahaiforums.com/media/bahai-inspired-ruhi-arbab-school-in-jamundi-robles-colombia.154/.

Ruhi Institute. *Ruhi Institute Overview: Main Sequence of Courses, for Those 15 and Older*. https://www.ruhi.org/materials/list.php.

Ruhi Institute. *Ruhi Institute Statement of Purpose and Methods*. https://www.ruhi.org/institute/.

Ruhi Institute. *Song Prefer Your Brother*. https://www.ruhi.org/resources/songs2/EN_Prefer_Your_Brother.pdf.

Ruhi Institute. *The Ruhi Institute—Programs and Materials*. https://www.ruhi.org/materials/list.php.

Saiedi, Nader. *Gate of the Heart: Understanding the Writings of the Báb*. Ottawa, ON: Association for Bahá'í Studies and Wilfrid Laurier University Press, 2008.

Saiedi, Nader. *Logos and Civilization*. Bethesda, MD: University Press of Maryland, 2000.

Saiedi, Nader. "Replacing the Sword with the Word: Bahá'u'lláh's Concept of Peace." *The Bahá'í World* (April 2019). https://bahaiworld.bahai.org/articl es/replacing-sword-word/.

Schaefer, Udo. "An Introduction to Bahá'í Law: Doctrinal Foundations, Principles and Structures." *Journal of Law and Religion*, 18(2) (2003): 307–372.

Schaefer, Udo. *Bahá'í Ethics in Light of Scripture. Volume 1: Doctrinal Fundamentals*. Oxford: George Ronald, 2007.

Schaefer, Udo. *Bahá'í Ethics in Light of Scripture. Volume 2: Virtues and Divine Commandments*. Oxford: George Ronald, 2009.

School of the Nations (Brasilia, Brazil). https://www.schoolofthenations.com.br/.

School of the Nations (Macau). https://www.facebook.com/schoolofthenati onsmacau/.

Shoghi Effendi. *The Advent of Divine Justice*. Bahá'í Reference Library. https://ww w.bahai.org/library/authoritative-texts/shoghi-effendi/advent-divine-justice/.

Shoghi Effendi. *Bahá'í Administration*. Bahá'í Reference Library ("BRL"). https://www.bahai.org/library/authoritative-texts/shoghi-effendi/bahai-administration/.

Shoghi Effendi. *This Decisive Hour* (originally published under the title, *Messages to America*). Bahá'í Reference Library. https://www.bahai.org/library/authoritative-texts/shoghi-effendi/decisive-hour/.

Shoghi Effendi. "The Faith of Bahá'u'lláh: A World Religion" (1 July 1947). https://www.bic.org/statements/faith-bahaullah-world-religion

Shoghi Effendi. *God Passes By*. Bahá'í Reference Library. https://www.bahai.org/library/authoritative-texts/shoghi-effendi/god-passes-by/.

Shoghi Effendi. *The Promised Day is Come*. Bahá'í Reference Library. https://www.bahai.org/library/authoritative-texts/shoghi-effendi/promised-day-come/.

Shoghi Effendi. *The World Order of Bahá'u'lláh*. Bahá'í Reference Library. https://www.bahai.org/library/authoritative-texts/shoghi-effendi/world-order-bahaullah/.

Shoghi Effendi. *Unfolding Destiny*. Bahá'í Reference Library. https://reference.bahai.org/en/t/se/UD/.

Smith, Peter. *An Introduction to the Bahá'í Faith*. Cambridge: Cambridge University Press, 2008.

Stockman, Robert. *'Abdu'l-Bahá in America*. Wilmette, IL: Bahá'í Publishing, 2012.

Supporting Community Leaders (SCL), a program of FUNDAEC (Colombia). https://www.fundaec.org/.

Taherzadeh, Adib. *The Covenant of Bahá'u'lláh*. Oxford: George Ronald, 1992.

Taherzadeh, Adib. *The Revelation of Bahá'u'lláh, Volume 1: Baghdád 1853–63*. Oxford: George Ronald, 1976.

Taherzadeh, Adib. *The Revelation of Bahá'u'lláh, Volume 2: Adrianople 1863–68*. Oxford: George Ronald, 1977.

Taherzadeh, Adib. *The Revelation of Bahá'u'lláh, Volume 3: 'Akká, The Early Years 1868–77*. Oxford: George Ronald, 1984.

Taherzadeh, Adib. *The Revelation of Bahá'u'lláh, Volume 4: Mazra'ih & Bahjí 1877–92*. Oxford: George Ronald, 1987.

Tahirih Justice Center. *Tahirih Justice Center*, 2019. https://www.tahirih.org/.

Townshend International School (Czech Republic). https://www.townshend.cz/.

UNESCO. "Bahá'í Holy Places in Haifa and the Western Galilee." 2019. http://whc.unesco.org/en/list/1220.

United Nations. *Situation of Human Rights in the Islamic Republic of Iran*, 2019. https://undocs.org/A/C.3/74/L.27.

Universal House of Justice, The. *18 January 2019: To the Bahá'ís of the World*. Bahá'í Reference Library. https://www.bahai.org/library/authoritative-texts/the-universal-house-of-justice/messages/20190118_001/1#276724432.

Universal House of Justice, The. *26 November 1992: To the Bahá'ís of the World*. Bahá'í Reference Library. https://www.bahai.org/library/authoritat ive-texts/the-universal-house-of-justice/messages/19921126_001/1992112 6_001.xhtml?196d5e17.

Universal House of Justice, The. *A Widening Embrace*. https://www.bahai. org/widening-embrace/.

Universal House of Justice, The. *April 2002: To the World's Religious Leaders*. Bahá'í Reference Library. https://www.bahai.org/r/047519634.

Universal House of Justice, The. *Framework for Action: Selected Messages of the Universal House of Justice and Supplementary Material 2006–2016*. West Palm Beach, FL: Palabra Publications, 2017. https://www.bahai.org/lib rary/authoritative-texts/the-universal-house-of-justice/framework-action/.

Universal House of Justice, The. *Letter to an Individual: 27 April 2017*. Bahá'í Reference Library. http://www.bahai.org/r/657409828.

Universal House of Justice, The. *October 1963: To the Followers of Bahá'u'lláh throughout the World*. Bahá'í Reference Library. https://www.bahai.org/ library/authoritative-texts/the-universal-house-of-justice/messages/19631 001_001/1#572517632.

Universal House of Justice, The. *October 1985: To the Peoples of the World*. Bahá'í Reference Library. https://www.bahai.org/library/authoritative-t exts/the-universal-house-of-justice/messages/19851001_001/1.

Universal House of Justice, The. *Riḍván 2010: To the Bahá'ís of the World*. Bahá'í Reference Library. https://universalhouseofjustice.bahai.org/rid van-messages/20100421_001.

Universal House of Justice, The. *Riḍván 2018: To the Bahá'ís of the World*. Bahá'í Reference Library. https://www.bahai.org/library/authoritative-t exts/the-universal-house-of-justice/messages/20180421_001/2018042 1_001.xhtml.

Universal House of Justice, The. *The Constitution of the Universal House of Justice*. ("*Constitution*.") Bahá'í Reference Library. https://www.bahai.or g/documents/the-universal-house-of-justice/constitution-universal-hous e-justice.

Universal House of Justice, The. *The Institution of the Counsellors*. Bahá'í Reference Library. https://www.bahai.org/documents/bwc/institution-co unsellors.

Universal House of Justice, The. *Turning Point*. Bahá'í Reference Library. https://www.bahai.org/library/authoritative-texts/the-universal-house- of-justice/turning-point/.

Vahman, Fereydun. *175 Years of Persecution: A History of the Babis & Bahá'ís of Iran*. London: Oneworld Publications, 2019.

Vance, Anthony. "Personal Interview." 2019.

GLOSSARY
KEY BAHÁ'Í TERMS

ABBREVIATION:

- BWNS: Bahá'í World News Service. "Media Information: Style Guide, Glossary and Pronunciation Guide." https://news.bahai.org/media-information/style-guide/.

KEY BAHÁ'Í TERMS

- **'Abdu'l-Bahá (1844–1921)**: "The son of Bahá'u'lláh who was the head of the Bahá'í Faith from 1892 to 1921. Bahá'u'lláh in His will had designated 'Abdu'l-Bahá as His successor. 'Abdu'l-Bahá occupies a special station as the authoritative interpreter of the writings of Bahá'u'lláh and as the perfect example of how a Bahá'í should live. 'Abdu'l-Bahá traveled widely through Europe and North America from 1911–1913, explaining his Father's teachings in talks, interviews, and addresses at universities, churches, temples, synagogues, and missions for the poor." (Source: BWNS)
- **Acre**: "English rendering of the name of the city north of Haifa where Bahá'u'lláh was exiled in 1868. He lived in or near the city until His passing in 1892. Bahá'ís often use the Arabic name, 'Akká, which was the name in general use during the time of Bahá'u'lláh. In Hebrew the name is Akko." (Source: BWNS)

- **Administrative Order**: "International system, originating in Bahá'í scripture, that governs the affairs of the Bahá'í Faith, which has no clergy and no professional learned class; a framework based on elected councils that hold legislative, executive, and judicial authority and on appointed individuals whose role is to protect, advise, and influence the Bahá'í community; the embryonic form of the future world order envisioned by Bahá'u'lláh." (Source: Glenford E. Mitchell, "Administration, Bahá'í," *Bahá'í Encyclopedia Project*. http://www.bahai-encyclopedia-project.org/attachments/Administration_Bahái.pdf)

   "Today the Universal House of Justice is the central governing body of the Administrative Order. Under its guidance, elected bodies, known as Local Spiritual Assemblies and National Spiritual Assemblies tend to the affairs of the Bahá'í community at their respective levels, exercising legislative, executive, and judicial authority. An institution of appointed individuals of proven capacity—the institution of the Counselors—also functions under the guidance of the Universal House of Justice and exerts influence on the life of the Bahá'í community, from the grassroots to the international level. The members of this Institution encourage action, foster individual initiative, and promote learning within the Bahá'í community as a whole, in addition to offering advice to Spiritual Assemblies." (Source: Bahá'í International Community, "The Bahá'í Administrative Order." https://www.bahai.org/beliefs/essential-relationships/administrative-order/)

- **'Akká, Akko**: See entry above for "Acre." (Source: BWNS)

- **Animator**: See "Junior Youth Spiritual Empowerment Program."

- **Arc**: "An area on Mount Carmel in Haifa, shaped like an arc, where the major international administrative buildings of the Bahá'í Faith, including the Seat of the Universal House of Justice, are situated." (Source: BWNS)

- **Báb**: "The title, meaning 'Gate,' assumed by Siyyid 'Ali-Muhammad, the Founder of the Bábí Faith and the Forerunner of Bahá'u'lláh. Considered by Bahá'ís to be one of the twin Manifestations of God associated with the Bahá'í Faith. Born on 20 October 1819, the Báb proclaimed Himself to be the Promised One of Islam and said His mission was to announce the imminent coming of another Messenger even greater than Himself, namely

Bahá'u'lláh. Because of these claims, the Báb was executed by firing squad in the public square in Tabriz on 9 July 1850. His remains were hidden in Iran for many years before being taken to Haifa/Acre in 1899 and buried on Mount Carmel in 1909. For more information, see bahai.org." (Source: BWNS)

- **Bábí Faith**: "The religion founded by the Báb. After 1863 and the announcement by Bahá'u'lláh that He was the Messenger whose coming had been foretold by the Báb, the Bahá'í Faith gradually became established and most followers of the Báb began to call themselves Bahá'ís." (Source: BWNS)

- **Badí' Calendar**: "The Bahá'í calendar, consisting of 19 months of 19 days each, with four intercalary days (five in leap year). The first day of the year corresponds to the spring equinox. The Bahá'í era (B.E.) begins with 1844, the year of the Báb's declaration." (Source: BWNS)

- **Bahá'í**: "(1) A noun referring to a member of the Bahá'í Faith. The plural is Bahá'ís. (2) An adjective describing a person, place, or thing related to the Bahá'í Faith. Examples: a Bahá'í book, the Bahá'í community, a Bahá'í holy day, a Bahá'í holy place." (Source: BWNS)

- **Bahá'í Era (BE)**: "The Bahá'í era (B.E.) begins with 1844, the year of the Báb's declaration." (Source: BWNS)

- **Bahá'í Faith**: "The correct term for the religion is the Bahá'í Faith. It is an independent, monotheistic religion established in virtually every country of the world. It is not a sect of another religion. In a list of major religions, it would look like this: Hinduism, Zoroastrianism, Buddhism, Judaism, Christianity, Islam, the Bahá'í Faith." (Source: BWNS)

    "[A] world religion, destined to evolve in the course of time into a world-embracing commonwealth, whose advent must signalize the Golden Age of mankind, the age in which the unity of the human race will have been unassailably established, its maturity attained, and its glorious destiny unfolded through the birth and efflorescence of a world-encompassing civilization." (Source: Shoghi Effendi, "The Faith of Bahá'u'lláh: A World Religion" (1 July 1947). https://www.bic.org/statements/faith-bahaullah-world-religion)

- **Bahá'í International Community**: "The Bahá'í International Community is a non-governmental organization that represents the worldwide Bahá'í community. It has been registered with the United Nations as a nongovernmental organization since 1948. It currently has consultative status with the United Nations Economic and Social council (ECOSOC) and the United Nations Children's Fund (UNICEF), as well as accreditation with the United Nations Environmental Program (UNEP) and the United Nations Department of Public Information (DPI). The Bahá'í International Community collaborates with the UN and its specialized agencies, as well as member states, inter- and non-governmental organizations, academia, and practitioners. It has Representative Offices in Addis Ababa, Brussels, Geneva, Jakarta, and New York." (Source: BWNS)

- **Bahá'í World Centre**: "The spiritual and administrative center of the Bahá'í Faith, comprising the holy places in the Haifa–Acre area in northern Israel and the Arc of administrative buildings on Mount Carmel in Haifa. The Bahá'í World Centre itself uses the spelling 'Centre'; elsewhere both 'Centre' and 'Center' are used, depending on the custom of the country." (Source: BWNS)

- **Bahá'u'lláh (1817–1892)**: "The founder of the Bahá'í Faith, who lived from 1817 to 1892, considered by Bahá'ís to be the most recent divine Messenger, or Manifestation of God, in a line of great religious figures that includes Abraham, Buddha, Jesus, Krishna, Moses, Muhammad, Zoroaster, the Báb, and others. Bahá'u'lláh was born in Tehran in present-day Iran, and passed away near Acre, in what is now Israel. 'Bahá'u'lláh' is a title that means the 'Glory of God' in Arabic; His name was Mírzá Husayn-'Alí. His writings, which would equal about a hundred volumes, form the basis of the Bahá'í teachings. For more information, see bahai.org." (Source: BWNS)

- **Bahjí**: "The place near Acre where the Shrine of Bahá'u'lláh (His burial place) is located, as well as the mansion that was His last residence and surrounding gardens. It is a place of pilgrimage for Bahá'ís. The word 'Bahjí' is Arabic for 'delight'." (Source: BWNS)

- **Children's classes**: "Classes in moral education that are provided for children, operated at the community level by the Bahá'í training institute. Open to all, they are considered a core activity. (See 'core activities.')" (Source: BWNS)

- **Cluster**: "[A] manageable geographic area consisting of villages and perhaps a small town or of a large city and its suburbs.

The main objective in each cluster is strengthening, through the application of Bahá'í teachings, the three main protagonists in the processes of change: the individual, the community, and the institutions. This work includes raising, through the institute process, growing numbers of people capable of promoting spiritual and social progress; building vibrant local communities where 'individuals, families and institutions … [work] together with a common purpose for the welfare of people both within and beyond its own borders'; and developing institutions with the capacity to mobilize, canalize, and unify the energies of many friends who are eager to serve. Clusters necessarily are at different stages of development based on the number and effectiveness of those labouring for change and the strength and advancement of the local communities and institutions. In some, efforts of the Bahá'ís to build a new society are yet to begin." (Source: Bahá'í International Community, "Community Building and Fostering Mutual Support." https://www.bahai.org/action/youth/community-building-fostering-mutual-support)

- **Consultation**: "[A] process of collective inquiry called consultation, which serves as the basis for deliberation and decision-making in Bahá'í communities around the world. Consultation is an approach to collective inquiry that is unifying rather than divisive. Participants are encouraged to express themselves freely as they engage in discussion, yet take care to do so in a dignified and courteous manner. Detachment from one's positions and opinions regarding the matter under discussion is imperative—once an idea has been shared, it is no longer associated with the individual who expressed it, but becomes a resource for the group to adopt, modify, or discard. As consultation unfolds, participants strive to identify and apply moral principles relevant to the matter at hand. These may include the equality of men and women, stewardship of the natural environment, the elimination of prejudice, the abolishment of the extremes of wealth and poverty, and the like. This approach, unlike those of partisan confrontation or debate, seeks to shift the deliberation towards a new center, maneuvering away from competing claims and interests to the arena of principle, where collective goals and courses of action are more likely to surface and prevail." (Source: Bahá'í International Community, "Transforming Collective Deliberation: Valuing Unity and Justice." https://ww

w.bahai.org/documents/bic/transforming-collective-deliberati
on-valuing-unity-justice)

- **Core activities**: "Bahá'ís currently use the term 'core activities' to refer to devotional meetings, children's classes, classes for young adolescents (termed 'junior youth'), and study circles that use a specific curriculum." (Source: BWNS)
- **Counselor**: "An adviser appointed by the Universal House of Justice who serves in a particular geographic area or at the Bahá'í World Centre in Haifa. At present, there are 81 counsellors assigned to specific countries or regions, and nine counsellors who form the membership of the International Teaching Centre at the Bahá'í World Centre. Appointments are for five years." (Source: BWNS)
- **Devotional Meetings**: "Gatherings, often in people's homes, for prayers and to read the sacred writings of the Bahá'í Faith and other religions. Usually undertaken as an individual initiative. Considered a core activity. (See core activities.)" (Source: BWNS)
- **Fast**: "A period during which Bahá'ís abstain from food and drink from sunrise to sundown during the Bahá'í month of 'Alá', from 2 March to 20 March. Bahá'u'lláh enjoined His followers to pray and fast during this period. The sick, the traveler, and pregnant women, among others, are exempt." (Source: BWNS)
- **Feast**: "See 'Nineteen Day Feast'." (Source: BWNS)
- **Guardian of the Bahá'í Faith**: "See 'Shoghi Effendi'." (Source: BWNS)
- **Haifa**: "The city in northern Israel that along with nearby Acre is the location of the Bahá'í World Centre. The international administrative buildings of the Bahá'í Faith (including the Seat of the Universal House of Justice), the Shrine of the Báb, and surrounding terraces and gardens are all located on Mount Carmel in the heart of Haifa." (Source: BWNS)
- **Holy Days**: "Eleven days that commemorate significant Bahá'í anniversaries. The nine holy days on which work is suspended are the Birth of Bahá'u'lláh, the Birth of the Báb, Declaration of the Báb, Ascension of Bahá'u'lláh, Martyrdom of the Báb, Naw Rúz, Riḍván (a 12-day festival, of which the first, ninth and 12th days are holy days). The other two holy days are the Day of the Covenant and the Ascension of 'Abdu'l-Bahá." (Source: BWNS)
- **Holy Land**: "The area associated with present-day Israel, which is holy to a number of religions, including to Bahá'ís. The resting

places of Bahá'u'lláh near Acre and of the Báb in Haifa are, to Bahá'ís, the holiest spots on earth." (Source: BWNS)

- **International Archives Building**: "One of the buildings at the Bahá'í World Centre on Mount Carmel in Haifa. The repository of many sacred relics of the Bahá'í Faith, it is visited by thousands of Bahá'í pilgrims each year." (Source: BWNS)

- **International Bahá'í Convention**: "A gathering every five years of delegates from around the world to consult on the affairs of the Bahá'í Faith and elect the members of the Universal House of Justice. Members of the National Spiritual Assemblies serve as delegates." (Source: BWNS)

- **International Teaching Centre**: "One of the institutions at the Bahá'í World Centre in Haifa. The International Teaching Centre has nine members, all counsellors appointed by the Universal House of Justice. Appointments are for five years." (Source: BWNS)

- **Junior Youth Spiritual Empowerment Program**: "The junior youth spiritual empowerment program … continues to evolve through experience worldwide. Beyond instructions in the simple mechanics of reading and writing, the program seeks to endow young people in this age group with the capabilities of reading with good comprehension and expressing thoughts clearly and eloquently. Emphasis is placed on the need for positive words and thoughts to be accompanied by pure deeds. … The program, then, aims at awakening the junior youth to their own potential, developing their talents, and directing their new abilities toward service to humanity. It is organized around the concept of a junior youth group, which serves as an environment of mutual support for its members. Guided by older youth, who serve as 'animators,' junior youth study materials based on moral and spiritual concepts, engage in artistic activities, and carry out acts of community service. At present, the program is being carried out in some 165 countries involving more than 160,000 junior youth in over 17,000 groups. (Source: Bahá'í International Community (Office of Social and Economic Development), "For the Betterment of the World: The Worldwide Bahá'í Community's Approach to Social and Economic Development," p. 46. https://www.bahai.org/documents/osed/betterment-world.pdf)

- **Local Spiritual Assembly**: "At the local level, the affairs of the Bahá'í community are administered by the Local Spiritual Assembly.

Each Local Assembly consists of nine members who are chosen in annual elections. As with all other elected Bahá'í institutions, the Assembly functions as a body and makes decisions through consultation. The responsibilities of the Local Spiritual Assembly include promoting the spiritual education of children and young people, strengthening the spiritual and social fabric of Bahá'í community life, assessing and utilizing the community's resources, and ensuring that the energies and talents of community members contribute towards progress." (Source: BWNS)

- **Manifestation of God**: "Throughout the ages, humanity's spiritual, intellectual and moral capacities have been cultivated by the Founders of the great religions, among them Abraham, Krishna, Zoroaster, Moses, Buddha, Jesus Christ, Muhammad, and—in more recent times—the Báb and Bahá'u'lláh. These Figures are not simply ordinary people with a greater knowledge than others. Rather they are Manifestations of God, Who have exerted an incomparable influence on the evolution of human society. ... With the coming of each Manifestation, new forces are released that, over time, increasingly permeate human affairs, providing the main impulse for the further development of consciousness and society. This process—in which the Manifestations of God have successively provided the guidance necessary for humanity's social and spiritual evolution—is known as 'progressive revelation'." (Source: Bahá'í International Community, "Manifestations of God." https://www.bahai.org/beliefs/god-his-creation/revelation/manifestations-god)

  "Author's note: According to 'Abdu'l-Bahá's "Tablet to Amír Khán," indigenous Manifestations of God were sent to the Americas in the Western Hemisphere as well:

  Extract from a Tablet of 'Abdu'l-Bahá

  In ancient times the people of America were, through their northern regions, close to Asia, that is, separated from Asia by a strait. For this reason, it hath been said that crossing had occurred. There are other signs which indicate communication. ...

  Undoubtedly in those regions the Call of God must have been raised in ancient times, but it hath been forgotten now.

  (Source: "Extract from a Tablet of 'Abdu'l-Bahá" (otherwise known as the "Tablet to Amir Khan"), Additional Tablets, Extracts and Talks, online at www.bahai.org/r/760585775)

- **Mashriqu'l-Adhkár**: "The term Mashriqu'l-Adhkár is used in the writings of Bahá'u'lláh, 'Abdu'l-Bahá, and Shoghi Effendi to refer to a gathering of Bahá'ís worshiping and praising God through use of sacred scripture, especially at dawn; to a building dedicated to such worship; to the complex of buildings surrounding a central House of Worship that Bahá'u'lláh ordained to be at the heart of every Bahá'í community and that is to include educational and humanitarian service institutions open to people of all religions; and to the central House of Worship, or Temple, itself. Only Bahá'ís may contribute funds to the building and operation of a Mashriqu'l-Adhkár. As is generally the case with Bahá'í institutions, the development of the Mashriqu'l-Adhkár as an institution is both gradual and evolutionary." (Source: Julie Badiee and the Editors, "Mashriqu'l-Adhkár (Arabic: 'Dawning Place of the Praise of God')," *Bahá'í Encyclopedia Project*. http://www.bahai-encyclopedia-project.org/attachments/Mashriqul-Adhkar.pdf)
- **Mount Carmel**: "In Haifa, Israel, site of the Bahá'í World Centre, including several Bahá'í holy places, the most important of which is the Shrine of the Báb, and the buildings housing the offices of the Bahá'í World Centre administrative offices." (Source: BWNS)
- **National Bahá'í Convention**: "In each country, the annual gathering of elected delegates to discuss the affairs of the Bahá'í Faith in their jurisdiction and to elect the members of the National Spiritual Assembly." (Source: BWNS)
- **National Spiritual Assembly**: "At the national level, the affairs of the Bahá'í community are administered by the National Spiritual Assembly, a nine-member elected council responsible for guiding, co-ordinating, and stimulating the activities of Local Spiritual Assemblies and individual members of the Bahá'í community within a given country. The responsibilities of a National Spiritual Assembly include channelling the community's financial resources, fostering the growth and vibrancy of the national Bahá'í community, supervising the affairs of the community including its social and economic development activities and its properties, overseeing relations with government, resolving questions from individuals and Local Spiritual Assemblies, and strengthening the participation of the Bahá'í community in the life of society at the national level." (Source: BWNS)

- **Nineteen Day Feast**: "An administrative gathering at the local level. The term refers to a spiritual 'feast' of prayers, consultation and fellowship. It is held every 19 days, on the first day of each Bahá'í month." (Source: BWNS)
- **Pilgrimage**: "Each year thousands of Bahá'ís undertake pilgrimage, during which they forge a profound and lasting connection with the spiritual and administrative centre of their Faith, located in the Haifa–'Akká area of what is now northern Israel. Bahá'í pilgrims pray and meditate at the Shrine of Bahá'u'lláh and the Shrine of the Báb, as well as in the beautiful gardens that surround them. They also draw inspiration from the time spent at various historical sites associated with the lives of Bahá'u'lláh, 'Abdu'l-Bahá, and Shoghi Effendi, as well as from visits to the edifices dedicated to the worldwide administration of the Bahá'í Faith." (Source: BWNS)
- **Progressive Revelation**: "The central belief that Manifestations of God have successively provided the guidance necessary for humanity's social and spiritual evolution." (Source: BWNS)
- **Public Discourse**: "At the level of the cluster, involvement in public discourse can range from an act as simple as introducing Bahá'í ideas into everyday conversation to more formal activities such as the preparation of articles and attendance at gatherings, dedicated to themes of social concern—climate change and the environment, governance and human rights, to mention a few. It entails, as well, meaningful interactions with civic groups and local organizations in villages and neighbourhoods." (Source: UHJ: The Universal House of Justice. Riḍván 2010: To the Bahá'ís of the World. Bahá'í Reference Library. https://universalhouseofjustice.bahai.org/ridvan-messages/20100421_001
- **Reflection Meetings**: "A reflection meeting is an opportunity for a group of people in a small geographic area to discuss the progress of the community-building activities that Bahá'ís and their friends have initiated, form a united vision and identify immediate steps forward." (Source: Bahá'í Community of Toronto, "A space to study, reflect and consult." https://www.bahaitoronto.org/reflection-meeting/)
- **Regional Bahá'í Council**: "In some countries, the National Spiritual Assembly assigns certain of its functions to Regional Bahá'í Councils, which serve a designated geographical area within the land in question. The responsibilities of a Regional Council may

include carrying out policies of the National Spiritual Assembly, supervising progress of particular plans and projects, and taking steps to stimulate and coordinate the growth of the Bahá'í community within the region." (Source: BWNS)

- **Shoghi Effendi (1897–1957)**: "The head of the Bahá'í Faith from 1921 to 1957. His title is Guardian of the Bahá'í Faith. He is the grandson of 'Abdul-Bahá and the great-grandson of Bahá'u'lláh. For more information, see bahai.org." (Source: BWNS)
- **Shrine of Bahá'u'lláh**: "The resting place of the mortal remains of Bahá'u'lláh, located near the city of Acre in what is now Israel. The shrine is the holiest spot on earth to Bahá'ís and a place of pilgrimage." (Source: BWNS)
- **Shrine of the Báb**: "The resting place of the mortal remains of the Báb, located on Mount Carmel in Haifa, Israel. It is a sacred site to Bahá'ís and a place of pilgrimage." (Source: BWNS)
- **Study circles**: "A study circle is one of the principal elements of the process of distance education offered by the Bahá'í training institute. It is a small group that meets regularly to study the [training] institute course materials." (Source: BWNS)
- **Training Institute**: "[T]he concept of the 'training institute' was introduced by the Universal House of Justice in the mid-1990s. Its purpose is to assist individuals to deepen their understanding of the Bahá'í teachings, and to gain the spiritual insights and practical skills they need to carry out the work of the community. ... We may think of the work of the training institute, then, as maintaining a system of distance education to fuel and facilitate this evolving conversation. The principal elements of the system include the 'study circle', the tutor, and a set of materials, grounded in the Bahá'í writings, that express the spiritual insights and the knowledge gained in the process of translating Bahá'u'lláh's teachings into reality. The materials help the individual enter into the discussion of what the Bahá'í community has learned through experience as it has tried to contribute to the advancement of civilization. More crucially, they seek to involve him or her in this process of learning and in the diffusion of relevant knowledge." (Source: Bahá'í International Community, "The Training Institute." https://www.bahai.org/action/response-call-bahaullah/training-institute)
- **Tutor**: "The group [study circle] is brought together by a tutor associated with the training institute. Tutors do not hold any special

status. They are simply those who are further along in their study of the materials. Everyone can potentially serve as a tutor on some occasions, while taking part as a member of a study circle on others. All those participating are seen as active agents of their own learning, and tutors strive to create an atmosphere that encourages individuals to assume ownership for the educational process in which they are engaged." (Source: Bahá'í International Community, "The Training Institute." https://www.bahai.org/action/response-call-ba haullah/training-institute)

- **Universal House of Justice**: "The international governing council of the Bahá'í Faith. It is the supreme administrative body ordained by Bahá'u'lláh in His book of laws. The Universal House of Justice is elected every five years at the International Bahá'í Convention, where members of the National Spiritual Assemblies around the world serve as delegates. The Universal House of Justice was first elected in 1963. Its permanent seat is on Mount Carmel in Haifa." (Source: BWNS)

INDEX

Printed in the United States
by Baker & Taylor Publisher Services